KU-524-345

e Manufacturing

Just-in-Time Manufacturing

An introduction

T.C.E. Cheng
Head of the Department of Management
Hong Kong Polytechnic
Hong Kong

and

S. Podolsky
Department of Acturial and Management Science
University of Manitoba
Canada

CHAPMAN & HALL
London · Glasgow · New York · Tokyo · Melbourne · Madras

Published by Chapman & Hall, 2–6 Boundary Row, London SE1 8HN

Chapman & Hall, 2–6 Boundary Row, London SE1 8HN, UK

Blackie Academic & Professional, Wester Cleddens Road, Bishopbriggs, Glasgow G64 2NZ, UK

Chapman & Hall Inc., 29 West 35th Street, New York NY10001, USA

Chapman & Hall Japan, Thomson Publishing Japan, Hirakawacho Nemoto Building, 6F, 1-7-11 Hirakawa-cho, Chiyoda-ku, Tokyo 102, Japan

Chapman & Hall Australia, Thomas Nelson Australia, 102 Dodds Street, South Melbourne, Victoria 3205, Australia

Chapman & Hall India, R. Seshadri, 32 Second Main Road, CIT East, Madras 600 035, India

First edition 1993

© 1993 T.C.E. Cheng and S. Podolsky

Printed and bound in Great Britain by Clays Ltd, Bungay, Suffolk

ISBN 0 412 45690 7

Apart from any fair dealing for the purposes of research or private study, or criticism or review, as permitted under the UK Copyright Designs and Patents Act, 1988, this publication may not be reproduced, stored, or transmitted, in any form or by any means, without the prior permission in writing of the publishers, or in the case of reprographic reproduction only in accordance with the terms of the licences issued by the Copyright Licensing Agency in the UK, or in accordance with the terms of licences issued by the appropriate Reproduction Rights Organization outside the UK. Enquiries concerning reproduction outside the terms stated here should be sent to the publishers at the London address printed on this page.

The publisher makes no representation, express or implied, with regard to the accuracy of the information contained in this book and cannot accept any legal responsibility or liability for any errors or omissions that may be made.

A catalogue record for this book is available from the British Library

Library of Congress Cataloging-in-Publication data available

HERTFORDSHIRE
LIBRARY SERVICE

No.		
Class		
Supplier	Price	Date
JMLS	£35.00	3/95

♾ Printed on permanent acid-free text paper, manufactured in accordance with the proposed ANSI-NISO Z 39.48-199X and ANSI Z 39.48-1984

This book is dedicated to two great practitioners of JIT manufacturing – my beloved parents – who, over the years, have been giving me the right advice in the right dose at the right time.

T.C. Edwin Cheng

To my loving parents whose guidance and support has made this all possible.

Susan Podolsky

Contents

Preface   xi
1   Introduction   1
1.1 History and development of JIT manufacturing   2
1.2 Elements of a JIT manufacturing   4
     1.2.1 People involvement   5
     1.2.2 Plants   6
     1.2.3 Systems   7
1.3 The goals of JIT   7
1.4 Advantages and limitations of JIT   10
     1.4.1 Advantages of JIT   10
     1.4.2 Limitations of JIT   11
1.5 The rationale for implementing JIT   12
1.6 Prerequisites to a JIT program   17
     1.6.1 Plant evaluation   17
     1.6.2 Management influence   18
     1.6.3 Housekeeping activities   18
     1.6.4 Organizational flexibility   19
1.7 Layout of the rest of the book   19

2   Just-in-time production   20
2.1 Workplace organization   21
     2.1.1 Clearing and simplifying   21
     2.1.2 Locating   23
     2.1.3 Cleaning   23
     2.1.4 Discipline   23
     2.1.5 Participation   24
2.2 Visibility   25
2.3 Preventive maintenance   28
2.4 JIT production planning   39
     2.4.1 Customer orientation   41
     2.4.2 Plant arrangement for JIT production   46
     2.4.3 Linking demand pull with cellular manufacturing   59
     2.4.4 Automation   70
     2.4.5 Flexible plant   71
     2.4.6 Focused factory   77
2.5 JIT production control   82
     2.5.1 The kanban system   83
     2.5.2 Rules for kanban operation   84

2.5.3 Preparing the plant for the kanban system   85
2.5.4 Lead time and cycle time reduction   89
2.5.5 Implementing the kanban system   91
2.5.6 JIT and MRP   92

3   Just-in-time logistics   99
3.1 JIT purchasing   99
   3.1.1 Contrasts between JIT and traditional purchasing   99
   3.1.2 Supplier selection   103
   3.1.3 Supplier education   109
   3.1.4 Supplier commitment and customer dependency   109
3.2 JIT delivery   115
   3.2.1 Increasing delivery frequency through production related
       elements   116
   3.2.2 Improving customer delivery through problem
       identification and resolution   118
   3.2.3 Improving customer delivery through forecasting and DRP   120

4   Total quality management   123
4.1 Quality and quality costs   124
   4.1.1 Quality: a systems perspective   125
   4.1.2 The cost of quality   129
   4.1.3 A general guideline to quality improvement   129
   4.1.4 Defining employee roles in the quality improvement process 131
   4.1.5 Quality improvement through employee ownership   133
4.2 Quality of design   136
   4.2.1 Defining quality of design   136
   4.2.2 Improving the quality of design   137
4.3 Quality of conformance   140
4.4 Quality of services   146
4.5 Quality issues in JIT   152
   4.5.1 Increasing customer responsiveness   152
   4.5.2 Continuous improvement   152
   4.5.3 Total employee involvement: the key to JIT success 153
   4.5.4 Total quality control   154
   4.5.5 Quality circles   156
4.6 Managing in-process quality   160
   4.6.1 Brainstorming and NGT   160
   4.6.2 The 5 'whys'   161
   4.6.3 Pareto charts   161
   4.6.4 Histograms   163
   4.6.5 Check sheets   163
   4.6.6 Flip charts   164
   4.6.7 Analysis of cause and effect   164

5   Total employee involvement   168
5.1 Teamwork   168
     5.1.1 Management commitment to teamwork   171
     5.1.2 Employee education and training   173
     5.1.3 Factors of successful training and education programs   173
     5.1.4 Incentives for employees   175
5.2 JIT discipline   178
     5.2.1 Employee work ethic   178
     5.2.2 JIT and employee motivation   180
     5.2.3 JIT work procedures   181
     5.2.4 JIT vs. traditional work practices   181
     5.2.5 JIT standards and measurements   183

6   Implementing JIT manufacturing   184
6.1 Developing an implementation strategy   184
6.2 An operational plan for implementation   185
6.3 Data collection and measurement systems   187
6.4 Pilot projects   189
6.5 Dealing with employee resistance and unions   190

7   Industrial case study   194
7.1 Introduction   194
7.2 TQM project   195
     7.2.1 Development of the TQM project   195
     7.2.2 The repair and overhaul process   196
     7.2.3 Implementation of TQM   197
     7.2.4 Measuring and monitoring progress   202
     7.2.5 Preparing employees for TQM   204
7.3 TQM production issues   205
7.4 Quality issues   208
7.5 Teamwork building issues   211
7.6 Learning experience with TQM   212

References   217

Index   222

Preface

The contemporary organization is faced with an environment in which the ability to prevail in the face of increasing levels of competition, changing economic conditions and consumer attitudes is redefining a successful business. More than ever, organizations must find a way to adapt to this changing environment and many are becoming modern trail blazers through replacing traditional methods with ideas relatively new to North America. Just-in-time (JIT) represents such an alternative for North American businesses within manufacturing and non-manufacturing industries. With successful implementation, JIT offers an organization an effective means of fully utilizing its workforce, cutting costs and satisfying the customer.

JIT Manufacturing: An introduction presents a comprehensive summary of the ideal methods of implementation, as well as a practical illustration of its adaptation within an organization. Through focusing on the implementation aspects of JIT, this book will assist many who embrace the concept with its ongoing implementation within the firm. What sets success apart from JIT simply becoming another romantic idea within a firm is the knowledge, awareness and experience of those involved in the implementation effort. The breadth of the book functions to provide the reader with these necessary tools for successful implementation.

The first part of the book provides the reader with a comprehensive overview, introducing the basic concepts underlying the functions and goals of JIT. Specific concepts dealing with JIT production, total quality management, total employee involvement and implementation issues are presented. The nature of JIT as being a 'people system', is stressed through discussion on employee involvement within each of these varying aspects of JIT implementation.

The book exemplifies the role of commitment within a JIT environment as it demonstrates to the reader the kind of approach necessary for success. Inherent in this approach is the attitude toward implementation and the ongoing commitment of all managers and employees toward problems as well as successes. *JIT Manufacturing: An introduction* brings to the reader something new in implementation books, as it is carries the reader through the incremental process of JIT implementation while enabling the reader to comprehend and assess its impact upon the organization as an integrated whole.

The final chapter of the book presents an illustration of JIT within an organization, through an industrial case study. The case study compliments the preceding ideal concepts as it provides the reader with an excellent opportunity to examine the 'real world' of JIT. Presented through discussion is the adaptation of these ideal principles within a specific organization. Such an example leaves the reader with a realistic picture of what to expect from JIT, the problems one may encounter with implementation, and the commitment and learning experience of others who have taken on such an endeavour. The learning experience of others cannot be over-emphasized, as a wealth of information provided through the trials and triumphs of others can key us into the very nature of JIT.

JIT Manufacturing: An introduction is written to assist those in industry who aspire to learn about JIT, to broaden their understanding of its underlying concepts or to assist them with specific elements of implementation. *JIT Manufacturing: An introduction* was written with those in mind who are determined to make JIT successful within their own organization.

Acknowledgement

Thank you to the Canadian Labour Congress and the American Federation of Labour for their time and assistance.

The authors wish to extend a special thank you to the employees and management of Company A, particularly Brian Lanoway for his involvement and effort in coordinating this study. Thank you to NSERC for financial funding, as well as family and friends for their support and encouragement.

1

Introduction

Just-in-time (JIT) manufacturing is a Japanese management philosophy applied in manufacturing which involves having the right items of the right quality and quantity in the right place and at the right time. It has been widely reported that the proper use of JIT manufacturing has resulted in increases in quality, productivity and efficiency, improved communication and decreases in costs and wastes. The potential of gaining these benefits has made many organizations question and consider this approach to manufacturing. For these reasons, JIT has become a very popular subject currently being investigated by many North American organizations.

Just-in-time management involves the application of old management ideas; however, their adaptation to the modern manufacturing firm is a relatively new practice. Presently, many North American firms are considering the JIT approach in response to an ever more competitive environment. North American organizations are beginning to feel the pressure placed upon them by the success of their Japanese competitors at obtaining phenomenal levels of productivity. In order to remain competitive and experience economic success, these companies have focused on increasing productivity, improving the quality of their products and raising the standards of efficiency within their firms. The ability to achieve higher standards of productivity without sacrificing quality is also an important goal of a manufacturing firm. Over the long run, application of JIT manufacturing may assist these companies in achieving these goals of manufacturing excellence.

This text discusses in depth the implementation of JIT manufacturing. The objectives are twofold. The first objective is to acquaint the reader with the overall JIT concept and the factors necessary for its implementation; the concepts presented here represent the ideal principles and methods of implementation. The second objective is to illustrate an actual case study of a manufacturing firm, involving the discussion of specific problems and adjustments which are required in order to implement JIT manufacturing successfully in an organization. The use of a case study will provide the opportunity to observe, test and discover if the claims of higher productivity, efficiency and quality are practical and realizable benefits associated with the use of JIT manufacturing. Discussion of the overall planning and effects of JIT will also be presented.

1.1 History and development of JIT manufacturing

JIT is a Japanese management philosophy which has been applied in practice since the early 1970s in many Japanese manufacturing organizations. It was first developed and perfected within the Toyota manufacturing plants by Taiichi Ohno as a means of meeting consumer demands with minimum delays (Goddard, 1986). For this reason, Taiichi Ohno is frequently referred to as the father of JIT.

The Toyota production plants were the first to introduce JIT. It gained extended support during the 1973 oil embargo and was later adopted by many other organizations. The oil embargo and the increasing shortage of other natural resources were seen as a major impetus for the widespread adoption of JIT. Toyota was able to meet the increasing challenges for survival through an approach to management different from what was characteristic of the time. This approach focused on people, plants and systems (Goddard, 1986). Toyota realized that JIT would only be successful if every individual within the organization was involved and committed to it, if the plant and processes were arranged for maximum output and efficiency, and if quality and production programs were scheduled to meet demands exactly.

JIT had its beginnings as a method of reducing inventory levels within Japanese shipyards (Goddard, 1986). Today, JIT has evolved into a management philosophy containing a body of knowledge and encompassing a comprehensive set of manufacturing principles and techniques. JIT manufacturing has the capacity, when properly adapted to the organization, to strengthen the organization's competitiveness in the marketplace substantially by reducing wastes and improving product quality and efficiency of production.

There are strong cultural aspects associated with the emergence of JIT in Japan. The development of JIT within the Toyota production plants did not occur independently of these strong cultural influences. The Japanese work ethic is one of these factors. The work ethic emerged shortly after World War II and was seen as an integral part of the Japanese economic success. It is the prime motivating factor behind the development of superior management techniques that are becoming the best in the world. The Japanese work ethic involves the following concepts.

- Workers are highly motivated to seek constant improvement upon that which already exists. Although high standards are currently being met, there exist even higher standards to achieve.
- Companies focus on group effort which involves the combining of talents and sharing knowledge, problem-solving skills, ideas and the achievement of a common goal.
- Work itself takes precedence over leisure. It is not unusual for a Japanese employee to work 14-hour days. This contrasts greatly when compared to the North American emphasis on time available for leisure activities.

- Employees tend to remain with one company throughout the course of their career span. This allows the opportunity for them to hone their skills and abilities at a constant rate while offering numerous benefits to the company. These benefits manifest themselves in employee loyalty, low turnover costs and fulfillment of company goals.
- There exists a high degree of group consciousness and sense of equality among the Japanese (Cheng, 1990). The Japanese are a homogeneous race where individual differences are not exploited or celebrated.

In addition, JIT also emerged as a means of obtaining the highest levels of usage out of limited resources available. Faced with constraints, the Japanese worked toward attainment of the optimal cost/quality relationship in their manufacturing processes. This involves reducing waste and using materials and resources in the most efficient manner possible.

Furthermore, Japanese firms tend to focus on enhancing the long-run competitiveness rather than emphasizing the realization of short-term profits. They are willing to experience opportunity costs by introducing and implementing innovative ideas within their firms. Stockholders and owners of Japanese companies also encourage the maximization of long-term benefits. This enables them to experience the rewarding long-term profits as a result of their efforts.

JIT management has a high degree of cultural aspects imbedded in its development. Heiko (1989) has suggested several relevant Japanese cultural characteristics which may be related to JIT as follows.

- JIT management allows an organization to meet consumer demand regardless of the level of demand. This is made possible through the use of a pull system of production. The Japanese cultural characteristic which relates to the demand pull concept involves a great deal of emphasis on 'customer orientation'. Satisfying consumer needs quickly and efficiently is a priority for most Japanese business organizations.
- The degree of time lapse between material arrivals, processing and assembly of the final product for consumers is minimized by the JIT production technique. Production lead time minimization is possibly the result of the Japanese cultural emphasis on speed and efficiency. This may be due to the overcrowded living conditions which exist in Japanese cities.
- JIT allows a reduction in raw material, work-in-process and finished goods inventories. This frees up a greater amount of space and time between operations within plants. The corresponding cultural characteristic is concern for space due to a very dense population.
- The JIT production technique uses containers for holding parts. This allows easy identification and monitoring of inventory levels. The use of designated containers within the production process may be due to the emphasis placed upon the types of packaging which exist when goods are purchased by consumers.

- An element of JIT production requires that the plant be clean, i.e. there should be no wastes present which may hinder production. Japanese are concerned with the cleanliness of their environment which may be due to limited space. A clean and uncluttered environment may give the illusion of greater area.
- JIT production involves the use of 'visible signals' to display the status of machinery. The corresponding cultural characteristic involves the use of many signs displaying various products. Another contributing factor to the use of visible signals is the high literacy rate among Japanese people as compared to other countries.

The differences which exist between North American and Japanese cultures have led to the belief that JIT cannot work effectively within North American manufacturing organizations. The cultural differences which contribute most to this belief include the Japanese work ethic and the role of unions within the North American work environment. Unions typically play a large role in manufacturing or 'blue collar' organizations which would be more apt to adopt a JIT approach to manufacturing. In addition, unions tend to exert influence upon management in developing policies which are more favorable to labour. Therefore, issues such as increasing leisure time for labour would be contradictory to the Japanese work ethic. This may explain some of the beliefs that JIT and North American firms are incompatible.

The claim that JIT cannot be effective in North American firms has not been substantiated as several organizations have successfully implemented JIT. Many organizations realize some of the benefits of JIT in the early stages of implementation (Lubben, 1988). It should be noted that in organizations where a union plays an active role in bargaining for employee concerns, it is beneficial to consider union involvement in the beginning stages of implementation.

Although focus has been directed toward inadequacies within the North American environment, the Japanese are subject to change as well. North American culture has to some extent being adopted by many Japanese people. For this reason, much of the Japanese youth have rejected their elders' work ethic and replaced it with one that apes that of North American culture. Despite this abandonment and change in attitudes, Japan is still able to attain productivity and quality standards which far exceed those of North America.

1.2 Elements of JIT manufacturing

JIT manufacturing consists of several components or elements which must be integrated together to function in harmony to achieve the JIT goals. These elements essentially include the human resources and the production, purchasing, manufacturing, planning and organizing functions of an organization. In short, these elements can be grouped together into the above-mentioned Toyota production system of people, plants and systems (Goddard, 1986).

1.2.1 People involvement

Obtaining support and agreement from all individuals involved in the achievement of organizational goals is a fundamental *sine qua non* for JIT success. Obtaining support and agreement will require involving, and informing, all groups who have an interest in the company. This can greatly reduce the amount of time and effort involved in implementing JIT and can minimize the likelihood of creating implementation problems. Support and agreement should be obtained from the following groups:

- *Stockholders and owners of the company* Emphasis should be placed on the long-term realization of profit, and so short-term earnings should be plowed back into the company to finance the various changes and investment commitments necessary for JIT success. It should be made clear that most of the benefits associated with JIT will only be realized over the long run.
- *Labour organizations* Labour unions and members should be informed about the goals of JIT and made aware of how the new system will effect the employees' work practice. This is important in winning the union and workers' support to assist with the implementation and to remove potential problems and difficulties. Failure to involve labour organizations will result in a lack of understanding of management motives and causing fears of job loss on the part of the labour. This can lead to impediments such as non-cooperation and resistance to change. Union support is also vital in achieving elimination of job classifications to allow for multi-skilled workers and company-wide focus.
- *Management support* This involves the support of management from all levels. It also requires that management be prepared to set examples for the workers and initiate the process to change attitudes. Striving for continuous improvement is not only required of the employees on the shop floor, but must also be inherent in management's attitudes.
- *Government support* Government can lend support to companies wishing to implement JIT by extending tax and other financial incentives. This can provide motivation for companies to become innovative as it bears some of the financial burden associated with the costs of implementing JIT (Lee and Ebrahimpour, 1987).

Organization theory suggests the hypothesis that people will be more compelled to work toward goals when they are included in the development of the goals. Onto this hypothesis JIT builds the idea of involving employees at different levels in the organization. The introduction of **quality circles** and the concept of **total people involvement** are examples of the avenues available for attempting to maximize people involvement through the use of JIT.

The introduction of changes in an organization has the potential to elicit reactive behaviours from the individuals who may be subjected to these modifications (Gray and Starke, 1988). JIT represents one of these changes and can cause substantial organizational transformations. Although these changes may affect the organization in very positive ways, reactive behaviours such as resisting the change by working against organizational goals may develop. Involving people becomes increasingly important at this point. Communication, training and increasing the values of the workers' jobs can help alleviate reactive behaviours.

1.2.2 Plants

Numerous changes occur about the plant which encompass plant layout, multi-function workers, demand pull, kanbans, self-inspection, MRP and MRP II and continuous improvement. Each of these will be explained separately with relation to how they tie into JIT production.

Plant layout

Under JIT production, the plant layout is arranged for maximum worker flexibility and is arranged according to product rather than process. This type of layout requires the use of 'multi-function workers', i.e. the focus shifts towards training workers and providing them with the skills necessary to perform many tasks rather one or two highly specialized tasks.

Demand pull production

The concept of demand pull involves the use of demand for a given product to signal when production should occur. Use of demand pull allows a company to produce only what is required in the appropriate quantity and at the right time.

'Kanban' is a Japanese word meaning signal and is usually a card or tag accompanying products throughout the plant. Indicated on the kanbans is the name or serial number for product identification, the quantity, the required operation and the destination of where the part will travel to. The use of kanbans assists in tying or linking the different production processes together.

Self-inspection

The use of self-inspection by each employee is done to ensure that their production input adds value to the product and is of high quality. Self-inspection allows mistakes and low quality work to be caught and corrected efficiently and at the place where the mistakes initially occur.

Continuous improvement

The concept of continuous improvement involves a change in attitudes toward the overall effectiveness of an organization. Continuous improvement is an integral part of the JIT concept and, to be effective, must be adopted by each member of the organization, not only by those directly involved with the production processes. Continuous improvement requires that with every goal and standard successfully met, these goals and standards should be increased but always in a range that is reasonable and achievable. This will allow a company to constantly improve upon its operations, product and, ultimately, its customer satisfaction.

1.2.3 Systems

Systems within an organization refer to the technology and processes used to link, plan and co-ordinate the activities and materials used in production. Two such systems are MRP (material requirements planning) and MRP II (manufacturing resource planning).

MRP is 'a computer-based method for managing the materials required to carry out a schedule'. It is a 'bottom-up' or 'consolidation' approach to planning, i.e. it involves the planning of lower level products within the product family such as component parts (Dilworth, 1989). Planning for MRP can be broken down essentially into two parts. These include a production plan, which is a broad plan indicating the available capacity and the manner in which it is to be allocated about the plant, and a master production schedule which is a detailed plan of what products to produce in specified time frames.

MRP II is a computer-based program which can be used to provide information on financial resources available to carry out the plans of MRP. An example of the information MRP II provides is inventory investment. Other systems within an organization include those that provide linkages with suppliers and assist with the co-ordination of the overall functioning of the organization.

Given the nature of JIT, quality will assume an increasing importance. The use of total quality control is an additional element of JIT and is important in ensuring that the quality standards set for production are achieved. JIT quality involves 'quality at the source' (Hay, 1988). Quality at the source means there is an emphasis on producing products correctly the first time. Quality at the source contrasts greatly with the traditional 'after the fact' approach to quality or producing the product then inspecting it. This approach does not allow for minimizing inventory levels and rework costs. Thus, it does not tie into the goals of JIT to eliminate wastes.

1.3 The goals of JIT

JIT management can be applied to the manufacturing processes within any company. It is also being adapted to organizations within the service industry (Hay, 1988). JIT, when successfully implemented, can reduce the fluctuations which many manufacturing firms experience contingent upon changing economic conditions. Goddard (1986) suggests that a company can achieve the 'competitive edge' by competing on the basis of cost, service and quality. These three elements are the distinguishing characteristics that set products apart from one another. JIT allows companies to filter out the wastes in the production process, improve upon quality and satisfy consumer demands in an efficient and reliable manner.

There are three main manufacturing objectives for JIT (Suzaki, 1987). These objectives are universal or homogeneous in nature, i.e. they can be applied and adapted to a diversity of organizations within industries that differ greatly from one another.

1. *Increasing the organization's ability to compete with rival firms and remain competitive over the long run*   Organizational competitiveness is enhanced through the use of JIT as it allows organizations to develop an optimal process for manufacturing their products. There are differences between the production processes for conventional and for progressive organizations.

   The conventional organization is one which adheres to the well-practised forms of production. The progressive organization is one that can respond to changes within the environment and adapt its manufacturing processes to these changes. Frequently, these types of organizations are the first to develop or implement innovative methods of production. Thus, the progressive organization is one that would be more apt to adopt JIT management. The progressive organization is one that is able to remain competitive through adaptation to environmental changes.

   The progressive organization will have a well-integrated system of manufacturing which involves shared organizational values, co-ordinated flow of manufacturing techniques, people involvement and the opportunity to use potential skills. The differences which exist between the conventional and progressive companies involve operational and organizational characteristics.

   The operational characteristics include set-up time, lot size, inventory, floor space, transportation, lead time, defect rates and machine trouble. It is typical for conventional companies to experience long set-up times, transportation and lead times. Inventory, floor space and lot sizes are likely to be large. In addition, defect rates and machine trouble will be high for the conventional firm as well.

   The progressive company will have short set-up, transportation and lead times. Inventory, floor space and lot sizes will be small and defects and machine trouble low for these organizations. The overall functioning of production will be smoother and more efficient than for the conventional firm.

   The organizational characteristics include the structure, orientation toward goals, communication, agreement, union focus, skill base, suppliers and education and training. The structure of the progressive organization allows greater flexibility. Orientation is toward total optimization of the whole company while avoiding departmental focus which tends to work against the achievement of organization-wide goals.

Communication within the progressive firm is open and there is not a long chain of command to follow. Also, agreement among members is trust based as compared to contract based. Union focus is company based rather than skill based. The skill base tends to be broad or flexible in contrast to narrow or highly specialized skills. The level of supplier involvement is narrowed down to include a selected few and the education and training aspects constitute a significant role. These types of organizations are more likely to invest more resources in training employees.

2. *Increasing the degree of efficiency within the production process* Efficiency will concern itself with achieving greater levels of productivity while minimizing the associated costs of production.
3. *Reducing the level of wasted materials, time and effort involved in the production process* Elimination of unnecessary wastes can significantly reduce the costs of production.

The above three universal objectives are applicable to any firm; however, there exist several other goals which may be specific to organizations.

In order for JIT management to work and be profitable, it must be fully adapted to the organization. Every organization is unique in its production processes and the goals it aims to achieve. In addition, every organization will be at a different stage in its development. The goals for each organization are unique in their priority and importance. The goals of JIT are useful in assisting the organization to define, direct and prepare for implementation. There exist short- and long-term goals, which include the following.

- *Identifying and responding to consumer needs* This goal will assist the organization in focusing on what is demanded from customers and required of production. The fundamental purpose of the organization is to produce products which its customers want, therefore, developing a manufacturing process which produces quality products will ensure the organization's viability.
- *Aiming for the optimal quality/cost relationship* Achieving quality should not be done to the point where it does not pay off for the organization. Therefore, emphasis should be placed on developing a manufacturing process that aims for zero defects. This may seem like an unrealistic goal; however, it is much less costly to the firm in the long run as it eliminates redundant functions such as inspection, rework and the production of defective products.
- *Eliminating unnecessary wastes* These are wastes that do not add value to the product.
- *Aiming for the development of trusting relationships between the suppliers* Also, relationships with just a few or even one supplier, if possible, should be focused upon. This will assist in the creation of a more efficient company in terms of inventory and materials, timeliness of deliveries and reassurance that the materials will be available when required.

- *Designing the plant for maximum efficiency and ease of manufacturing* This involves the use of machinery and labour that are absolutely essential to the manufacturing process.
- *Adopting the Japanese work ethic of aiming for continuous improvement even though high standards are already being achieved* This will ensure that the organization remains competitive by continually striving for means of fulfilling consumer demand.

Although several North American plants have adopted JIT management techniques, these firms are in the beginning stages and have not yet realized the full potential of benefits. It has taken Toyota ten years to perfect the JIT technique within its plants. Therefore, JIT is a long-term process which cannot be implemented in a short period of time, nor can its rewards be realized overnight.

JIT can offer organizations a competitive advantage which can take the form of offering consumers higher quality products than those offered by the rival firms, or providing a superior service or developing a superior means of production which allows the organization to become increasingly efficient or productive. Lubben (1988) suggests three ways JIT can assist management in obtaining a competitive advantage.

1. *Integrating and optimizing* This involves reducing the operations and resources which do not facilitate production.
2. *Improving continuously* This involves continually trying to improve processes and systems.
3. *Understanding the customer* This entails reducing the cost of products and satisfying consumer needs.

Hall (1989) suggests four areas that contribute to efficiency gains: 30–60% reductions in quality rejects, decreased production time of 50–90%, reduction of capital expenditures of 25–30%; and significant decreases in inventory costs. Another possible benefit which may be realized is the discovery of problems inherent in the production process that may surface due to streamlining or to reduction of slack within the process.

1.4 Advantages and limitations of JIT

Considerable attention has been focused on the benefits associated with the use of JIT. However, in order to properly implement JIT within an organization, managers should be aware of the limitations and short-comings of JIT which may be applicable to their organizations. An overview of the potential advantages and limitations follows.

1.4.1 Advantages of JIT

The advantages of using JIT are numerous. Several advantages mentioned already are those of waste reduction and increased ability to remain competitive. Other advantages include improved working relations between employees, stronger and more reliable working relations with suppliers, higher profits and improved customer satisfaction.

1.4.2 Limitations of JIT

Although the benefits of using JIT are numerous and cited more frequently than any potential limitations, several short-comings have been identified as follows.

- North American and Japanese cultural differences have been cited as a possible limitation of JIT. There exist many cultural differences which may be intrinsically tied to JIT success. These will be problems that may be difficult to overcome or work around without changes in attitudes and worker philosophy. The magnitude of their impact may be difficult to measure because of their nature (Hall, 1989).
- The traditional approach to manufacturing involves the use of large inventories with safety stocks. Safety stocks can act as a buffer for companies to fall back on to offset inaccurate demand forecasts. This has the potential to cause problems for the organization which relies heavily on safety stocks to absorb any increases in demand (Hall, 1989).
- The benefits associated with increased employee involvement and participation resulting from the use of quality circles may be evident in Japanese organizations. However, North American ideas of participation involve largely 'empowering' the workforce with respect to decision making. This suggests that the level of involvement established within Japanese organizations using JIT is not compatible with the degree of employee participation required to satisfy North American workers. The benefits associated with JIT may be culturally bound and somewhat limited to the Japanese environment (Klein, 1989).
- Loss of individual autonomy has been suggested as another possible short-coming of JIT. Loss of autonomy has largely been attributed to limited cycle times or the 'time between recurring activities'. Buffers such as slack or idle time are significantly reduced resulting in greater amounts of stress and pressure placed upon the worker to perform. The time which would otherwise be present would allow the worker more freedom to perform 'vertical tasks' which constitute administrative tasks or team meetings. In addition, reduced cycle times force workers to adjust immediately to changes in demand without taking their needs into consideration (Klein, 1989).
- Loss of team autonomy is a possible result of reducing or eliminating buffer inventories. This serves to reduce the flexibility of workers to discuss possible solutions to problems. This is a function of quality circles, which are an important part of JIT. Reduced buffer inventories and worker flexibility contradict the other aspects of JIT concerning quality circles (Klein, 1989).

- Loss of autonomy over methods involves the idea that, under JIT, employees must adhere to strict methods of production in order to maintain the system. This idea diminishes the 'entrepreneurial spirit' which many workers may have previously enjoyed prior to JIT implementation (Klein, 1989).
- JIT success may be 'industry specific', i.e. craft-oriented businesses are considered to be better candidates of a JIT program than organizations producing commodity-type products (Hall, 1989).
- Resistance to change (Gray and Starke, 1988) may be experienced since JIT involves an organizational level of change which will affect almost every member of the organization. Employees may resist the change based on two different levels: emotional and rational resistance. Rational resistance occurs when an individual is deficient of the necessary information and facts pertaining to the degree to which the change will affect them. Emotional resistance refers to the psychological processes of fear, anxiety and suspicion which arise from inducing change and cause resistance.

  Several common examples of these types of resistance which arise are fear of losing job security and not being provided with the necessary training to facilitate the change. However, these sources of employee resistance can be eliminated with better communication and a willingness on behalf of management to fulfill employee needs. Organizational level changes such as JIT have a significant impact upon the entire organization, therefore, a slow and well-planned implementation will assist in reducing resistance to change.

In addition to improving communication and informing employees, Hall (1989) has suggested several precautions managers can take to help avoid or diminish the negative impact of introducing JIT. First, managers should understand and become fully aware of the short-comings of JIT and how these could possibly affect their organization during implementation. It should also be realized that JIT is not a remedy for all problems, but a means of lowering costs and improving efficiency of production. Therefore, the goals an organization sets for itself should be in line with JIT capability.

Then the organization should allow for changes and flexibility once JIT is fully implemented. Successful implementation does not mean that changes will no longer occur; changes must occur for JIT to remain successful over the long run. Finally, managers must recognize that JIT involves changes in attitude which must affect or influence the organizational culture and reflect the values which are required to make JIT successful.

1.5 The rationale for implementing JIT

The impetus for implementing JIT lies largely in attaining the productivity and quality standards that many Japanese organizations enjoy. Economic conditions such as increased competition, fluctuations in the economy and consumer demands for high quality products also play a role. Stiff competition has created an environment in which only the most effective and productive firms will survive. The organizations which are quick to apply innovative ideas to their manufacturing processes will have a competitive advantage over those which do not. These firms will be able to survive and make profits over the long run.

Use of JIT manufacturing is not adversely affected by fluctuations in the economy as production is readily flexible to meet variable consumer demand. The use of JIT is appropriate in both economic upswings and downturns as it can be adjusted rather painlessly to meet any consumer demand. This is possible as it operates on a pull system where demand acts as the impulse calling the production process into action. During economic booms firms and individuals have higher demands, and production with JIT can be easily increased to meet these demands. Similarly, in economic downturns, production can be decreased to meet lower levels of consumer demand.

Other reasons for adopting JIT are the potential cost savings associated with its use. Consider the profit formula: profit = selling price × sales volume — cost. This formula represents the components of profit. Most organizations are unable single-handedly to influence the selling price of their products as the selling price is determined by market forces of supply and demand and industry standards. Therefore, if organizations wish to increase their profits, they must focus on increasing the sales volume and decreasing the cost. To increase sales volume requires better quality and delivery while reducing costs calls for reducing any unnecessary operations and wastes. JIT can assist organizations to improve the sales volume, reduce the cost component of their manufacturing processes and provide the opportunity to realize increased profits.

The savings associated with cost reductions include reduced manufacturing costs, material costs, costs of lost sales and customer goodwill. The manufacturing costs which can be reduced include costs for inspection which are necessary for products of less than 100% quality. With achievement of 100% quality levels, there is no reworking and testing required to improve quality. The cost of quality is also lowered by avoiding lost consumer goodwill, lost sales and production line stoppages. In addition, there will be less waste of time and effort in searching for flaws in the process which may be responsible for defective items.

JIT focuses on the 'value added' to products. This involves only conducting the activities and processes which build in product quality. To illustrate the concept of adding value, consider the following: the use of high quality components, assembling of these components and self-inspection of work-in-process. These activities focus on adding value. Operations such as reworking, scrapping materials and excess handling do not add value to a product. They do not change the level of quality of a product in any way, therefore these activities involve unnecessary financial costs and effort invested in production and should be avoided. They may also serve to reduce productivity levels because of the extra time required to perform these tasks. Figure 1.1 presents graphical illustrations of the waste associated with the activities which are commonly performed, without adding value to the product (Suzaki, 1987). The percentage of labour hours, material and machine usage which constitutes value added activities represents a relatively small fraction of the total.

Closely associated with the value added concept is the idea of reducing wastes. Waste can best be defined as 'anything other than the minimum amount of equipment, material, parts and working time essential to production' (Hay, 1988). There are seven categories of wastes which have been identified in several North American production plants. These wastes are the most common and occur frequently, resulting in excess costs of production. The fundamental concept underlying waste reduction requires that machinery and people do not need to be fully used at all times. They should be used only when necessary to meet demand. These seven categories are discussed below.

1. *Waste from over-production*   JIT manufacturing allows a company to produce only what is needed, operating on the demand pull concept. Therefore, in many plants that do not use the demand pull concept, over-production will occur. The wastes caused by over-production involve employee effort and time wasted in producing products which are not required.

   Excess materials require handling and movement to and from inventory. Thus there will also be large amounts of handling of the products which are not required. The more a product is handled, the greater the possibility that it will become damaged. Therefore, the less amount of handling the better it is. Over-production also involves over-usage of machinery and equipment used in the production process. Over-usage is responsible for machine breakdowns and major repairs which can impede or halt the production process. These repairs involve unnecessary costs and significantly reduce the life of machinery and equipment. Over-usage can result in an organization having to invest significant amounts of resources in capital expenditures to replace worn out machinery and equipment.

2. *The waste of motion*   Motion study involves beliefs and practices developed through scientific management. The application of scientific management to JIT involves the idea that excess handling of materials and equipment to meet over-production demands requires inefficient levels of motion and involvement on behalf of employees. The motions required to move this excess of material around the plant represent waste.

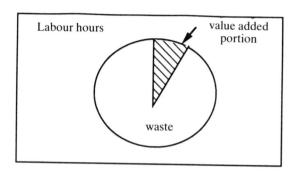

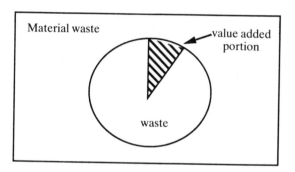

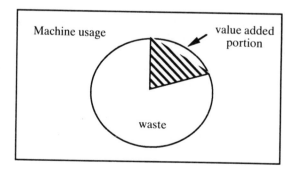

Figure 1.1 Value added pies.

3. *Transportation wastes*   These are the wastes associated with the movement of materials from inventory to different work stations. This arises from inefficient plant layout.
4. *Processing wastes*   These include the processing of parts that affect the final or finished product. These parts may or may not be a necessary step in the completion of the product. They also may not contribute to the value of the product.
5. *The waste of waiting or queuing time*   This involves the length of time inventory in transit is idle and waiting to enter the next operation. Queuing time is largely the result of inefficient work flow and can cause uneven lot sizing.
6. *Product defects*   The use of inspection after the product is made or partially completed does not allow the source of the defect to be eliminated. Inappropriate methods of monitoring quality may misguide a company into believing they are manufacturing acceptable products, when in fact they are not. A direct result of this is completion of batches of defective products.
7. *Inventory costs*   Excess production will be transferred to inventory where it runs the risk of becoming damaged or obsolete. Other unnecessary costs included are the costs of excess raw materials and component parts not required to produce the final product. The cost reductions associated with materials are estimated to be 30–50% of total operating costs. These cost reductions include the following.
   (a) *The elimination of holding inventory*   The cost savings from this are threefold: reduction of storage facilities, reduced dangers of obsolescence and of potential theft and damage to the inventory.
   (b) *The elimination of bulk breaking*   This involves the breaking down of large shipments into smaller lots which can be readily used for production purposes.
   (c) *Reduced number of suppliers*   JIT requires the use of only a few suppliers. The success of this depends upon the development of a trusting relationship between customer and supplier. It also requires supplier dependability with respect to the stock arriving when it is needed in order to fulfill consumer demands.
   (d) *The development of long-term contracts*   This helps to ensure that supplies needed for production will be received. It also removes the risk of a company not being able to negotiate a contract with a supplier in terms favorable to both. This helps to create a win–win situation for both the supplier and the manufacturer.
   (e) *Reduction in receiving inspection*   This can also be achieved as the supplier contract establishes and enforces the quality of supplies to be received.

1.6 Prerequisites to a JIT program

Prerequisites to a JIT program encompass all the actions and preparation that are required of the organization prior to embarking upon a JIT program. These typically involve plant evaluation, management influence, housekeeping activities and organizational flexibility. Each of these will be discussed separately below.

1.6.1 Plant evaluation

This is required of the organization to determine exactly where the organization stands in terms of production and workforce capability. The success of JIT management requires the organization to be able to assess its present condition and to be instrumental in making changes in the following areas.

- A flexible workforce will be a requirement; this entails workforce capability to respond to changes in demand. In addition, the workforce will have to become acquainted with the skills and knowledge required to perform a number of various tasks of production.
- There must be commitment from all involved in the organization and willingness to adapt to change.
- The idea of continuous improvement must be adopted into the philosophy and goals of the company.
- The use of teamwork becomes critically important to the development of a co-ordinated system.

In addition, evaluation becomes crucial in determining the degree of change and difficulty required for JIT implementation. The type of manufacturing process an organization engages in will allow for variations in the level of assessed change to be required. The flow of products through the manufacturing process is one factor which can determine the level of difficulty.

There are three ways in which products flow through the manufacturing process: continuous production, repetitive manufacturing and job–shop manufacturing (Lubben, 1988). Generally, the smoother the products flow through the production process, the easier it will be to adopt JIT to the existing flow system. Irregular or unpredictable flow will present a greater level of difficulty.

Adaptation of JIT is easiest with continuous production as it is typical in involving the production of a single product with only a minimal amount of interruption in the process flow. Companies which operate in a continuous production environment possess a streamlined flow process with little or no fluctuations, set-up changes and product variability. Changes which will present greater levels of difficulty will be those involving relationships with suppliers and employees and those monitoring inventory levels.

Repetitive manufacturing involves continuous manufacturing but with short production runs. Generally, the production process is not continuous as there is no demand requirement to maintain continuous production. The production process is called into action by consumer demand. Two means of adapting this process to JIT exist. The first involves converting the short runs into a continuous production process. This is accomplished by increasing volume or decreasing the rate of production to match that of the consumer requirements. The second method of adaptation involves reducing set-up times. This method allows for a reduction in excess inventories and an increase in available machine time.

Job–shop manufacturing involves production to meet variable demand, with small lot sizes and frequent set-ups. This method of manufacturing cannot easily be converted into a continuous flow form due to the random nature of customer orders. Furthermore, customer orders are usually very low in volume. Adaptation of this method to JIT will require the use of work cells arranged by product, quick and easy set-ups and procedures which minimize production costs. Establishing close relationships with customers facilitates this conversion process as demand can more accurately be assessed in a timely fashion. Accurate assessment will allow for superior scheduling and levelling of production.

1.6.2 Management influence

This will be instrumental in persuading and motivating the employees toward a JIT orientation. This is an important aspect as JIT success depends upon the degree to which employees are motivated and committed to making the process work as a co-ordinated system. To a certain extent, organizational attitudes and culture will have to be modified to mirror the beliefs that are integral to JIT success.

1.6.3 Housekeeping activities

These include management and employee efforts to reduce and eliminate the visible waste, clutter and obstacles from the production area. Unnecessary materials may present an obstacle to efficiency, safety and quality of production. The removal of unnecessary materials can also aid in the detection of other problems which may impede performance.

Housekeeping activities are closely linked to improvement activities (Suzaki, 1987). Improvement activities are those actions carried out by management and employees which, both directly and indirectly, lead to an increase in productivity and enhancement of the value of the firm's products. Housekeeping activities are associated closely with the number of defective products, level of employee morale, frequency of machine breakdowns, flow of materials, employee suggestions and inventory levels. Understanding this relationship may contribute to higher levels of production and assist improvement activities.

1.6.4 Organizational flexibility

Flexibility on the part of the organization planning to adopt JIT will also be a prerequisite. The organization may be required to respond to situations which are very different from those it is accustomed to, as JIT may inflict very new and foreign experiences on the organization. Ability to accommodate these experiences will be measured by the organization's capacity to respond quickly to these experiences and demands.

The organization should consider flexibility on four levels: adjustment to changes in volume, modification of the product mix, choice of equipment and people flexibility (Hall, 1987). These are explained below.

1. Flexibility to adjust to changes in volume pertains to the organization's willingness to plan carefully and to analyse future capital expenditures. Capital expenditures should be engaged when such purchases will assist in meeting the purposes of operations and complement the overall manufacturing processes. Flexibility of this nature also implies that organizations should strive to maintain low levels of overhead, process costs and equipment in order to achieve a low break-even point.
2. Flexibility to modify the product mix will require an organization to employ multi-skilled workers, low inventory levels with a wide variety of parts and reduced set-up times for operations.
3. Flexibility in choice of equipment for operations will be a consideration of the organization when it is faced with specific tasks. The first approach to meeting the demands of specific tasks is to adapt the existing general purpose equipment to those tasks. In the event that this approach proves to be inappropriate, equipment designed to perform the specific tasks should then be purchased or built, but at the lowest cost possible to the organization.
4. Development of employees to acquire multiple skills, or of specialists willing and able to accommodate the needs of production, should be focused on as a means of creating an organization with greater flexibility. Employing such people will allow the organization to meet variations in demand and ensure that production can continue in a smooth and steady manner. An organization which fails to cultivate flexible employees may be characterized by such occurrences as production line stoppages. Line stoppages result from employees who are hesitant to perform a necessary task because it is not directly related to their job function.

1.7 Layout of the rest of the book

The first chapter of this book on JIT management has introduced the concept of JIT with a summary of its historical background and relevance to the contemporary organization. The subsequent chapters introduce specific topics of JIT and its effects upon manufacturing processes. The literature presented describes what is considered to be 'ideal' methods and approaches to JIT implementation within an organization.

2

Just-in-time production

JIT production focuses on the elements of plant, equipment and input from employees. It encompasses the modification, rearrangement and assessment of the means of production to achieve the goals of JIT. Figure 2.1 depicts the elements of JIT production. The dedicated firm will evaluate their processes and adjust them to be compatible with the philosophy of JIT. The rest of this chapter addresses several of the components of JIT production.

Figure 2.1 JIT production.

2.1 Workplace organization

Workplace organization is a process whose purpose is to bring hidden problems to the surface and eventually eliminate these problems within an organization. It involves all units of a company, however, it commences with the plant. Once workplace organization has been initiated within the plant, it will gradually extend to other areas of the company. The concept of workplace organization is included in the policies of the organization and reflects its values and beliefs. Workplace organization commences at a rapid pace, but it slows down in response to the problems which arise during its course. There are five steps necessary to execute workplace organization. They are explained in the following sections (Buker, 1988; Hall, 1987).

2.1.1 Clearing and simplifying

This step involves removing any unnecessary materials which may hinder performance of employees and machines. Unnecessary materials include wastes and garbage, as well as tools and items which are not used in production at that point in time. Only the materials which are to be readily accessed for production should be included in the work area.

The clearing up of the work environment should not just be confined to areas affected by the build-up of unnecessary materials. It should extend into other areas and management issues, such as 'material on hold', back-up equipment, gauging, tooling and schedule stability. These issues should be brought up in an attempt to uncover the fundamental reasons behind the presence of unnecessary materials.

'Material on hold' refers to the material present on the shop floor while waiting for the next operation to commence. This deals with the issues concerned with the length of time required to make decisions and the purpose of these decisions.

Back-up equipment is often present to compensate for heavy loads of production or, if it is new equipment, to remove any 'bugs' which could impede the performance of the machines. Management should be aware as to why there is back-up equipment on the shop floor and differentiate between the functions of the plant and the engineering department.

Gauging equipment which is inaccurate and unsuitable for production needs should be removed from the plant floor. This is done to assist in maintaining appropriate and reliable measuring instruments at ready access to the employees when required.

Tooling refers to the equipment used in the various operations of production. Exactly what tools will be required for immediate use and which tools will not be used immediately should be determined. Only the tools required should be available for use. Pursuit of this goal can lead to an examination of the existing storage and categorization of tooling. An outcome of this step is to develop a superior storage area that is efficient for production use. A superior storage area is one which provides for easy access with short travelling time and tools and equipment specifically categorized for use.

Suzaki (1987) provides an illustration of how superior storage can be achieved through focusing on several aspects of the plant. These include provision of racks for the tools which are used frequently, placing operator's instruction sheets at the equipment sites, providing a visual status report by each machine indicating the status of the machine and any problems associated with its use in the past, storing tools where they are going to be used, hanging tools where they can be easily identified and labelling areas for inventory and equipment storage. Figures 2.2 and 2.3 provide an illustration of a drill press function and storage markings, indicating how operator's instructions, visual status reports, tool storage bins and labelling areas for easy identification can be located to facilitate storage.

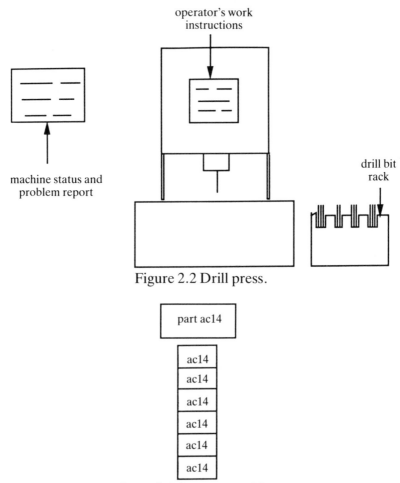

Figure 2.2 Drill press.

Figure 2.3 Storage markings.

Schedule stability offers an ideal application of the demand pull concept to organizational practices. Schedule stability requires the company to examine its customer needs in great detail in order to determine what is necessary to be present on the shop floor. This requires a company to be flexible and able to meet demand through the development of specific company practices.

2.1.2 Locating

Locating refers to the layout of operations by function and of the employees carrying out those functions. There are general rules which apply to organizations such as developing standards for proper storage places. These standards should be adhered to by all employees to ensure that tools are returned to their designated areas. For example, tools which are used for specific operations should be returned to those designated areas and tools used for operations which are of a more general nature should be returned to the general storage areas. Thus, storage areas can be sub-categorized into two broad areas of general and specific functions.

The success of locating largely depends upon the employees' willingness to comply with the standards on a continuous basis. The general rule for locating is really one of common sense. An analysis of a plant will provide the organization with the necessary information which will enable it to develop a storage area that benefits all the operations.

2.1.3 Cleaning

The purpose of cleaning is to provide a working environment which promotes quality work, safety and avoids maintenance problems. The cleanliness standards will differ from organization to organization depending upon the type of manufacturing engaged in. However, each organization should direct its cleaning efforts to achieving the above-mentioned goals. Cleaning serves two functions: to promote visibility and as preventive maintenance.

2.1.4 Discipline

Discipline requires that both employees and management at a plant should adhere to the standards and rules of workplace organization. In order that all members of an organization comply with the standards and rules, everyone should be able to participate in their creation. Provision of an opportunity for employees to assist in the development of the rules and standards will increase the chances of success as people are more apt to work toward the fulfillment of goals when they are allowed some control over their development. In addition to the success of the goals through participation, it becomes equally important that the quality of the goals developed through a participative process is increased.

2.1.5 Participation

Participation in workplace organization is not limited to one step. It is an integral part of each step and is fundamental to a successful clean-up of the organization. Participation not only includes those members of an organization who contribute on a daily basis, but members such as executives, repair people and engineers who must comply with the established rules of the organization.

The success of a company in achieving JIT production depends upon many interrelated factors. Development of appropriate and effective workplace organization standards is one such factor which will determine the level of success of manufacturing under JIT. An important factor which a company should concern itself with is soliciting ideas from employees directly involved on the plant floor. Ideas should address the development of standards and convey the importance of these standards to all employees involved with manufacturing operations. Co-ordinated and consistent effort is required to make workplace organization an operational step in the overall JIT concept.

Table 2.1 provides a checklist of duties and elements of workplace organization which should not be disregarded (Suzaki, 1987). The chart

Table 2.1 Workplace organization activities and key concepts

Activities	Key concepts
Clearing and simplifying	• removal of unnecessary tools • back-up equipment and gauging • focus on tooling, superior storage area • schedule stability
Locating	• adhere to standards • appropriate placement of tools and equipment
Cleaning	• environment of safety and quality enhancement • maintenance problem reduction • promote visibility and preventive maintenance • provide charts, logs and signals • limits inventory • periodic reassessments (disposal notice cards, monthly reviews)
Discipline	• participative processes • adherence to rules
Who participates	• internal and external members of the organization

represents a brief summary of the steps and key concepts presented in each phase of workplace organization.

2.2 Visibility

Visibility refers to the cleanliness of the workplace atmosphere, where activities and parts can easily be identified without obstruction. Preventive maintenance refers to the general organization of the workplace and how it functions as a whole to maintain facilities and avoid mishaps. Achieving a clean environment offers employees immediate feedback of the current status of the plant. Visibility is achieved by posting schedules which inform everyone. All employees and supervisors will have ready access to the same information.

The layout of the plant under JIT production takes on work cells which allow all employees working within those cells to see what is occurring during various stages of the manufacturing process. Therefore, the layout of the plant in itself assists in promoting visibility. The use of charts and logs can convey to employees the important and immediate actions which must be taken first.

Machinery and equipment which is furnished with signal lights can indicate to employees the immediate malfunction of machinery. This allows problems to be recognized and corrected with minimum delays. Signal lights can also be used to indicate to employees when equipment should be changed or when quality checks should be carried out. Provision of signal lights on machinery and other processes which allow the immediate detection of malfunctions is known as a 'fail-safe method' and will be discussed further in this book.

Visibility is facilitated through the use of colour coded containers for storing parts and tools (Potter and Buker, 1988). Colour coded containers serve to perform several functions. One is to designate material used in specific work areas of a plant. Another is to assist in identifying parts unique to a specific product in a mixed model assembly and simultaneously safeguard the process against possible errors. Empty colour coded containers may, in certain organizations, act as a signal to replenish inventory. Work-in-process inventory is monitored by the quantity of containers present on the plant floor. Finally, empty colour coded containers may serve as a means of identifying the quantity of product to be produced.

Another form of visibility system used by many organizations is known as a signal marker. Signal markers are 'flags placed within a stack of containers holding a particular part in an outbound stock point', (Potter and Buker, 1988). Signal markers act as a mechanism for replenishing inventory. During the production process inventory is withdrawn from a stock point. Once the signal flag is reached, employees realize the inventory from the stock point has been depleted and the flag serves as a warning sign to restore inventory to the pre-established level. The use of clearly marked outbound stock

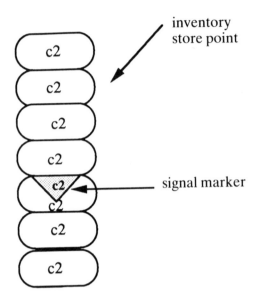

Figure 2.4 Signal markers.

points is essential to synchronizing the product flow and requires a minimum amount of supervision. Figure 2.4 illustrates the use of a signal flag to replenish inventory.

In addition to the benefits a company receives from the use of visibility systems with respect to production control, Potter and Buker (1988) identify six ways in which visibility is capable of relaying the status of the production process to management, and communication of status is accomplished.

1. Control boards, indicating the achievement of daily production goals, are capable of displaying production goals achieved on shorter than a daily basis, such as up-to-the-minute goals.
2. Fail-safe methods such as colour coded ranges on gauges and control charts display the status of the production processes. These charts and gauges indicate if the processes are operating in control.
3. Operator instructions indicating the preventive maintenance procedures and the daily start-up routine accompany each machine.
4. Diagrams and pictures in the plant serves two purposes. The first is to illustrate the steps of product assembly. The second is to indicate the nature of defects to employees. An awareness of defects allows employees to readily identify when production processes are out of control.

5. Boards equipped with lights, otherwise known as 'Andon', identify the status of production processes. For example, when the boards are showing all green lights, this indicates to the employees that the processes are running correctly. Red lights often indicate that machines are shut down. Boards indicating yellow lights indicate that a process requires operator assistance.

6. Visibility systems are useful in relaying the achievement of goals and improvements in the production processes. Visibility systems are also instrumental in identifying the level of waste reduction, defects, work-in-process inventory, lead time reduction and reduced work space. Knowledge of plant status allows the employees to identify the areas which require improvement.

Finally, there should be limits placed on the level of inventory which is allowed to build up prior to operations. Areas within the plant should be chosen specifically for the purpose of storing inventory. The use of designated areas for holding inventory can provide stopping signals for production once the inventory within the area has been depleted.

Reassessing the need for tools should occur on a periodic basis to ensure that parts which were once thought to be, but are no longer, of primary importance to the manufacturing process are removed from the plant work areas (Suzaki, 1987). Examples include the use of disposal notice cards and monthly reviews.

Disposal notice cards

This entails the use of cards on a plant-wide basis by workers from different departments. The process is initiated by identifying all goods and tools which are not necessary. Cards are subsequently attached to these potentially useless items indicating what the item is, why it is present on the plant floor, which unit it belongs to and when to dispose of it. The disposal or

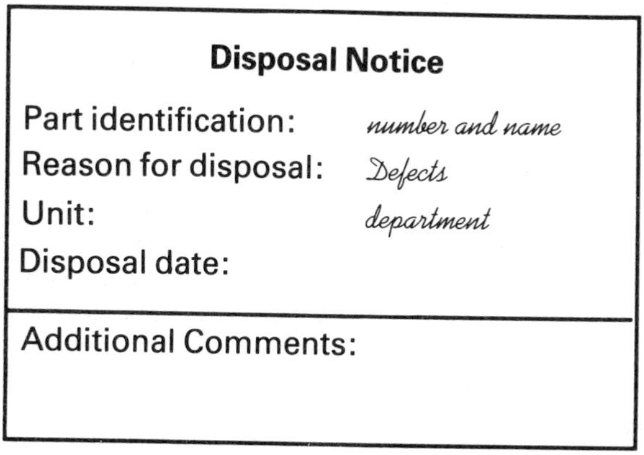

Disposal Notice

Part identification: *number and name*
Reason for disposal: *Defects*
Unit: *department*
Disposal date:

Additional Comments:

Figure 2.5 An example of disposal notice cards.

probation period should be long enough (approximately one to three months) to ensure that the item is in fact unusable and its elimination will not place undue stress upon any operation in the manufacturing process.

Once the one to three month period has ended, all cards should be evaluated to identify which parts should be kept and which should be eliminated. Deciding whether a part will be kept or not is determined by employees' written suggestions stating there is a need for that particular part. If no such response is received, the part will be eliminated. Refer to Figure 2.5 for an example of a disposal notice card.

Monthly reviews

Monthly reviews entail the introduction of teams or groups, composed of several employees from various disciplines in the company, to tour and evaluate areas of the plant in accordance with workplace organization standards. Results of monthly reviews are made available to the plant employees and the areas which have exhibited superior workplace organization practices are rewarded for their efforts.

2.3 Preventive maintenance

Preventive maintenance is another important aspect of workplace organization. It has been viewed as a necessary ingredient in the pursuit of manufacturing excellence. An organization without preventive maintenance runs the risk of facing accidents and safety problems, substantial repair costs and out-of-control manufacturing processes. Preventive maintenance procedures should be an ongoing and integral part of the workplace. Maintaining the operating ability of machines encompasses the majority of preventive maintenance activities, therefore; a significant portion of these activities should be the responsibility of the machine operators. Machine operators work on a regular basis with equipment and have developed a certain familiarity or 'feel' for the machines. Familiarity with machine functioning allows operators to recognize when a process will need adjusting to avoid the production of defective products. Furthermore, those who work on a regular basis with machines possess a deeper understanding of machines and are less likely to mishandle them (Hall, 1987).

Preventive maintenance is not solely the responsibility of one individual or a single department in a plant. Effective maintenance policies are implemented and practised by a number of employees on a plant-wide basis. Employees who play an active role in preventive maintenance procedures are machine operators and maintenance crews. The combined effort of operators and maintenance crews should be evident with everyday maintenance practices as well as the development of solutions to problems when they arise (Suzaki, 1987).

Procedures for conducting preventive maintenance

Preventive maintenance can be compared to a mechanic giving a car a spring tune-up or to a yearly visit to the doctor. The whole purpose underlying preventive maintenance is to intercept the small problems before they develop into big problems. Many organizations fail to recognize the importance of preventive maintenance and the significant role it plays in allowing organizations to achieve manufacturing excellence.

An organization should 'aim for zero failure, zero trouble, and minimum waste' (Suzaki, 1987). The initial step to achieving this is to realize that people are responsible for problems. It follows that, if people are responsible, then something can be done to prevent the problems from recurring. Preventive maintenance activities will be applied to machines, safety and accident-proofing of the plant. The main overall goal of a maintenance program is to ensure that machines are capable of operating at all times within specified tolerances (Darress, 1988).

Factors which directly influence the effectiveness of preventive maintenance programs include the size of the plant, labour force, approach to maintenance, number of machines to be maintained and the nature of inventory (Darress, 1988). The application of computer programs to disperse information, such as the timing of work orders, can simplify the process of preventive maintenance. Work order catalogues permit the prioritizing, categorizing, planning, cost estimation, releasing and execution, and comparison of actual and estimated labour and material costs. The allocation of tasks, material and labour, and the assignment of due dates are examples of the functions of work orders.

There are several categories of work orders and they include the following.

- *Preventive* work orders, such as inspections and machine maintenance. Additional work orders are issued to upgrade machines operating outside specified tolerance levels.
- *Scheduled* work orders, which includes the extra work orders initiated to repair machines with inadequate operating capability.
- *Unscheduled* work orders, initiated to complete emergency repairs such as when a machine breaks down, and for which documentation is required.
- *Emergency* work orders, issued when the plant is in a disastrous condition. This type of work order is not initialized to repair machines, but rather to upgrade safety conditions. All documentation is returned subsequent to the completion of repairs.
- *Predictive* work orders, which involve the use of sensors, artificial intelligence and the collection of information to interpret and determine when preventive maintenance activities should be performed on machines.

- *Project or major maintenance* work orders, which address the overhauling of machines and major repairs. Projects are planned and executed to upgrade equipment and improve processes.

The activities which apply to preventing machine breakdowns entail three steps: maintaining normal machine conditions, detecting abnormal conditions as early as possible and developing and implementing counter-measures to recover the normal conditions.

Maintenance of normal machine conditions requires several activities which should be carried out by employees and maintenance crews. The activities involve inspection and cleaning of machines, tightening loose bolts and maintaining proper operating procedures.

Detection of abnormal conditions relies upon the accuracy of measuring and gauging equipment, as well as the ability of operators to sense when machines are not functioning normally. Detection is made possible through the use of operators' five senses: seeing the process is out of control, smelling unusual odours, the feel that certain parts such as belts may be unusually tight or loose, or hearing the machine make unfamiliar sounds; in the case of food or drink production, the machine may be producing a product which does not taste right. Application of inspection and diagnostic equipment can detect any abnormalities in the process which may be overlooked by human senses.

Counter-measures can be applied to the process in an attempt to return operations to their normal conditions. Development of counter-measures is possible by asking oneself 'why' five times. This is a practice suggested by Taiichi Ohno (Suzaki, 1987). Asking why five times increases the possibility of correctly identifying the cause of the abnormalities in the process. Once the cause is determined, new standards can be developed addressing the issue of prevention.

Determining the correct cause of abnormalities is not an easy task, as in most cases the problems are not obvious. Machine problems can be categorized into two groups of problems: suddenly exposed problems and chronic problems. Chronic problems present more difficulties even after the cause has been identified. This type of problem may reoccur subsequent to the implementation of counter-measures. For this reason, it benefits the firm to maintain an ongoing awareness of chronic problems affecting machines. In the event that more than one cause is identified, counter-measures should be developed for each.

Five of the most common causes of machine problems are:
1. failure to maintain machines, i.e. cleaning and minor repairs;
2. failure to maintain operating conditions, i.e. temperature, speed;
3. insufficient skills such as improper operation and errors;
4. machine deterioration, i.e. bearings, belts; and
5. poor design such as the wrong materials, sizes.

Awareness of these potential problems may assist employees and maintenance crews with identifying problems associated with their machines.

Maintenance procedures

There are several maintenance procedures which can be applied to machines and tools. The most significant of these activities is cleaning and inspection. These two activities can occur simultaneously. Other activities which address machine and tool maintenance focus on the care and prevention of problems rather than finding solutions to problems.

Four steps are applied to preventive maintenance for machines, as identified by Suzaki (1987). Each of these steps involves the participation of machine operators. The first step includes cleaning and inspection activities which deals with machine deterioration. The activities required at this step include minor adjustments such as oiling, and tightening bolts. Larger, more encompassing activities will involve the restoration of machines to their original condition, in the event deterioration has occurred.

The second step of preventive maintenance again addresses deterioration. However, this deterioration is 'natural' to the machines; it will occur regardless of whether preventive maintenance activities were performed or not. This is the stage where the benefits of preventive maintenance activities carried out in step one will be realized.

The third step is concerned with continuous action against machine deterioration. Operators continue to play an active role in preventive maintenance procedures. Their function at this point is to apply their knowledge to identify abnormalities in the functioning of the processes and repair these whenever possible. In addition to this, operators' skills are relied upon to safeguard against machine misuse and to improve machine design so as to further 'foolproof' the system.

The fourth step involves condition-based maintenance procedures. Machines are initially monitored by operators, then diagnostic equipment is applied to the machines for further monitoring. The success of monitoring through the use of diagnostic equipment is only realized when machines are operating under prescribed conditions. Diagnostic equipment functions to monitor the quality and life of manufactured parts through the use of pulse and ultrasonic meters.

The relationship between JIT and preventive maintenance

JIT and preventive maintenance procedures are closely linked. Preventive maintenance functions as a sub-structure for the realization of JIT goals. Many elements of preventive maintenance are interdependent with JIT. The relationship which exists between the two serves to substantiate the importance of preventive maintenance for firms undergoing JIT implementation. The dependency relationship is expressed through sixteen elements, identified by Darress (1988) and presented in Table 2.2.

Table 2.2 PM/JIT Chart

Element	Preventive maintenance	JIT
Machine availability	periodic maintenance	demand pull
Elimination of waste	machines operating	simplification of process
SPC, TQC	improve process	regulation of process
	TQC	
SPC, JIT, TQC	team effort	improved set-ups
	improved set-ups	
Reduction of inventory	problems surface	problems surface
	easy identification of operations outside of tolerance	
Demand pull process	reduce machine downtime	level loading
Machine maintenance	emergency repairs	first stage maintenance such as minor repairs and cleaning conducted by operators
	PM activities and scheduling	
Maintenance initiation	procedural activities	kanbans sent into process by operator observation
Preventive maintenance scheduling	co-ordinated with JIT	co-ordinated with PM
	measure machine downtime with throughput	
Reduction of cycle time	frequent, less time-consuming set-ups	reduce lot sizes
Reduce unit costs	lower overheads	eliminate waste

Engineering excellence	operators communicate machine specifications to engineering	process control data relayed to engineers
Firefighting	reduce emergency situations increase PM activities	demand pull reduction of scrap and rework
Customer relationships	teamwork increased productivity	downstream employees
Vendor relationships	equipment and tools	improve product and process quality
On-time performance	increases due to less waste, rework, scrap	increased manufacturability

Implementing preventive maintenance

Preventive maintenance, when successfully integrated and managed within a plant, assists a company with the achievement of JIT goals. Many organizations search for quick fix ideas to resolve organizational deficiencies. Preventive maintenance is not a quick-fix answer. Tackling implementation can prove to be taxing on the ingenuity and resourcefulness of a company as there is no single method which is exclusively correct. Successful implementation is dependent upon a company's ability to deduce organizational specifics with the greatest relevance towards preventive maintenance.

Although no specific implementation algorithm exists, Darress (1988) has suggested several general elements essential to successful implementation:

- management commitment to the activities;
- fostering a sense of employee ownership in the activities;
- provision of an awareness and education of JIT, total quality control (TQC) and statistical process control (SPC) issues;
- conducting employee surveys to determine individual needs awareness;
- studying customers;
- determining specific areas within the plant to carry out pilot projects for preventive maintenance procedures;
- eliminating waste and simplifying processes;
- documenting all activities and results;
- automating all the processes which are in their most simplified state;
- planning and developing time frames and establishing employee responsibilities for implementation;
- questioning all activities; and
- extending beyond the pilot projects and establishing preventive maintenance throughout the rest of the plant.

Preventive maintenance is largely a quality issue as it encompasses all activities carried out to ensure the production of products which meet quality standards. Preventive maintenance activities can be extended to safety issues at a manufacturing plant. Its application to safety becomes especially important when hazardous materials are a necessary ingredient of the manufacturing process. The activities which can be applied to hazardous chemical use include holding in inventory only the quantity of the chemical required for immediate use, and using the oldest material first to avoid leakages and damage to containers.

Total productive maintenance

Total productive maintenance (TPM) is defined as 'a partnership between the maintenance and production organizations to improve product quality, reduce waste, reduce manufacturing cost, increase equipment availability, and improve the company's overall state of maintenance' (Rhyne, 1990). The numerous definitions of TPM contain common elements which, when extracted, apply to the maintenance and improvements in machinery, labour and maintenance systems. These elements have been identified as:

- upgrading and maximizing equipment effectiveness;
- applying computer-aided technology to assist equipment;
- developing schedules to increase equipment availability;
- developing preventive maintenance programs for equipment; and
- total employee involvement.

Total employee involvement will be required in different areas throughout the plant. Participation in TPM is not exclusive to any single department or operation. Work teams or the formation of small groups are representative of the types of employee involvement strategies used within the TPM sphere. The use of work teams is instrumental in achieving improvements and promoting TPM issues. The main participants in carrying out TPM methods are mechanics, repair crews and machine operators. These three groups actively participate in TPM methods such as:

- performing routine maintenance tasks;
- operators assisting mechanics and repair crews with minor repairs;
- mechanics assisting operators with equipment shut-downs and start-ups;
- reserving highly skilled workers for special tasks, while delegating the routine tasks to less skilled employees;
- using groups or teams to promote TPM activities;
- using teams to identify areas in the plant for improvement activities; and
- upgrading employees' knowledge of maintenance, equipment and manufacturing.

Employees of the production department assume an important role under a TPM perspective. Training should be provided to enhance the functioning of TPM and should be directed toward teaching production employees to carry out housekeeping activities and minor maintenance

Table 2.3 TPM/TQC Chart – solutions to potential problems

	TPM	TQC
	machine breakdowns	defective products
traditional approach	replace the damaged part	final product inspection, rework, defect goes to scrap
improvement	preventive maintenance activities	in-process inspection
	condition-based maintenance	fail-safing the process
	maintenance prevention	quality design
monitoring	machine problems	SPC charting
basic approaches	training and education	training and education
	employee involvement	employee involvement
	'maintenance is free'	'quality is free'

procedures, learning how to operate machines properly, and identifying possible deterioration problems before they cause serious damage to equipment. Maintenance employees take on the tasks of assisting production employees with maintenance, adjusting, inspecting and restoring deteriorated machines, altering machine designs to compensate for weaknesses and increasing operators' maintenance skills.

TPM contrasted to preventive maintenance is comparatively novel in its impact upon an organization. An organization becomes 'cultured' to the beliefs and attitudes characteristic of TPM methods. The employees within a company which adheres to TPM will have strong beliefs in directing the organization toward accomplishing permanent improvements in productivity and preventive maintenance activities will assume a new level of importance. Due to the significance of its impact upon an organization, TPM cannot be undertaken and successfully implemented within a short period of time. The process of implementation may take two or three years to complete. There are significant differences between the approach toward traditional maintenance procedures and TPM. The following characterize TPM (Rhyne, 1990).

- TPM is included in the organization's business strategy.
- The goal is to eliminate equipment breakdowns.
- Expenses are planned and controlled.
- Machinery selection and design is executed with TPM as a guideline.
- Inventory is made increasingly more compatible with the manufacturing processes with respect to availability and timing of the correct parts.
- Quality becomes every employee's concern.
- Teams who assume an active role in organizational concerns are introduced.
- Total quality control (TQC) and total people involvement (TPI) are combined.
- TPM is an integral part of manufacturing.
- 100% quality is pursued 100% of the time.
- Manufacturing processes are arranged in conjunction with preventive maintenance activities.
- Continuous improvement is adopted.

Provision of the right material at the right time, pursuit of 100% quality, 100% of the time and the focus on continuous improvement are goals integral to JIT. Therefore, the use of TPM complements the activities which are endorsed through JIT manufacturing. Total quality control (TQC) is also an integral part of JIT. Strong emphasis on the level of quality of the products produced under JIT manufacturing substantiates the importance of total quality control. Numerous similarities as illustrated in Table 2.3 can be drawn between TPM and TQC (Suzaki, 1987).

The implementation of TPM involves considerable time, effort and ingenuity on part of a firm. Planning plays an important role in the success of such an endeavour to co-ordinate and integrate processes into a finely tuned system. Planning should address the events which can send operations out of synchronization or unbalance product flow. Consideration should be given to the following (Rhyne, 1990).

- Machine downtimes such as equipment breakdowns and those associated with the time required to adjust operations following set-ups.
- Losses on the rate of production such as that due to idling and stoppages and reduced speed as a result of design differences.
- The level of manufacturing defects and decreased yields. Process defects include scraps and repairs. Decreased output of the process is the result of the extended measure of time required for a machine to engage in stable production beginning with start-up.

The potential benefits to be realized through the use of TPM overshadow those received from the use of a traditional approach to preventive maintenance. The benefits of such a system are reduced product costs, improved quality, employee empowerment over their jobs, increased employee flexibility, a co-ordinated work effort, lowered levels of emergency work and reduced equipment downtime.

Implementing TPM

The goal with respect to maintenance is to develop employee skills and initiative toward caring for equipment. Once employees have mastered their skills to reach beyond simply cleaning machines to the application of an innovative approach to maintenance, then TPM has taken effect. This transition is termed 'autonomous maintenance' (Rhyne, 1990). Seven steps have been developed to assist employees with achieving autonomous maintenance work activities.

1. *Initial cleaning*, which includes removing dust from the equipment, oiling, tightening loose belts, bolts etc., identifying minor problems and repairing them.
2. *Counter-measures* at the source of problems, which requires employees to determine the cause of dust, suggest possible means to improve difficult to clean and maintain parts and reduce the length of time needed to perform these activities.
3. *Cleaning and lubrication standards*, which should be developed and which address opportunities to improve daily activities such as cleaning.
4. *General inspection*, in which employees correct minor defects identified during inspection, in accordance with instructions.
5. *Autonomous inspection* in which an autonomous inspection worksheet is developed and applied to operations.
6. *Orderliness and tidiness* involving the standardization of the workplace and systemization of maintenance and apply to inspection standards, cleaning and daily maintenance, recording of data and parts and tool maintenance.

Table 2.4 Factors responsible for machine trouble

Machines	Operators	Maintenance crews
Dirt in the machine Dirt in the oil	• lack of concern over dirt	• repair the machine, do not question the cause
Flooded oil pan	• mistakes occur in operation	• fail to work with and inform operators on machine maintenance
Leaking oil Empty oiler	• lack of inspection knowledge	• lack of effective communication with operators
Motor overheating Motor is noisy	• maintenance is difficult	
Vibration Scattered chips	• lack of machine knowledge	• tend to emergencies, ignore ongoing quality issues
Inspection difficulties		
Dirt on floor	• do not pursue help for maintenance or problem assistance	• attitude that machine deterioration will occur regardless
Cluttered work area	• emphasize production, not maintenance procedures	
Poor organization	• lack of control over machines	• ignore available resources to solve problems, look for new ones

7. *Full autonomous maintenance*, enhancing organizational maintenance policies and engaging in improvement activities on a continuous basis.

Preventive maintenance applies to machines as well as to the tools which are used to maintain the machines. Software is a tool which has applications to many machines, although it is not frequently recognized as a tool. The advent of sophisticated equipment for production purposes is one determinant of increased software usage. Examples of software uses in the plant include numerical control tapes and downloading programs to machines.

Preventive maintenance with respect to software closely resembles the preventive maintenance issues which concern complex equipment. Hall (1987) outlines five issues relating to software:

1. *Substantiation of existing machine and conditions status.* This can be accomplished by documentation on the software itself. Separate documentation can be used, however, this will require periodic updating, simplifying and standardizing. This also applies to complex machinery.
2. *Preventive maintenance for software.* This will require continuous attention to preserve its compatibility with hardware, and also applies to complex machinery, especially if machinery requirements include the need to be flexible. The functioning of preventive maintenance is to ward against obsolescence.
3. *The presence of several individuals who possess the ability to interpret and diagnose software.* This is an advantage to the firm, and further applies to the use of complex machinery, though while benefiting a firm, training of this nature can place stress on valuable company resources.
4. *Understanding and mastering the ability to use several programming languages.* This is an important aspect of co-ordinating the system, and not all programmers possess this ability. Training can be difficult.
5. *Storing software.* The closeness to processes is an important aspect of its flexibility, but however numerous the benefits may be, there are potential disadvantages; storing software close to the operations increases the risk of it being damaged or stolen.

Several common factors which lead to machine problems have been identified (Suzaki, 1987). Table 2.4 provides a comprehensive list of factors and the roles that machines, operators and maintenance crews play in allowing these problems to appear.

2.4 JIT production planning

JIT production planning involves the elements which most closely affect the actual production method. They include the various components of the production system such as the type and role of machinery and equipment and the function of the workers. JIT production planning will demand changes in the physical flow of products through the production lines, as the firm seeks to adopt a customer-oriented approach. Other elements of JIT production planning include altering the configuration of the plant and

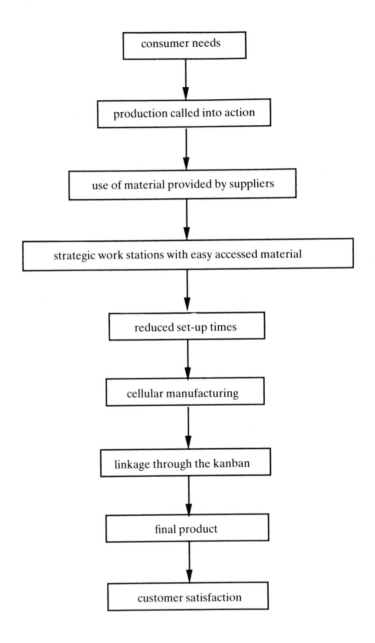

Figure 2.6 The demand pull concept.

equipment, changing the role of workers, scheduling manufacturing to match the demand pull concept, reducing set-up times and adopting a total approach to quality. Reduction of manufacturing lead times and inventory levels is necessary to realize the real potential of JIT manufacturing. Each of these elements of JIT production planning will be discussed in detail in the following sections.

The different elements of JIT production planning, which involves considerable plant changes and adoption of innovative production techniques, can be explained by using the concept of demand pull production and having all other elements stem from this idea. The demand pull concept refers to the manner in which materials are 'pulled' through the production process. The items necessary for production in a workstation are pulled from the preceding workstation only as required. This is in stark contrast with traditional manufacturing where items from one workstation are 'pushed' onto the succeeding workstation indiscriminately, regardless if this workstation is ready to receive and process the items. Following this method of product flow, the formation of long waiting lines and bottlenecks are likely to occur.

The elements of JIT production planning can best be explained pictorially as in Fig. 2.6, which illustrates the application of the various manufacturing techniques and plant arrangement designed to facilitate the flow of products. Every action a company takes to change its existing manufacturing practices in order to accomplish JIT manufacturing must be taken with the concept of demand pull in mind.

2.4.1 Customer orientation

The customer-oriented approach applies to JIT manufacturing from two perspectives. The first perspective imposes a 'symbolic' role on the employees who perform the manufacturing functions. Each employee views all other employees as customers. Parts or components are passed from one employee to the next employee to meet his processing demands, just as the final product is passed to the customers to fulfill their requirements. Most organizations undergoing a JIT program adopt and assign this symbolic role to their employees. The second perspective involves meeting customers' needs outside the organization. The role of demand pull in this sense is to determine the quantity of goods which external customers will purchase. Thus the demand pull system is a customer-oriented approach. In summary, the function of demand pull serves two purposes: to direct production flow and to determine the quantity of goods to be produced.

The use of a demand pull system is a relatively simple concept, however, it can impose difficulties upon an organization. The source of these difficulties arises from viewing production from an old-fashioned perspective. Emphasis in production planning from a North American point of view has been largely from the perspective of a push system – 'how much can we get the customer to buy?' – rather than trying to find out and satisfy the customer's needs. Under the push mode of manufacturing, parts are pushed onto the next operation once they are through with the prior operation. It assumes a 'ready or not' position (Kinsey, 1987). On the contrary, the pull mode of manufacturing only allows parts to be moved from the previous operation to the next when the subsequent operation is ready to process.

Several advantages and disadvantages of the push and pull systems have been identified (Civerolo, 1990). The main advantages of using a push system are spreading overhead costs and continuous utilization of people and equipment. Other advantages are that:

- push systems do provide visibility within the plant allowing the comparison of actual to planned production;
- push systems allow for the development of cohesive, well-integrated production plans, which are encompassing and reflect ideal plant conditions, although they are frequently inoperable;
- push systems are most familiar to employees due to their past and continued use in manufacturing plants; and
- the flexibility of push systems allows production of various product types.

The major disadvantages of the push system include increases in work-in-process inventory due to poor linkage between operations and lack of co-ordinated teamwork. Other disadvantages are given below.

- Significant capital investment in employees and information processing equipment to prepare the system for operation.
- Inventory will be expensive to maintain and is laden with inaccuracies due to the method with which it is stored and accessed under a push system.
- Numerous assumptions about production processes concerning set-up times, cycle time and machine downtime are made which frequently do not realistically reflect actual operations. Another assumption is made about the steadiness of production processes, while in practice they can and frequently do vary from time to time.
- Push systems are unable to meet the idiosyncrasies of production. They lack the level of responsiveness required to maintain a smooth production run. For example, push systems disregard the production of defective products, machine breakdowns, labour shortages and other problems which arise in the normal course of operations. Failure to recognize and work with these problems leads to stockpiling of inventory on the plant floor.

The main advantages of pull systems are to link various production operations, keep a low and stable level of inventory and add value to units which are required to meet demand. Other advantages are given below.

- Pull systems are relatively inexpensive as they do not require a comprehensive entourage of employees and information processing equipment to be functional.

- Inventory is not perpetual, therefore, documentation is kept to a minimum and few ínaccuracies arise.
- Production control is executed through the use of kanbans. It does not operate under a number of inaccurate assumptions. Pull systems do not treat production as fixed. Accordingly, the production model reflects the actual production.
- Pull systems by far outreach the responsiveness of a push system. The responsiveness of the system to changes and problems which arise in upstream processes allows the downstream processes to be shut down. This prevents the accumulation of inventory on the plant floor.

The main disadvantages of pull systems are that people and equipment may not be fully in use at all times and the inventory cost may not be spread among all operations. Other disadvantages include the factors considered benefits with push systems.

- Pull systems do not provide the same degree of visibility as push systems because there is no development of detailed plans. Furthermore, employees are required to observe and take actions on the floor.
- The majority of organizations are unfamiliar with a pull system.
- Pull systems do not maintain the same level of flexibility as push systems. They are most successful with repetitive manufacturing systems. Thus, the production of a wide range of products would not be facilitated.

Weighing the advantages with the disadvantages of the pull system, one would discover that such a system has beneficial impact upon the efficiency and productivity of the plant. Another key advantage of the demand pull concept, due to the linking of operations through kanbans, is the ability to stop the entire production line at once in the presence of production problems. This becomes especially favorable when quality problems arise or when employees experience difficulties with a process.

Accompanying the demand pull concept is the notion that idle workers and processes will become an essential functioning of operations. This may be a difficult idea to accept given the traditional emphasis on reducing idle time. However, this mode of thinking has its advantages. Engaging workers and equipment only when necessary frees up workers to focus on different tasks and lessens the load placed on equipment which would otherwise be used continuously. Increased availability of workers provides time to participate in team problem solving and engage in multi-task operations. Reducing the strain on equipment and machinery decreases the maintenance and replacement costs of worn-out parts.

Demand pull is also known as 'pure kanban'. It is especially applicable to repetitive manufacturing where the same parts are produced over and over again. Pure kanban for repetitive manufacturing indicates when and what to manufacture, not how much to manufacture. However, a demand pull system may not be appropriate for producing parts characterized by infrequent or seasonal demand. This is where the 'hybrid method' comes into play (Civerolo, 1990). The hybrid method overcomes the short-comings of the demand pull system when applied to non-repetitive manufacturing. One of the short-comings includes indicating which part is required for the various products, not only indicating when it should be made. This method is aptly named, as it involves a combination of kanbans and schedules. Pure kanban does not differentiate between the types of products being manufactured.

Advantages which are common to both the pure kanban and hybrid methods include the following (Civerolo, 1990).

- Each technique is relatively easy to understand.
- Both techniques are capable of signalling when to call operations into action.
- Reduced inventory levels allow previously hidden problems to surface. Problems are easily identified and operations are easier to put back on track.
- Out-of-balance capacity is easily identified. This is known as visual capacity control.
- The use of demand pull can assist an organization in reducing queues indirectly, upon the resolution of queuing problems.
- Lead times, overhead activity and inventory are reduced. Inventory is handled by those directly involved in the production processes.

To implement the pull system, a number of prerequisites, as suggested by Civerolo (1990), should be considered. An awareness of the prerequisites should aid managers in understanding the requirements and their impact upon the plant and people. The prerequisites include the following.

1. *The pull rule is in effect* This rule maintains that production only occurs as needed and, in order to make the system succeed, everyone must obey it. Production is controlled by the downstream workstation and authorized through a signal. If no signal to produce is received, the internal supplier should produce nothing. This prerequisite also addresses the issue of not keeping workers busy all the time. Demand pull acknowledges that it is necessary to have idle workers and machines, and line stoppages are no longer forbidden, sometimes even desirable. In order to have the rule fully adhered to, it is crucial to communicate to workers that idle time does not mean future lay-offs. The purpose of demand pull is not to reduce labour. Idle employees can be further put to use in other areas of the plant.

2. *Repetitive usage* With repetitive usage, the assumption that whatever is used is repeated only holds true for repetitive manufacturing. Seasonal demand, infrequent usage and 'one-time specials' can lead to excess inventory build-up. The hybrid technique should be used in these circumstances.

3. *Separation of products*   Manufacturing of products distinct from one another requires inventory of each item and storage space for each. The hybrid technique should be used to deal with some of these problems.
4. *Lot sizing*   This addresses the question of how many parts should be made. Under demand pull the objective is to make lot sizes as small as practical. The benefits of reducing lot sizes include reduced queue and lead time, and reductions in scrap and waste. This can be successfully accomplished; however, there are obstacles which the organization should effectively remove first. These obstacles include long set-up or changeover times, increased paperwork for inventory and purchase orders, increased material handling and disagreement among employee opinions regarding large versus small lot sizes.
5. *Short lead times*   Parts are required to be ready and available when needed by the internal customer. If parts are not ready to enter the next operation when they are required, inventory can build up.
6. *Reliable processes*   They are required to reduce inventory buffers or safety stock. Defect-free parts must be produced in each process in order to avoid delays. Poor quality will create scrap, rework and delays, and increase lead times and overall costs.
7. *Excellent material planning*   This means the provision of the right material in the correct amounts at the required work station. Prerequisites to the attainment of excellent material planning include a well-planned master schedule and bill of materials, inventory accuracy, supplier knowledge of requirements and a well-coordinated and timed set of operations.
8. *Excellent capacity planning*   This includes maintaining balance between different work stations. In the event that the system runs out of synchronization, there are a number of steps which can be executed to resolve the situation. These include increasing or decreasing the rate of operations on the upstream and downstream processes respectively, transferring more workers to the upstream processes, allowing for more overtime or extra shift work and increasing inventory buffers.
9. *Provision of a control mechanism*   Control mechanisms function as a means of linking operations and demand together.
10. *Standard containers* should be used at each workstation.
11. *Inventory and product flow* easily identified. Routings should be clearly designated to avoid delays in the process.
12. *Each part should have one original location*   This assists employees in determining where parts were extracted and allows inventory levels to be accurately estimated.
13. *Redesign the plant layout*   This is done to accommodate changes in demand and simultaneously avoiding major upsets in the production processes and balance of flow.

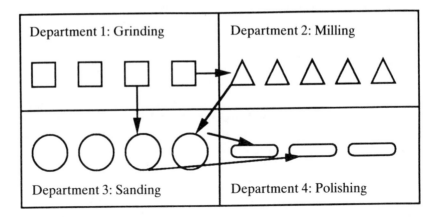

Figure 2.7 Cellular manufacturing.

2.4.2 Plant arrangement for JIT production

The implementation of a JIT production system requires that the plant layout be changed to facilitate worker flexibility and contact. The typical and widely practised plant layout of machinery and equipment involves specialization of activities and organization by processes rather than products. JIT production adopts a plant layout which is arranged according to product flows. Each product will be produced in a number of manufacturing stages following the required processing sequence. Parts delivered by suppliers enter the production process and become component parts upon intermediate processing. The component parts are then assembled into the finished product to be shipped to the customer.

The primary goal of JIT production is the achievement of a high standard of production efficiency. Efficiency encompasses the production of a better product with less time, waste and effort. Reducing manufacturing lead times and space required for inventory and operations are two necessary steps taken to accomplish JIT manufacturing. Reduction of space and time in production can be accomplished effectively through the application of cellular manufacturing. Cellular manufacturing can best be defined as 'the linking of operations according to their various part families, and likeness of manufacturing process, as opposed to the traditional groupings of machines according to functional capability, such as drills in one department and lathes in another' (Goddard, 1986).

Manufacturing by product is compatible with the ultimate goal of JIT manufacturing, i.e. to eliminate wastes. Several wastes associated with the traditional form of manufacturing by function have been identified as follows (Suzaki, 1987):

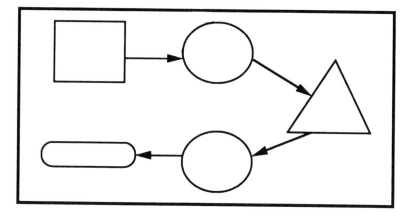

Figure 2.8 Layout of a cell under JIT production.

- Transportation wastes result from parts and component parts travelling from the various process areas.
- Co-ordination and scheduling of production is difficult to achieve.
- In-process inventory may build up and accumulate as it sits in queue waiting to be processed at the next operation.
- Materials may be handled repetitiously many more times than is required.
- The production lead time may be too long.
- The cause of defects is difficult to identify.
- The flow of material and operation times are difficult to standardize.
- Due to the lack of standardization, improvement activities are difficult to carry out.

Manufacturing by function impedes the communication and visibility between workers. This is largely the result of distance between the functional areas. There are incompatibilities which exist between a functional plant layout and a demand pull production system. The impedances created by poor communication and visibility prohibit applying the demand pull concept to product flow. They also hinder the development of the customer-oriented working relationship among workers, i.e. it is difficult for workers to view their fellow workers or the next manufacturing process as a customer.

A further disadvantage of manufacturing by function is the emphasis on achieving functional goals by individual departments. Each department may set goals which are incompatible with the overall manufacturing goal of the organization. For example, driven by the desire to minimize machine and worker idle time, a common departmental goal is to maximize

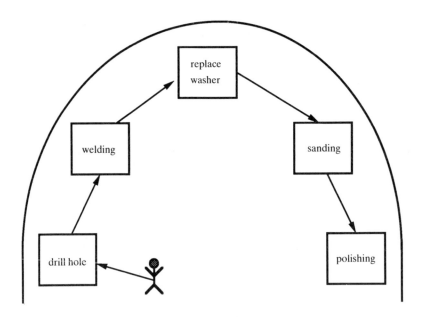

Figure 2.9 The 'rabbit chase'.

the quantity of parts produced. This emphasis on volume contributes to wastes if the quantity of parts produced exceeds that required to meet consumer demand.

The wastes identified with the functional approach to manufacturing are illustrated in Figure 2.7. The arrows indicate the amount of movement and handling which the parts receive. This movement is redundant as products flow to the many areas of the plant. Communication and visibility are also impeded as those functional areas which are situated in the extremes of the plant are not easily accessed by other areas. Figure 2.8 shows how these operations can be rearranged in a work cell. The work cell is organized in an efficient and logical manner.

Machines and equipment are organized in a cellular or U-shape with one or more workers operating inside the cell. There can be any number of work cells in a plant to carry out the manufacturing operations. Each worker moves from machine to machine performing the necessary tasks to complete the product. This is where training for multiple skills is crucial to achieve the required quality of the product.

The cellular, or U-shaped, lines assist worker flexibility and contact with various machines and other workers as the distance between machines is reduced and movement is not hindered. The machines and equipment are organized in a logical fashion according to the order of the task to be performed. Workers usually stand and rotate from machine to machine upon completion of each task. This method of worker rotation from task to task is also commonly referred to as the 'rabbit chase' and is illustrated in Figure 2.9.

Hay (1988) identifies the factors which distinguish a 'true' JIT work cell from a traditional one. Distinguishing JIT work cells from traditional cells entails some difficulties, as there are some aspects of true cells which are shared with traditional cells.

In order for a JIT work cell to qualify as a true JIT manufacturing cell, it must pass two tests. The first test involves establishing the flow of the product within the cell. True JIT work cells have products which flow one at a time from the various operations within the cell. There is no batch processing and the flow of one product at a time develops 'overlapping operations'. The part transferred from the initial operation becomes the work of operation two.

The second test involves the flexibility of cycle times. Cycle time is defined as 'the time between recurring activities' (Hall, 1987). This is an important concept as it relates to the idea of demand pull. Ability to vary cycle times between operations in the work cell will be necessary to meet variable customer demand.

Prior to developing work cells, the organization must establish what is required of the work cell and the number of employees needed to carry out the functions. Many organizations engage in the manufacturing of several products. Production of multiple products can complicate the smooth flow which is required in cellular manufacturing. Process analysis is often carried out to simplify the flow of materials through the plant. Suzaki (1987) has listed several steps which an organization can follow to improve the flow of materials in the plant. The organization should undertake the following steps.

- Product-quantity analysis constructs a product profile of all the items a company manufactures and it establishes a relationship between production unit size and dollar volume associated with each product.
- Process route analysis recapitulates which operations dictate the completion of each product listed in the product-quantity analysis.
- Subsequent to the completion of process route analysis, grouping of all products according to their sequence through the production process occurs. All similarly sequenced products are grouped together.
- Idea generation should occur to capitalize on the previous analyses. Areas of improvement which are important determinants for the development of a streamlined flow encompass the following: reducing set-up times and lot sizes, maintenance of machinery, machine capability, required processing times and the number of times tool changes are required. Other areas which should be addressed include reducing the distances between various processes for products grouped together, simplifying production flow to achieve one-piece flow production and

changing the physical arrangement of equipment. Opinions should be solicited from employees with a technical background, supervisors, operators, maintenance, quality and production control.

Suzaki (1987) has outlined several approaches to process improvement. These suggestions are the result of the actual findings in various organizations. Several organizations were observed and process improvement was applied to alleviate difficulties or improve upon the existing conditions. The results are discussed as a means of how process improvement can positively affect various plant areas.

1. *Layout improvement* Once an organization changes from a process-oriented layout to a product-oriented layout and introduces work cells in the plant, initial benefits may be realized. These benefits may take the form of reduced lead time and reduced inventory levels. The organization can further increase their benefits by reducing wastes in storage and transportation, solving quality problems and improving productivity.

2. *Application of the optimal number of operators* The use of work cells in true JIT manufacturing requires fewer workers. One operator may be responsible for several operations. Process improvement can identify when a plant may be employing too many workers to operate the machines. This situation can lead to poor visibility and communication, delayed feedback, the production of low quality or defective items and inefficient use of floor space. Adopting work cells can be advantageous as it can lead to significant improvements in these areas.

3. *Continuous improvement* This can prove to be beneficial through encouraging the participation of machine operators in improving the arrangement and utilization of equipment.

4. *Arrangement of parts storage* Two-piece flow production involves the use of two operators and the placement of parts and tools in an area which can be focused upon for improvement. Changing the arrangement of parts storage areas can lead to improvements in productivity and quality.

5. *Use of a feeder line* If the connection between a feeder line and the assembly line is poor, a plant can experience problems in communication which may lead to over- or under-production of parts, accumulation of inventory, over-handling of materials and under-utilization of the workforce. These problems can be overcome by changing the arrangement of the feeder line to the assembly line, depending on the specific layout which exists in an organization. The benefits received from rearrangement of the plant are improved communication, reduction of accumulated inventory and one-at-a-time production when required. Other advantages include increased productivity and ability to meet variations in demand.

6. *Linking a separate operation into the mainstream* The main purpose behind linkage is to ensure that the product flow is smooth. A common

reason why certain operations are held in reserve is that their inclusion in the line may result in adverse effects to the working environment such as increasing the level of heat and dust. These factors may contribute toward the creation of an unsafe environment. In these circumstances, production may be banded together in different groups, although grouping can cause disruptions in the smooth flow of production, communication, co-ordination and employee relations. The use of production control techniques can assist this situation by providing the necessary linkage for operations. Production control techniques will be discussed in a later chapter.

Cellular manufacturing with multiple machines
The purchase of equipment very often results in large capital outlays; therefore, many organizations limit purchasing new equipment and use one machine to perform a number of operations for manufacture of various products. A drawback to using true JIT work cells is that the equipment may become committed to one cell. There do exist, however, several means of using one machine to perform various operations in order to curtail the expenditure of new equipment.

There are a number of approaches to using equipment in a more flexible manner. Hay (1988) suggests three such approaches. The first approach involves 'semi-dedicating' equipment to a work cell in which the equipment is physically located in the work cell, but is only scheduled to work within that particular cell for a portion of the working day. During the part of the day in which the machine is not dedicated to the work cell, it could be used to perform separate operations. This approach requires flexibility in scheduling to satisfy all production needs.

The second approach relies upon the use of 'temporary work cells'. Work cells would be set up to perform manufacturing for specific operations. Once this work is completed, the work cell would be dismantled and set up again in a different sequence to provide manufacturing for other operations. The success of this approach rests heavily upon an organization's ability to execute quick and reliable set-ups. One limitation to this approach concerns the type of equipment contained in the work cells. This approach is only appropriate for equipment which is small and capable of being transported with minimum difficulty.

The third approach involves the use of JIT production control techniques such as the kanban, which is the subject of discussion in the ensuing section.

Benefits of cellular manufacturing
The use of JIT work cells benefits the organization in two broad areas, namely the improvement of production related activities and of employee related issues. A summary of the improvements in manufacturing activities

which are realized include the creation of a smooth flow of materials, one-at-a-time manufacturing, reduction of inventory, reduced storage areas, improvements in quality, increased visibility and communication and co-ordination of worker activities. These benefits were previously outlined in the discussion of the implementation of work cells in a plant and are representative of the more obvious outcomes of their use. Another benefit which is realized is related to quality. Inspection of product as a separate function is eliminated as the operator performing the manufacturing function is required to perform self-inspection.

The benefits of using cellular manufacturing include improved communication and worker flexibility; however, the benefits are not restricted to these areas. Toyota manufacturing developed and perfected JIT with three main goals in mind: 'quality control, quality assurance, and respect for humanity, while pursuing its ultimate goal of cost reduction' (Monden, 1983). Cellular manufacturing is conducive to the realization of these goals. Quality of products is enhanced, costs are reduced through waste reduction and respect for humanity is evident through the number of benefits which accrue to employees who work in a manufacturing cell. Work cells require employees to become an active part of the process. Workers are no longer required to perform one task repetitiously. They learn multiple skills and thus perform many operations. For example, cellular manufacturing may require workers to drill, weld, sand and polish work-in-process inventory.

Operators in motion may experience higher degrees of mental alertness (Hay, 1988). It is believed that workers are more alert and conscious of their tasks and the machines when they are required to stand, move frequently and perform various tasks. This assists in reducing possible work related accidents caused by workers becoming too relaxed at their jobs. In addition, ability to perform more than one task relieves the monotony associated with routine production jobs. As a result, increases in productivity, motivation, employee job satisfaction and enhancement of product quality are achieved.

Bundling machines together complements the manufacturing process by diminishing the queuing time between operations. An employee can perform one function and, upon its completion, will not have to wait for another employee to be free to perform the succeeding function. Thus, inventory in transit, equipment and available materials are ready for use.

Other advantages associated with the manufacturing by-product are the elimination of the wastes identified with the functional approach. Transportation and handling wastes are reduced as a result of efficient equipment layout, lead times become shorter, there is increased standardization and capacity to carry out improvement activities, the cause of defects is more readily identified, scheduling and co-ordinating production are simplified and the level of in-process inventory which tends to accumulate is significantly reduced.

Furthermore, communication and visibility among employees is achieved. Goal incompatibilities which previously existed are eliminated as demand is fully co-ordinated for the entire plant. One operation cannot run to the point where demand is exceeded as it is called into action only when the previous operation is completed.

Multi-functional skills

Cellular manufacturing allows a company to obtain improved communication, visibility in the plant, smoother production and other benefits as listed above. However, the effectiveness of cellular manufacturing is dependent upon the capability of workers in the cells to perform a variety of functions. Multi-functional skills prepare a company to respond to changes in market demand as workers become capable of responding to the changes in processing which reflect these market changes. Another factor which an organization should take into consideration is the degree of flexibility of the plant layout.

Multi-process handling requires workers to expand on their skills to enable them to handle many tasks. The use of foolproof mechanisms or 'pokayoke', which is the use of equipment developed with the capacity to indicate to the workers when a task is being performed incorrectly, aids in the development and application of multi-processing (Suzaki, 1987). Pokayoke will be discussed further in the chapter relating to quality. Other prerequisites to the development of multi-functional skills are standardization of work processes and use of checklists to familiarize employees with tasks. The degree of difficulty which an organization will experience in developing multi-functional skills will depend upon the existing level of employee skills and the degree of standardization which is present in the manufacturing process.

Employee skill levels can be enriched through training and job rotation (Suzaki, 1987). Suzaki identifies the results of training and job rotation through observing these two processes at manufacturing plants. The results indicated that there were many benefits to be received upon embarking on such enrichment projects. The employees who receive additional training are typically the supervisors and machine operators.

The benefits of upgrading employee skills and job rotation, ranging from improvements in employee satisfaction to efficient manufacturing are listed below.

- Employees can initiate individual goal setting to facilitate their own skill development.
- Improved employee concentration is a direct result of performing various tasks at stated intervals. Varying employee work patterns alleviates the monotony which is frequently associated with repetitive manufacturing.
- Work performed in short intervals alleviates employee eye and muscle strain. Overall, this contributes to improved physical well-being.

- Teamwork between supervisors and operators is promoted through the allocation of skills.
- Employees institute the sharing of ideas on such issues as problem solving and improvement activities. In addition, there is a sharing of interests in the plant, rather than interest directed solely toward an employee's immediate work area. Communication is another area which receives improvement as well.
- Standard work procedures are cultivated through the improved lines of communication.
- The development of teamwork transcends the concern for such issues as improving safety, product quality, cost reduction, customer delivery and housekeeping functions.

Implementing a flexible workforce depends upon a number of organizational factors. Each organization seeking to embrace the flexible workforce will encounter problems unique to it. Despite these difficulties, observation of an organization's attempt at flexible workforce implementation can assist others in identifying and avoiding potential problems in their companies. The following presents one company's approach to flexible workforce implementation (Wenzel, 1987).

A case study

The case study presents an analysis of the techniques used in a plastics company. They adopted a TEAM (together employees achieve more) approach to plant start-up. The team approach was chosen as it was deemed to have several advantages such as increasing employee participation, job satisfaction and efficiency of operations.

The initial step involved setting up a task force composed of a plant manager, human resource, plant, engineering and manufacturing managers and a corporate specialist. This task force was established prior to plant start-up activities and its main function was to identify the positive, functional aspects of the team approach and apply these concepts to the organization. Task force activities were supplemented with the aid of an external consultant. The outcome of their efforts resulted in the development of a team system known as the 'team technician system' (TTS).

The TTS assumed an active role in the development of a pay structure which facilitated plant efficiency and low costs. The pay structure applied to the five main skill groups in the company, including product assembly, distribution, process, quality and maintenance. Inauguration of employee cross-training within these five skill groups began with transferring employees to each group. Each employee received training within the particular skill groups, as they rotated from one to another.

Employees' demonstration of skill mastery within a specific skill group was directly tied to the salary they received. Salary increases, established at 6% or more, were proportional to the skill mastered and employees' responsibility in accordance with increments in pay level. Employees were regarded to have mastered a skill when they were able to complete 100% of the requirements of one skill or 50% of the requirements of two skills. The primary benefit received from rotating employees was a cross-trained, comprehensively skilled workforce. The main difficulty with such a system is lack of training for supervisors.

Three years into the implementation of the TTS, it was discovered that the system could not adapt to changing organizational needs and was devoid of any formal instrument to innovate change. The company introduced a second task force to analyse the TTS and bring forth recommendations. The second task force identified the following four areas as requiring improvement.

1. Supervisors needed supplementary training. Lack of supervisor training led to inconsistencies in conduct. Supervisors responded to situations based upon their own interpretations of the situation. Misunderstanding and misinterpretation led many employees to feel the system was inequitable and unfair. Thus, recommendations included the implementation of a formal supervisor training program.

    Further recommendations included training to address interpersonal communication skills, problem solving and the establishment of uniform methods of evaluation. In addition, to maintain consistency in supervisor interpretation and evaluation, it was suggested that meetings be held on a regular basis to address such issues as disciplinary action, attendance and time-keeping.

2. Technicians required training in addition to the two-week orientation they received upon hiring. The two-week training session addressed safety issues and the functioning of the five identified skill areas. Supplementary training regarding problem solving, presentation skills, group dynamics and decision making was also required. Quality circles became a useful resource of the organization and were used to address problem solving, presentations, group dynamics and decision-making skills. Activity teams were developed to address specific problems. The teams brainstorm, develop solutions to problems and implement the solutions. Training for the activity teams is a function of each department in the organization.

3. The most significant alteration of the existing pay structure and methods of evaluation entailed reducing the frequency of evaluations from quarterly to semi-annual. Preparing for quarterly reviews presented a difficulty on two levels: preparation for the quarterly reviews was a comprehensive task, almost impossible to satisfactorily accomplish, and attempting to prepare for quarterly reviews over-extended supervisors, reducing their objectivity and time available to engage in individual counselling.

    Recommendations also included increasing the flexibility of the system. Compensation is directly tied to the operator's skill level mastered at skill blocks. However, the level of skills required ignores the quality of worker's performance at a particular skill block. Employees who performed high quality work at a particular block were not given the opportunity to rotate to other skill blocks as supervisors were reluctant to transfer their best performers. In this sense, high quality workers were being penalized for superior performance. Thus, these employees did not receive the extra compensation linked with the acquisition of diversified skills. Recommendations addressed presenting supervisors with the discretion to award merit dollars where deserved.

4. Changing the subsisting control and audit system implicated the use of a task force to review and evaluate the functioning of the TTS on an annual basis. Necessary adjustments were made to maintain the current TTS activities.

Subsequent to the employment of the task force and enforcement of recommendations, the company transformed its organization by department to a focused factory approach to manufacturing. This transformation eliminated the departmental organization of quality, assembly, maintenance, distribution and processing. Task force involvement included the establishment of action plans to facilitate the transition.

The changes which occurred affected the arrangement of the plant as it was now systematized according to product. Specific areas within the plant were designated to the production of each product. Employees within the production areas acquired skills and were 100% responsible for the complete manufacture of a product. Employee responsibilities include the assembling, processing, maintenance, distribution, and quality of the product.

The benefits arising from the implementation of focused factories are numerous and include the following:

- the number of jobs available within each skill group has increased, providing the opportunity for operators to acquire several skills within a group;
- through simplification of rotations, operators are able to execute various tasks – performing a multitude of tasks is a contributory factor to employee development and job enrichment; and
- individual goals become harmonized with the overall factory production goals, and communication is enhanced throughout the factory with the elimination of obstructions and barriers.

Focused factories and TTS concentrate on the fragmented areas of the plant. Addressing the overall organizational needs is attained with the use of plant-wide team activities. Activities are carried out with the participation of employees from all organizational disciplines. Examples of plant-wide programs include a 'Total Quality Control' programme and a 'Customer Awareness Campaign'.

The 'Total Quality Control' programme focused on creating an awareness of the quality of products. Quality awareness was enhanced through various activities such as awarding quality work, contests and meetings. The 'Customer Awareness Campaign' focused on increasing employee consciousness of internal and external customers' needs through the use of meetings, publications, films and awards.

Cellular manufacturing allows for the elimination of tasks such as in-process inspection and transferring of the product over long distances from one operation to the next. These tasks become redundant or unnecessary with the use of work cells. The operators in each cell can fulfill the task of in-process inspection by checking their work subsequent to each operation performed on the product. Similarly, the need for another worker to carry the product to the next operation is eliminated as the in-process part need only travel a short distance to the next operation.

Achieving cellular manufacturing
The potential of cellular manufacturing cannot be fully realized without modifying related elements of production such as line balancing, reduced set-up times, economic feasibility, product design and flattening the bill of materials (Goddard, 1986). Other modifications which may be necessary, or occur naturally, as the plant gradually begins to resemble a JIT layout include improvements in activities and quality. Cellular manufacturing commands an increasing involvement and significant role of employees in order to experience success. The ability of workers to engage in a variety of tasks and complete high quality work represents a prerequisite to cellular manufacturing. Each of these elements required for work cells is now discussed.

Line balancing
Line balancing refers to the degree that the capacity requirements of each stage in a work cell meet the achieved capacity of each operation within the cell. Line imbalance often occurs when one operation runs slower than the other operations within a particular work cell. This imbalance can contribute toward long waiting lines and accumulation of in-process inventory. To combat this phenomenon, the equipment which runs at a faster rate can be slowed down to meet the rate of the slower operation, or the situation may correct itself without deliberate intervention in that the slower operations absorb some of the slack. In this sense, the slower operations can compensate for the discrepancy in synchronization.

Reduced set-up times
Short set-up times are required to enable the organization to produce the quantity of goods demanded and to produce a variety of products. Short set-up times allow a company to meet the changes in the product mix without requiring substantial periods of time. Set-ups refer to the changeover or

modification of existing equipment to produce a mix of products during the various phases of the production cycle.

Economic feasibility

Economic feasibility addresses the issue of suitability when equipment is used for the operations of one cell. Cellular manufacturing in this situation is appropriate when the volume produced by a cell supports the costs and use of the equipment within that given cell. Economic feasibility should be taken into consideration when an organization is embarking upon the purchase of new equipment. It may prove more feasible for the organization to purchase equipment which requires less technical support and knowledge.

Product design

Modifying product design is carried out to improve the manufacturability of products. Products must be designed to reflect the concepts of JIT. The development of products compatible with JIT is a responsibility of the engineering department. Members of the engineering department participate in an analysis of the stages of manufacturing to eliminate unnecessary processing steps.

Bill of materials

The bill of material lists the necessary parts for component parts or the final product which may be required and establishes the sequence of operations which must be performed to arrive at the final product. Changing the manufacturing process to reduce wastes or the number of steps involved in the manufacturing process may require the bill of materials to be altered. This step is performed consistent with the goal of waste reduction. Reducing the number of steps involved in the production process is known as 'flattening' the bill of materials. The benefits associated with flattening the bill of materials are reductions in the number of work orders and amount of paperwork, simplified scheduling and reduced inventory transactions.

Flow of materials

The flow of materials through the production process must be continuous and steady. Flow must also be uninterrupted by factors which needlessly impede its progress and thus the overall efficiency of the plant. A flow that is continuous is frequently referred to as 'developed' (Suzaki, 1987). Examples of the factors which may be present within a plant that interrupt the smooth flow of materials include inefficient plant layout and machine breakdowns.

Planning to prevent potential interruptions to a steady flow can be beneficial to the organization to the extent that these factors can be identified and if possible avoided. Several commonly identified problems which a manager should be aware of include the following (Suzaki, 1987):

- The use of a process-oriented plant layout. Inventory will tend to accumulate and operations are difficult to prioritize.
- Line imbalance refers to the degree that operations are not synchronized, resulting in accumulated inventory, long waiting lines and poor co-ordination of work effort.

- The production processes may be interrupted when low quality or defective parts are discovered.
- Breakdown of machines and equipment will cause the operations to come to a halt. Line stoppages as a result of machine breakdowns may contribute to the accumulation of in-process inventory.
- The absence of equipment operators will cause the production process to stop or slow down, especially if replacement workers are not available.

2.4.3 Linking demand pull with cellular manufacturing

Table 2.5 shows a method of linking the demand pull system to work cells (Hall, 1987). The rules presented apply to both straight (identical work pieces) and complex (multiple work pieces) flow parts.

Set-up time reduction

Levelling production requires reduced set-up times for machinery and equipment and small lot sizes. Reduced set-up time will allow for quick machine changeovers when production is mixed. Reducing the amount of time required for set-up also reduces the amount of time wasted between operations and the associated costs. Ability to set up machinery and equipment in less time requires training of labour and selection of the kinds of equipment which will make quick set-ups possible. Reduced set-up time works toward ensuring that the goals of production will be met in the required amounts at the appropriate times.

There are several reasons underlying the purpose of set-up time reduction, the main one being to more aptly meet the diversified needs of customers. The other purpose for reducing set-up time is internal to the organization. Set-up time reduction requires that employees be knowledgeable about their work, the work area well organized, equipment maintained and quality standards set by the organization achieved. Therefore, set-up time reduction is a factor which will contribute toward improving plant efficiency, especially if it becomes a standard of the organization.

There are three activities closely tied into the idea of set-up time reduction: the application of flexible manufacturing, the development of accurate data gathering and measurement techniques; and the establishment of problem-solving teams which address methods to reduce waste (Claunch, 1988).

Flexible manufacturing is defined as 'a system capable of responding or conforming to change or changes in the manufacturing environment which allows quick turnaround and requires minimal set-up' (Claunch, 1988). The main purpose of a flexible manufacturing system is to obtain world-class competitiveness. The ability of manufacturing companies to obtain set-ups which are made possible in a matter of minutes or, in some circumstances, seconds will enable these firms to outreach those in the market incapable of mastering quick set-ups. The ability to perform quick, 100% accurate

Table 2.5 Linking

Straight flow	Complex flow
Place workpiece in load position	Place workpiece in load position a) identify the workpiece b) determine the correct workpiece machine match c) if part skips a process, continue, if not then – apply the appropriate instructions to the machining process – choose the right tools
Carry out fail-safe checks on prior operations. Load the correct part or workpiece	Carry out fail-safe checks on prior operations. Load the correct part or workpiece. Also load any tools required
Operations performed and completed by the machine	Operations performed and completed by the machine
Machine and worker idle until the prior workpiece or part is required by the next operation	Machine and worker idle until the prior workpiece or part is required by the next operation
Man and machine idle until the next part or workpiece is ready for processing	Man and machine idle until the next part or workpiece is ready for processing

set-ups provides advantages to these firms with respect to increasing their efficiency. A firm incapable of quick, reliable set-ups will not only forgo the ability to readily meet consumer demands, but will also fail to capitalize on the benefits of inventory reduction. Inventory reduction occurs in finished goods and work-in- process inventory. Reductions in inventory are the result of setting manufacturing requirements based on consumer needs. The success of flexible manufacturing is dependent upon the reliable delivery of quality material from suppliers.

The development of accurate data gathering and measuring techniques becomes central to the process of set-up reduction through the provision of information identifying the status of the manufacturing processes. The information provided through gathering and measuring becomes a base from which progress can be monitored. The accuracy of data in a flexible manufacturing system should be nothing short of 100%. The acceptance of

Table 2.6 The ten-step plan

The ten-step plan
1 Avoid over-studying or over-planning projects.
2 Do not settle or limit the team to early successes.
3 Do not become a slave to the problem-solving techniques.
4 Strive for continuous goal improvement.
5 Problems, goals and accomplishments should be visible to all members.
6 Steps of team progress should be monitored.
7 Focus on small or streamlined ideas.
8 Focus on eliminating waste.
9 Implement solutions which are uncomplicated.
10 Establish objectives relating to inventory turnover.

anything less, say, 99%, would result in errors which could have a significant impact upon the operations of a company.

The use of problem-solving teams to address set-up time reduction issues is an effective method of identifying problems and finding solutions. A team is defined as 'a group of people dedicated to a common goal who have learned to build on each other's strengths and to compensate for each other's weaknesses' (Claunch, 1988). The use of teams should include members from the various disciplines in the plant and a primary role should be occupied by the operators of machines.

The formation of teams and application of problem-solving techniques represent complementary activities. Claunch suggests that company-wide goals be developed and he provides an outline, known as 'the ten-step plan', to serve as a guide for set-up reduction. Table 2.6 depicts the elements of this plan.

Subsequent to the ten-step plan, the team which is responsible for the implementation of set-up reduction techniques, designated as the task team, should evaluate the current plant conditions to establish which areas are to be affected and to identify existing opportunities. Table 2.7 provides an example of the areas which should be addressed. The list encompasses work improvement ideas. The work improvement activities should then be prioritized and a timetable developed defining and allocating an appropriate time frame to each activity. Use of an operational time frame allows the company to compare their progress against pre-established standards and to ensure these actions are being completed.

Claunch defines problem-solving techniques which a task team can follow to develop solutions to work improvement difficulties. A variety of problem-solving techniques is available, which share the common objective to steer the task team away from procedures which may lead to less than the most desirable solutions. Common procedures which should be avoided include:

Table 2.7 Work improvement

Assessment actions
1 Develop a statement of company-wide objectives.
2 Establish the improvement activities.
3 Structure the organization in a manner which leads to success.
4 Identify the existing skills and those which are needed to achieve success.
5 Evaluate the organizational climate and the political processes.
6 Assess the impact of the present organizational culture.
7 Formulate a plan to implement solutions.

- being over-anxious to reach a conclusion;
- forcing personal solutions on others;
- failure to fully resolve problems; and
- failure of the team to recognize their own short-comings and to admit they do not know the answers to all the questions.

These pitfalls can be avoided by identifying the causes and consequences of the problems, objectively and logically analysing the problem and identifying the fundamental root of the problem, rather than simply focusing on the symptoms alone.

The task team should not attempt to address all issues related to set-up time reduction. Rather, attention should be focused on the improvement issues which add value to the product and reduce the overall level of waste. The approach which task teams should take toward correctly identifying the problem is to question, five times, why the problem exists. This method of repeating 'why' five times, (the 5 'w's) will increase the likelihood of correctly identifying the root problem. Completion of the 5 'w's will then set the stage for brainstorming. The function of a brainstorming session is to generate a variety of solutions to the problem.

Effective work teams do not simply happen of their own accord. There must be management commitment to the creation and organization of task teams. Management commitment is instrumental in the provision of training in problem-solving techniques for task team members.

Set-up time reduction involves a lengthy process in order to ensure the setting up of machinery in an efficient and reliable manner. Goddard (1986) has identified four factors which are required for set-up time reduction. It requires input from operators and engineers, standardizing equipment, re-tooling time and practice by employees to learn and become efficient at set-ups. In short, set-up time reduction is an improvement activity of the organization.

Many specific set-up techniques have been developed and used in various organizations. There are, however, general ground rules which can be used as a guideline by any organization to assist in reducing set-up time. Hay

(1988) has listed several of these ground rules as they pertain to the definition of reduced set-up times. There are three sets of ground rules which, respectively, address the physical steps executed, the purpose of the set-ups and who is involved in the process of set-up reduction. These ground rules will be explained separately in the following paragraphs.

The physical steps or actions required for set-up time reduction are explained through the application of four phases.

1. *Set-up time reduction objectives*   The objective behind reducing set-up times encompasses the simplification of the procedures involved in increasing the organizational responsiveness to market demand. It does not aim to reduce or avoid the number of set-ups which are required.

2. *Measurement of time frames*   Measurement should focus on the two criteria of determining machine downtime during the set-up process and of the costs associated with this activity.

3. *The definition of set-up times*   The working definition of set-up time is 'the downtime of the operation to change from one part or product to another; but, to reduce set-up times, one should also remove the waste from the set-up process by reducing the labour required for them' (Hall, 1987). Measurement is applied at this step and commences at the time it takes once the last part or product comes off machinery until the machinery can start production for a different part. The factors which will be measured within this time span are the portion of time of the total that is consumed in teardown of the machinery, clean-up, commencing the new operation, preparing for the process to run correctly, inspection of the first part or product to run off the machine and achieving the rate of processing which is the set standard.

4. *Setting standards to achieve reduction in set-up time*   Measurement will focus on the two criteria of machine downtime during the set-up process and of the costs associated with this activity. The last step is to achieve a 75% reduction in set-up time. This can be accomplished by setting operational goals to initially achieve a reduction of 50%. Once this is achieved, reduction of a further 50% should be sought.

The second ground rule is for the organization to identify the purpose of reducing set-up times and relate its importance to the organizational goals. The main purpose behind set-up reduction is to aid in the elimination of wastes. The amount of time which is saved through executing a number of efficient set-ups can be applied to increasing the frequency of set-ups in order to reduce lot sizes or volume. Reducing the volume of products produced at any one time serves to fulfill two purposes of JIT:

- to develop a manufacturing process which is smooth and balanced; and
- to enable the organization to produce its product when necessary to meet demand, thus assisting in the reduction of inventory, space and wasted time.

Hay (1988) establishes two rules identifying what an organization ought not regard as purposes of set-up time reduction.

1. Set-up reduction should not be viewed as a means of reducing the number of employees within a plant. Although employee reduction is frequently an outcome of faster and efficient set-ups, set-up time reduction should not be initiated with this goal in mind.
2. An organization should avoid using set-up time reduction as a means for increasing production. This rule applies to organizations approximately 90% of the time. The remaining 10% applies to organizations who are turning away customers, i.e. organizations whose production capability is below consumer demands. Organizations which are able to meet consumer demand should not increase production with the time saved from set-up reductions. This would only contribute to excess inventory.

The third set of ground rules applies to those involved in the process of reducing set-up times. The best approach involves the use of teamwork, rather than an engineering-oriented approach. According to Hay (1988), a pure engineering approach is not practical given the nature of the task at hand. Engineering will tend to focus attention on the mechanics of the process rather than on the work which is required beforehand, or the 'administrivia'.

Time is consumed in changeovers in locating set-up people when they are required, determining the next job to be performed, finding the necessary tools and equipment and being able to set up machines correctly the first time. Items which are not contributing factors to set-ups are the machines themselves, the equipment and clamping methods.

Efficient set-ups will, however, involve the effort of all members of the organization and what they can contribute to the preliminary work. This approach is likely to be more successful than the engineering approach. The reasons for this are threefold. First, this approach will involve the 'experts' in the organization. The experts are defined as 'the set-up people or operators who know the most about the process and their machines' (Hay, 1988). The second reason involves the development of employees having a sense of ownership in the set-up process. This may arise through actively involving and soliciting input from a large segment of the organization's workforce. The third reason relates to the idea that the contributions of a large number of employees and the sharing of their input will present the organization with a multitude of thought and ideas, lending to the strengthening of its problem-solving ability.

The responsibility for set-up reduction is not confined to the role of the manager or supervisor in an organization. The role of the supervisor will be to encourage the free thought and ideas of the labour force which can be applied to the process of reducing set-up time. The use of a project team is an efficient approach to handling set-up reduction. Typical project teams are composed of two to four people who set up machines, two support people with a technical background, a team leader or facilitator and input from a shop floor supervisor. The use of technical support is necessary to ensure that the quality and safety standards are by no means adversely affected with equipment changes. The use of technical support is also instrumental in guaranteeing the changes are implemented in the most efficient and appropriate manner.

The role of the team leader is one of moderator between the different sub-groups of the project team. With this in mind, one may reasonably assume that the team leader will possess the ability to relate to the group members and will be knowledgeable about the political processes which exist in the organization.

The role of the shop floor supervisor will differ from organization to organization. Determining how actively the supervisor is involved with the project team depends upon the relationship between the supervisor and the group members. The supervisor's personality and the organizational circumstances are the two main factors which should be considered. In many organizations it may be appropriate for the supervisor to be a team member, in others it may not.

Hay (1988) has given two reasons why a supervisor should not become a project team member.

1. The personality of the supervisor may interfere with the project team members to take initiative towards set-ups. This may be especially evident if the supervisor has previously played a central role in directing and initiating actions.
2. Supervisors generally are more apt to have poor attendance records when it comes to team meetings. High supervisor absenteeism is the result of restricted time to spend on meetings due to other obligations. Repeated absenteeism by supervisors may convey negative messages to the other team members, leading members to conclude that management may not be committed to the team's success and thus question their own degree of commitment.

Project teams which do not include supervisors as full-time members will have extra responsibilities. These responsibilities usually fall on the team facilitators. Team facilitators will be required to inform the supervisors on a continuous basis, solicit their input on key issues and maintain them as a part of the process.

Hay (1988) describes a plan which will enable the organization to develop and implement a project team. This plan involves a series of steps which explain the role of management, choosing the team and the machine which will have its set-up times improved. The first step involves management understanding and agreement on the ground rules. Management must ensure that the project members understand and are willing to adhere to the rules as well. The second step concerns the selection of the operation or machine for the changeover. The third step involves choosing the team members and the fourth step deals with training the members.

Hay suggests that the activities of the project team be videotaped and then analysed. An analysis of the progress of the project team will allow the organization to assess their performance more accurately and suggest further improvements in the changeover process.

Techniques for set-up time reduction

Although set-up time reduction involves a lengthy process where the full benefits are only realized over a long period of time, many organizations are able to experience some of these benefits in the short run. For example, it has been estimated that a manufacturing company can reduce set-up times by up to 50% simply by being prepared for the process. Over the long run a company may expect to reduce set-up times by up to 90%. Organization is therefore a key element in determining success. Set-ups can be reduced to ten minutes by applying the skills of operators, technical staff, maintenance staff and quality people (Suzaki, 1987).

There are many methods for reducing set-ups, however, these models frequently are modified for the purpose of adapting them to the specific organization. Suzaki offers a broad or generalized approach for reducing set-up time, is outlined in a series of steps:

1. separating the internal set-up from the external set-up–internal set-up is defined as 'the work which must be done while the machine is stopped', while external set-up relates to the work which is carried out during operation of the machine;
2. focusing on transferring work from internal set-up to external set-up, which usually involves increasing the amount of preparatory work;
3. further reducing internal set-up by adding extra labour to the task when required, reducing or eliminating the number of adjustments to the process and simplifying.

The rule of focusing on machine downtime becomes important for separating the internal and external set-up times. The organization at this point is working toward reducing machine downtime through reducing internal set-up. Therefore, it is important to perform any activity that can be performed when the machine is still running during the machine's running time. This will cut back on the time the machines are not running by adding more activities to the external set-up. The activities which can be transferred from the internal set-up are usually external set-up activities, although not practised as such. Through common fault of many organizations, external activities are frequently categorized as internal set-up activities. Proper categorization of activities helps to substantiate the importance of step 1.

Step 2 involves the conversion of internal set-up activities to external set-up activities. Examples of an internal set-up activity which can be converted to an external set-up activity include preheating dies for plastic injection moulding machines and presetting tools for numerically controlled equipment.

The third step focuses on the activities which can be carried out to reduce internal set-up times even further. The emphasis is placed upon adjustments and how they can be reduced or completely eliminated. Adjustments are described as the necessary activities which must be engaged in to make the machine run well again subsequent to completed jobs.

Hay (1988) identifies several types of adjustments which are frequently carried out. The objective with adjustments is to eliminate internal set-ups whenever possible. The first adjustment technique described is one that is inefficient and therefore not appropriate for JIT, nonetheless, it is included in the discussion to create an awareness of what should be avoided in set-up time reduction. This technique involves the fine tuning of equipment, then running a product through the operation. This product is then inspected to ensure that the machine has been adjusted properly. In the event that it has been misadjusted, the product which has been run through will go to waste. The machine must be adjusted once again and another product is run through and inspected. This is known as 'one-at-a-time production and inspection' and this sequence of events will continue until it has been established that the machine is adjusted according to specifications. This is an ineffective approach and is not compatible with the goals of JIT.

A second type of adjustment relates to the type of equipment which many organizations employ. Most equipment allows for adjustments over a certain range. At the time of manufacturing it may not be known what specific task the machine will perform. Therefore, workers may be compelled to adjust the process, whether it requires adjustment or not.

Suzaki (1987) suggests possible means of eliminating these adjustment problems. Elimination of adjustments is necessary as it has been established that the time consumed in performing the adjustment activities may constitute 40–50% of the total set-up time. Standardizing fixtures eliminates the estimation that is necessary when parts are added. Frequently, specific co-ordinates or slots are built in and serve the purpose of standardizing equipment. This is illustrated in Fig. 2.10.

Another means of reducing set-up is through parallel operations, as shown in Fig. 2.11. Parallel operations entail the adding of extra labour or materials which can reduce the amount of travelling time required to obtain the tools necessary for set-ups. The use of an additional toolbox reduces the travelling time to obtain the tools. The use of parallel operations can contribute to improved co-ordination of work activities and an overall efficient process.

Parallel operations can be established through the application of PERT (Program Evaluation and Review Technique). PERT can assist an organization in two ways in determining how parallel operations can be used optimally and is helpful in determining which operations can be conducted

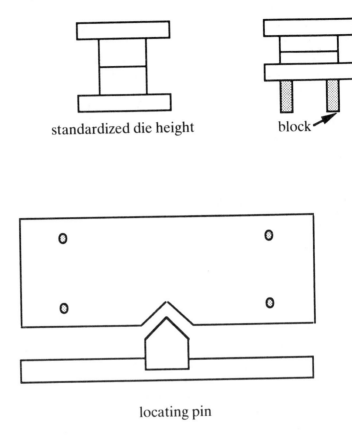

standardized die height   block

locating pin

Figure 2.10 Methods of eliminating adjustments.

simultaneously. This can reduce the amount of time that machines remain idle, since activities which were previously carried out one at a time can be doubled up. PERT can also be used to determine the critical path of activities. The critical path includes those internal set-up activities which will result in the smallest set-up time. PERT can establish the shortest critical path or reduce the existing path.

Clamping is another area of focus which can assist in the reduction of internal set-up times. Traditional use of clamps and other tools used in the clamping process such as threads and bolts require many motions to achieve proper working order. Their use contributes to inefficiency by increasing set-up times. Thus their use should be applied judiciously.

Other methods are available to reduce the amount of time invested in attachment and detachment activities. These methods should be selected

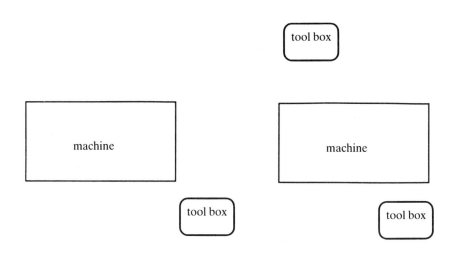

Figure 2.11 Parallel operations.

with two goals in mind: to eliminate the number of tools used in adjustments and to employ tools which require a minimum amount of motion. Other means of reducing adjustments include decreasing and standardizing the number of bolts used and trimming unnecessary threads.

The last step in the process of reducing set-up time involves improving the external set-up once the previous steps have been accomplished. Workplace organization represents the main focus of external set-up reduction. Workplace organization, as discussed previously, includes establishing designated areas for storing materials, placing tools in the appropriate storage areas and ensuring that frequently used materials such as dies are used and stored near machines where they can be readily accessed.

Internal and external set-ups, adjustments and clamping procedures represent activities which would be analysed in videotaped documentation. Other methods of reducing set-up time involve the use of a 'set-up performance chart' to relay management's concern for reducing set-up time to employees. The chart is also useful in providing feedback about progress. In summary, using videotape for objectively monitoring performance, standardizing material and parts, co-operation of employees and reducing the number of component parts can result in an efficient procedure to reduce set-up time.

2.4.4 Automation

Automation is an important issue in JIT manufacturing as it applies to the organization's capacity to manufacture in an efficient manner. It involves the changing or adaptation of machinery and processes to be fine-tuned to a company's specific manufacturing needs. The greater the degree an organization is able to automate, the greater the competitive edge this will offer them. There are several methods of improving and automating machines.

Low-cost automation

Low-cost automation requires the organization to become innovative and develop methods of using its machinery and processes at a relatively low cost. An example is adjusting a machine to automatically eject a finished piece of work, automatically load and switch on and off. The use of low-cost automation can improve the flow of products in the plant.

The presence of very large pieces of equipment or 'super-machines' may add to the overall inefficiency of the plant, despite the speed at which they tend to operate. Inefficiency results as super-machines are used for many different products in a plant. Inventory may accumulate as jobs begin to pile up. Thus, there will be long lead times, long queuing lines, excess storage space will be used and they may impair scheduling.

Autonomous control

Autonomous control or 'Jidoka' is another means of automating. Jidoka involves the 'adding of intelligent features to machines to start or stop operations as needed and emittance of signals for operators when necessary' (Suzaki, 1987). There do exist, however, certain limitations to the use of automated machines. Automated machines, for example, cannot detect when a machine malfunctions and they cannot automatically stop operating. Therefore, the use of manual labour to watch over machines will be required. This is an operation which does not add value to the product and therefore, according to the philosophy of JIT, should be eliminated. In response to this necessity, autonomous control builds in a special feature which enables the machines to exercise a certain degree of judgement. This added feature eliminates the need for operators to watch over the machines. These machines are equipped with a special light which will signal when the machine malfunctions. These signal lights are commonly referred to as 'Andon'.

Fail-safe methods

Purchasing of new equipment can also fulfill other goals such as ensuring quality. New machinery may come equipped with signal lights specifically designed to monitor the quality level of operations performed by a machine. In the event a machine malfunctions, the signal light will be activated, indicating to employees that there is a flaw in the process. The machine can then be shut down and repaired without setting the line back a great amount.

Early detection of low quality output reduces the amount of rework and inspection costs of work-in-process parts. Thus, costs are greatly reduced with this system compared to the use of a system where machinery is allowed to operate until the malfunction is manually detected or the proceeding work station becomes aware of the deficient quality of the parts. Manual detection may not occur until the final product is inspected.

2.4.5 Flexible plant

Ability to execute numerous tasks successfully does not occur on its own. Extensive education and training of employees is required to execute cellular manufacturing. Employees should develop skills enabling the attainment of 100% quality, 100% of the time. The ideal approach to employee education involves a broad overview of concepts, then emphasizing the narrower ideas directly related to task performance. JIT concepts can be taught to employees through the use of the following techniques (Sepehri, 1987):

- attendance in meetings;
- reading and understanding articles and journals;
- discussion groups and seminars;
- attendance at workshops; and
- training within specific departments to perform a number of tasks.

Employment of cross-trained employees is only one element of a flexible manufacturing plant. Other elements include: expeditious responsiveness to market changes such as volume and product mix, customizing a product and improving customer delivery (Garwood, 1990).

Responsiveness to market changes

Market changes are impossible to avoid and difficult to predict accurately. Quick response to demand and product mix changes entitles a company to prosper successfully when faced with circumstances beyond its control. A company is able to meet these changes quickly without experiencing setbacks through maintaining detailed production schedules, reducing lead times and reducing set-up times, and ensuring that visibility is a priority in the plant and that cross-trained employees are available.

The use of detailed schedules assists in communicating changes in volume quickly to suppliers and employees. The greater the detail of the schedule, including the identification of part numbers, the easier it is for employees to adjust the processes before them. Detailed schedules should be made available to the operators of work cells.

Shortened lead times are necessary to allow operators and suppliers to adjust to changed schedules. Short lead times tie into quick set-ups or changeover of machinery and small lot sizes. Once a company successfully reduces these, it follows that lead times can also be reduced. Lead times apply to the length of time it takes to produce a product and to the frequency of production of a particular product.

Volume flexibility also requires the type of equipment which allows for additions to and subtractions from the process. Equipment which is also capable of producing at the required quality level without delays will be desirable as well. The human element involved with reducing lead times speaks to employees who are able to respond quickly to changes in the schedules. Knowledge of operations and ability to set up equipment without having to make adjustments are characteristics of such employees.

The role visibility plays within the plant in meeting volume changes is to provide an environment where employees can readily identify what needs to be done. Immediate identification of parts and location of employees will reduce delays which interfere with responsiveness.

Customization of products

Customization of products to meet consumer needs involves two disciplines of the organization, the engineering and manufacturing departments. The efforts of these two departments should concur to develop a product compatible with a flexible manufacturing system. Ingenuity of repetitive manufacturing arms a company with the utmost ability to be responsive; however, it fails to fine tune the customers needs. Surmounting the disadvantage of operational obstructions associated with non-repetitive manufacturing implicates the use of standardization from a manufacturing perspective. Standardizing operations preserves the company's ability to meet unique consumer demands and is discussed in a later section of this book.

The idea of customizing products to consumer needs necessitates the concept of 'mixed model scheduling'. Mixed model scheduling is the production of several different products and its primary concern surrounds the allocation of inventory, machines and operators to complete scheduled requirements. Use of mixed model scheduling sustains a company's ability to meet productivity standards without inducing unnecessary costs.

Several techniques are available to secure mixed model scheduling. Thorne (1988) identifies one technique known as the 'Spreader Model Schedule'. This model was applied to the production of agricultural equipment, one product with several models. Mixed model scheduling, as compared to the traditional approach, possesses greater flexibility. For example, in the past this company used a schedule applicable to manufacturing processes on an 8-week basis and was frozen as such. The mixed model schedule contains each model to be manufactured on a weekly basis, allowing for changes in product mix during the following weeks. In addition to this, daily schedules are provided for the manufacturing of each model and allow the company to respond to daily demands. Another feature of the mixed model schedule pertains to the manufacturing of high level demand products which is intermixed with low level demand products. Manufacturing processes should be compatible with mixed model scheduling. For example, processing should occur with small lot sizes.

Benefits of mixed model scheduling embody manufacturing and process improvements. Less inventory and fewer alterations of original products are required as products are 'made to fit'. The task of reconciling inventory and consumer needs is eliminated with a well-executed mixed model schedule. Further benefits include increased productivity, responsiveness and reduced manufacturing costs. The chief result of mixed model scheduling is greater flexibility in meeting consumer demand.

Implementing a mixed model schedule is dependent upon how well a company prepares the plant. Actual implementation should commence at the point which requires the greatest amount of work. An organization can determine where the starting point should be by asking questions focusing on plant activities and company dedication to quality. Examples of questions include the following (Thorne, 1988).

- Is reducing set-ups an ongoing goal of the business, with aggressive action being taken?
- Is everyone in the company involved in and part of improving the quality and reducing the variability of the product and processes?
- Do both senior management and everyone else in the organization understand what needs to be done to be successful?

Discovery of a lack of commitment and understanding from management and other employees subsequent to the analysis places the organization at a new starting point: education and training for all.

There are several prerequisites to the preparation of the plant for mixed model scheduling implementation. Implementation is a conjunctive task and its success depends upon the weakest link in the process. Required prerequisites include detailed planning and performance mechanisms. Examples of the types of detailed planning required are development of master schedules, production plans and sales and operations plans. These plans demand review and updating.

Improving customer delivery
The time required from the point where a product idea is brought to life until production is completed and the product made available to customers may take several weeks or months. This length of time can be reduced by eliminating unnecessary delays. The delay which most commonly occurs includes production of goods which fail to appropriately meet consumer requirements. This is largely the result of inadequately identifying consumer needs. An array of associated problems arise with a failed initial attempt to confirm consumer needs, including the need to redesign the product in

accordance with consumer specifications, missed schedules, late deliveries from suppliers and incompatible or outdated manufacturing processes to accommodate the new product designs. The latter problem has a compounding effect upon plant activities which generates the following difficulties: required tools are not available, materials are in short supply, employees are unsure of which operations to execute, scrap and rework is common and is a driving force behind increasing wastes and costs.

Reducing product delays to the market may be achieved through the following steps.

1. View the product as a development endeavour rather than a design project. Focusing on product development transfers a vast amount of the responsibility onto other functions aside from design. The use of development teams as opposed to engineering project-oriented teams allows for concurrent, plant-wide input into product development.
2. The effort of design, involvement of suppliers and manufacturing processes should be combined to establish a product which is compatible with all constituents of the organization.
3. Involvement of engineering, suppliers, planning teams and plant floor operators should be sought during the initial stages of product development. Successful product development with respect to product flexibility and cost occurs within the incipient stages. Key decisions are frequently determined within the first 15% of discussion time.
4. The director of product development teams should not come from an engineering discipline. Direction through engineering may result in product development being regarded as an engineering adventure. Program managers should be assigned to direct the development team toward adopting an egalitarian approach to idea generation and scheduling.

Responsiveness is considered to be one of the key factors which innovative firms will embrace to achieve competitive advantages over rival firms. Traditional views toward competition focus upon gaining an edge through price, quality and service. Successful organizations will differ in how they use their resources to compete on this basis. In spite of the emphasis placed upon provision of service, many organizations have been unsuccessful in correctly identifying and measuring up to consumer expectations.

Several varying cycle times have been identified (Heard, 1987). Their significance within a manufacturing environment and the role they play in obtaining a competitive advantage provides two avenues of interest. Two types of competition have been distinguished, namely product-based and time-based competition. Product-based competition refers to the development of a product which competes on the basis of quality. Responsibilities for developing such a product largely rest with the engineering and manufacturing departments. Time-based competition focuses upon customer responsiveness. Responsiveness in this sense is defined as 'the ability to satisfy customer requirements quicker than one's competitors' (Heard, 1987). This definition can be interpreted on several levels, all of which are related through the common element of cycle time.

The following list of cycle times provides a summary of the areas in an organization where excess time and delays are responsible for reducing the level of customer responsiveness. Identifying areas where excess time is taken to fulfill customer orders and performing the necessary steps to reduce this time may assist a company in obtaining a competitive advantage.

1. *Book/bill cycle time*   It refers to the difference between the time customers want to have their product and when they will receive it. This discrepancy prevails as a result of the time required to identify customer needs, verifying customer credit and product price, transferring the sales order to open files, packaging and shipping. Other activities which account for this discrepancy include the assembling, configuration and fabrication of products when they are not readily available on the shelf.
2. *Purchase/produce cycle time*   It includes the activities such as document-ing purchase orders and releases sent to suppliers, shipping, unloading, receiving of materials from suppliers and storing materials in inventory. Other time-consuming activities concerned with stored materials include accessing or requisitioning the material for production. This in itself involves a series of activities comprising counting, issuing and preparing inventory release orders.

   The receipt of material on the plant floor sets the stage for a sequence of manufacturing events which consume an abundance of time. These activities include the processing of material, counting and shipping. Support activities for processing encompass preventive maintenance procedures, machine set-ups and changeovers, location of tools and inspection of the final product prior to shipping.
3. *Manufacturing cycle time*   This is defined as the critical path through internal manufacturing activities. Minimization of manufacturing cycle time is crucial to the competitiveness of an organization as it is tied into the level of inventory. The longer the cycle time, the greater amount of inventory that must be held. This is to compensate for the slack between operations. The relationship between holding of excess inventory and organizational competitiveness is inverse; inventory increases the cost of the product and organizational competitiveness declines in response.
4. *Design/develop cycle time*   It pertains to the time required to conduct a market analysis, design a potential product, develop a prototype, field test, process plan and conduct engineering and manufacturing process evaluations, to mention some of the design/develop activities.

   Long design/develop cycle times have a compounding negative impact upon organizational competitiveness. First, they are directly tied into the book/bill cycle time. The longer the design/develop cycle time, the longer the book/bill cycle time. Second, extended design/develop cycle times represent an opportunity cost to the organization with respect to market opportunities. Third, organizations which experience long design/develop cycle times will inadvertently experience a drain on profits. Profits will have to be dispensed to support these capital intensive activities.

5. *Spec/source cycle time*   The activities which comprise this stage include establishing the specifications for the materials to be used in production of the product. These activities include the evaluation and selection of suppliers, the development of product function, quality, price and delivery, and the formalization of supplier negotiations.

The spec/source cycle times do not have a singular impact upon an organization's competitiveness as they are directly tied into the design/develop and book/bill cycle times for customized products. The introductory stage of the product cycle is most apt to be affected by spec/source cycle times. Extended cycle times in this aspect are a contributory factor toward missed opportunities, as are long design/develop cycle times.

In addition to being able to distinguish the various types of cycle times, it will be useful to understand the implications of cycle times for customer responsiveness in the repetitive and non-repetitive manufacturing environments.

Cycle times in repetitive manufacturing

Organizations which engage in repetitive manufacturing achieve customer responsiveness through short purchase/produce cycle times. Efficient production is made possible through the nature of the product line; high volume and product standardization. Repetitive manufacturing firms have tenacious purchasing and manufacturing capability as a result of infrequent product modifications and rescheduling. The cycle times in which such an organization would be unable to obtain competitive advantages are the book/bill and design/develop cycle times. These are commonly undeveloped in such organizations and are the source of increasing costs, particularly during the introductory stage of the product cycle where design and development constitute many of the activities.

Cycle times in non-repetitive manufacturing

The cycle time in non-repetitive manufacturing organizations that tends to be highly developed and thus a contributing factor toward competitiveness is the design/develop cycle. It stands to reason that this is the cycle which would be most developed when one considers the activities which must be performed to manufacture a customized product. Customized products demand clear definitions, developed prototypes and specific operations for successful manufacture.

Flexible manufacturing systems

Flexible manufacturing systems (FMS) represent another element of a flexible plant. They pertain to the use of numerical control systems, which are the activation of motors and other means of operating equipment through the use of coded instructions which are translated into electrical currents (Johnson, 1986). The installation and application of FMSs is suitable for companies manufacturing a product which is capable of being altered with minimal planning and disruption to the function of normal plant operations. FMSs which are guided by computer control are especially applicable to operations which require few human interactions to be operational. For purposes of illustration, manufacturing operations that can be performed by FMSs include the transportation of material.

2.4.6 Focused factory

The focused factory is a grouping together of operations in pursuit of specific goals and is appropriate for the manufacture of several distinct products. Manufacturing operations are combined into a series of mini-factories, where lead times, set-up times, cycle times, inventory and manufacturing wastes are significantly reduced. Motivation for the replacement of conventional manufacturing techniques with a focused factory is to gain competitive advantages.

The concepts surrounding the focused factory are clearly explained through the use of an example. A case study outlining the transitional steps from the conventional manufacturing approach to the focused factory is presented by Kapoor (1987). This particular organization produced several products for customers with highly individualized needs. Manufacturing under the conventional approach allowed the company to compete with rival firms; however, the traditional approach left room for improvement in their manufacturing processes. Set-up times, inventory accumulation, cycle times and warranty costs were too high and customer satisfaction was not being met.

Rearrangement of the plant involved the establishment of five mini-assembly plants, a master store room and a common feeder plant. The company's products consisted of high, medium and low voltage assemblies and control panels for the American market.

The traditional approach to the medium voltage assemblies gives rise to the following:

- layout consisted of six distinct locations;
- each location had its own supervisor; and
- each of the six locations had its own production schedules.

In contrast, the focused factory approach to the medium voltage assembly results in the following:

- the six operations are combined into one large area;
- the machinery is repositioned;

- one production schedule is required;
- there is streamlined production flow; and
- the above four elements were repeated with four other areas with the creation of a common feeder plant, four mini-assemblies and a master storeroom.

The use of mini-factories removes the ambiguity of managing the whole and presents management with a clearer picture of specific segments of the organization. Segmentation facilitates achievement of manufacturing goals. Once the goals were identified, focus was directed toward improving operations in the mini-factories. Specific goals were set to address the issues of on-time performance, cycle times, product quality and profitability in each of the mini-factories.

Focused factories also have an impact upon product manufacture, material availability, information flow, quality improvement, organizational structure and business strategy. Each of these will be addressed separately below.

Product manufacture

Product manufacture is illustrated through the processes involved with low voltage assemblies. The low voltage assembly area is a mini-factory with its own storeroom, twelve workstations and a packaging area, all connected with the use of conveyors. Kits containing electrical components, wire harnesses and sub-assemblies are transferred from the storeroom to the workstations where assemblage, wiring and testing are performed. Employees are cross-trained to perform these three functions.

Kanbans are used to moderate the flow of material and reduce machine idle time. Two units are present at each workstation; one being worked on and one waiting in the kanban queue. Each workstation has tools, containers and testing equipment to perform the necessary tasks, simultaneously reducing the movement of work-in-process parts.

The benefits received from adopting a focused factory approach permitted the company to realize a 90% improvement in on-time performance, reduce cycles times by 50%, reduce product warranty and space by 20% and 40%, respectively, and improve productivity by 50%.

Material availability

Figure 2.12 illustrates the flow of material within each of the mini-factories. Material is placed in the storerooms once it is received from the feeder plant, master storeroom or the assembly villages. The materials flow from the storerooms to many areas around the mini-factories. Steel enclosures from feeder plants are not processed in large batches to avoid long cycle times, inventory accumulation and poor customer responsiveness. Specific orders are made for specific parts, regardless of whether the same style has to be produced twice per shift. Increasing customer responsiveness in this situation was accomplished through set-up reduction and equipment rearrangement.

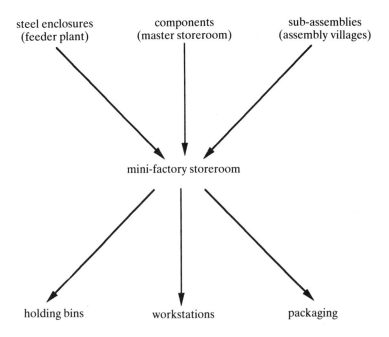

Figure 2.12 The focus factory.

Flow of components from the master storeroom is regulated though the use of kanbans. The kanbans function as a signal for material replenishment. Operations are guided with the direction of a material processor and a material co-ordinator. Suppliers are chosen in accordance with the goals inherent in JIT purchasing. The suppliers sought are those willing to schedule daily deliveries, produce 100% defect-free products and produce in small lot sizes.

Material availability with respect to assembly voltages serve to replenish mini-storerooms with sub-assemblies and harnesses. Assembly voltages are located and designed to work well and fulfill the requirements of mini-assembly plants.

Information flow

The purpose of information flow in the focused factory is to eliminate the errors associated with the traditional manufacturing approach. Errors such as shipping of wrong parts and quality problems arise with inadequately designed channels for information flow. Elimination of errors is addressed on an individual product basis.

The traditional manufacturing approach manifested itself in providing three main functions of information flow, failing to regard individual product dissimilarities: the first of these functions included provision of minimal informational requirements; the second, presenting of information in a manner which was designed to assist shop floor personnel; and the third, simplifying functions to reduce errors and delays.

Information flow in the focused factory is designed to reduce the steps and the amount of information required to execute production on a product-by-product basis. For example, standardized products are broken down and identified by numbers. Identification numbers are fed into a computer accompanying costs and manufacturing methods for the product. This information is given to product assemblers along with product assembly diagrams. Following this method of information flow, identification numbers and the quantity desired for manufacturing are required.

Employees assume an active role in the process. For example, product assemblers are required to anticipate future problems with meeting customer deliveries on a daily basis. This is the format followed for standardized products. Products manufactured to customized needs are addressed by teams consisting of marketing, engineering and manufacturing personnel. Teams were successful in developing the following system from communicating with customers to determine individual needs of product manufacture. Initially, forms are completed for documenting the customers' needs. The use of a standardized form allows team members to determine what information is still required from the customer. Standardized forms allow for the manufacture of a complete product, compatible with customers' needs.

Information present on the standardized form is then loaded into a computer to complete a bill of materials. The computer runs a fail-safe program to prevent the processing of erroneous information. Once the bill of materials is received by shop floor personnel, all the parts required for manufacture are transferred to the assembly area where the product is completed. Upon completion, shipping papers and invoices are documented.

The use of this informational approach to meeting diversified customer needs has benefited the company. Quality improvements, cycle time reduction to between two and six times and a 71% reduction in the number of employees required to produce the products were realized. This increased the overall productivity and efficiency of the plant.

Quality Improvement
Quality improvement is facilitated through the use of mini-factories by five main factors.

1. Products are completed in specific plant areas which are smaller than the manufacturing areas used by the traditional approach. This assists employees in identifying areas for improvement or the areas where quality problems are likely to arise. Employees are able to bypass the elimination process in determining the cause of problems.
2. Employees in a specific manufacturing area are responsible for the product produced in it. The use of mini-factories fosters a sense of employee ownership. Therefore, responsibility to create a defect-free product will be greater than that found within a traditional manufacturing environment.
3. The length of time required to identify the cause of product defects is substantially reduced. This is directly related to the reduced size of the segmented work areas.
4. Quality is further enhanced by another aspect of manufacturing under a focused factory environment. Employees are required to perform all tasks, from the initial stages of manufacturing to product assembly and testing. Successful task performance of this nature depends upon the cross-training of employees. Employees in training programs are immersed in an orientation of the product and forced to become familiar with it completely, rather than focusing upon one specific stage of product manufacture. They become more knowledgeable and question the manufacturing processes of the product in greater detail. Cross-training fosters quality consciousness.
5. Mini-factories require cohesive groups which are frequently well informed. Information concerning the product is conveyed to each employee within the group. Uniformity of information in the group allows product changes to be rapidly implemented. In summary, increased employee responsibility and the environment created in a focused factory provide the foundation for quality improvements.

Organizational structure

The organizational structure undergoes several changes when focused factories are implemented. Elimination of key departments such as packaging, shipping, receiving and inspection of incoming products is feasible. Mini-factories perform each of these tasks in totality. Maintaining separate departments to execute such tasks would be redundant.

The organizational structure becomes flatter as a level of general supervisors can be eliminated. Mini-factory supervisors, who perform several different functions, are employed. Organizational structure is further modified by the changes which occur in the supporting departments. For example, four departments were established to support the activities of the mini-factories: order management, customer order engineering, materials and technical services.

Business strategy
The effect upon the organization's approach to business strategy is multi-faceted. The transition from the traditional manufacturing approach to that of the focused factory requires increasing involvement of the employees in the company. Concern becomes focused around the development of products, not parts. Thus, needless inventory accumulation is averted.

Focused factories define the organization by product. Therefore, problems and opportunities become readily identifiable. Visibility is enhanced as the work areas are well defined. Housekeeping activities also obtain a new importance in the organization and they are pursued with vigour. The focused factory approach is analogous to the profit centre concept. Profit centres provide information concerning product performance; which products are competitively superior and which ones require improvement.

2.5 JIT production control

JIT production control is concerned with the elements of the system which link, co-ordinate and direct the actions of workers and machines. The two elements of JIT production control which stand out more readily than others and are most frequently used are the use of the kanban and MRP II. In many manufacturing organizations, MRP II has become a functional part of the manufacturing environment and its integration in a company frequently precedes the implementation of JIT. In these instances, it has assumed a permanent position in the organization, warranting further discussion of its functioning within a JIT environment. MRP and kanbans are used to establish the scheduling of operations, the quantity of product to be produced and direction of production flow.

The concept of demand pull was presented earlier and is an integral part of production control. Production is called into action by the demand of consumers and the flow of material is stipulated according to the demand pull concept. This concept, when applied to manufacturing, allows organizations to produce only the quantity of product that is required. Employees will work to produce this quantity and will avoid the manufacturing of products which are not demanded.

The application of demand pull can eliminate unnecessary inventory which would otherwise stockpile following the traditional approach to manufacturing. Organizations which adhere to the traditional manufacturing will push machinery and employees to work to produce as much as possible, regardless of the level of demand. The excess material and product will be stockpiled in inventory until it can be sold. There are numerous costs associated with traditional manufacturing. The majority of these costs will be incurred as inventory costs. Stockpiling inventory subjects products to the risk of becoming obsolete prior to unloading the excess. However, other costs which could be incurred are those created from low quality outputs such as scrap and rework costs.

2.5.1 The kanban system

The word 'kanban' when translated into English means signal. It is usually a card or tag accompanying work-in-process parts. There are two types of kanbans which are used as a tool in the JIT production system. The 'withdrawal' kanban is used to indicate the type and amount of product which the next process should withdraw from the preceding process. The 'production-ordering' kanban specifies the type and quantity of product which the next process must produce (Monden, 1983).

The functioning of the kanban is best explained through the use of an example. Hay (1988) and Suzaki (1987) use a supermarket analogy to illustrate the use of the kanban. Consumers determine the amount of goods which a company will have to produce by the quantity of goods they remove from shelves. Withdrawal tags attached to the products are removed at the checkout and placed into a kanban post or container for holding the tags. The withdrawal tags are picked up and taken to a warehouse where new products used to fill the supermarket shelves are removed. Production-ordering tags attached to these goods are replaced with withdrawal tags. These goods are brought back to the supermarket shelves. The production tags are then placed into another kanban post which are picked up and transported to a manufacturing plant. Production of new products will occur in the quantities specified by the production cards. Once the production of new goods is complete, production cards are attached and the goods are transported back to the warehouse shelves. The cycle is then complete and these actions are repeated on a continuous basis to meet consumer demands.

The functions of the kanban

The functions of the kanban are twofold. They are used as a means for production control and for process improvement. The role played by the kanban in production control is to tie the different manufacturing processes together and to ensure that the necessary amounts of material and parts arrive at the appropriate time and place. The use of the kanban in process improvement includes improving the operations used in the production process with emphasis on reducing inventory costs.

The use of the kanban may not be appropriate for every organization applying JIT to its manufacturing processes. Kanbans are appropriate if the following circumstances are present in a manufacturing plant (Hay, 1988):

- Sub-assembly and final assembly are carried out in separate plants or at distances which would not permit moving a product one at a time for practical reasons.

- Changeover times between feeding and using operations involve a great amount of time. This will not allow one-at-a-time flow especially if the feeding operation does not run at a faster rate than the using operation. Sufficient time to accommodate long changeovers will not be provided.
- There are a number of different work cells which must share a piece of equipment. The kanbans become important in this situation for linking the machine with the various work cells.
- The use of a machine which is responsible for work cell stoppages due to the requirement of a high degree of maintenance and repair work. The kanban can be used in this situation to link the machine to a work cell rather than risking the stoppage of an entire cell. This method allows the machine to be used separately and avoids it becoming an indispensable part of a work cell.
- The existence of problems such as low quality work and bottlenecks or other problems which may impair the steady flow of operations.

2.5.2 Rules for kanban operation

The use of the kanban involves specific rules to ensure it is being applied properly and is maintaining a production flow which is smooth and steady. The following rules should be considered and practised in order for the kanban to serve the purposes of the organization (Monden, 1983; Suzaki, 1987).

1. Parts from a downstream process should be obtained from a preceding process in the quantity, type and timing as described on the kanban. In order for this to be fully carried out the following steps must occur:
   (a) the kanban must always be attached to the product;
   (b) withdrawal of a product should never occur unless a kanban is attached; and
   (c) the number of withdrawals should never exceed the number of kanbans.

2. The parts should be produced corresponding to the information provided on the kanbans. Therefore, the quantities produced in the preceding process should match the quantities produced in the subsequent process. In order for this to occur, the following sub-rules will apply:
   (a) production should never exceed the number of kanbans;
   (b) when manufacturing involves different kinds of parts, the quantity and sequence of their processing should be followed as specified in the preceding operation.

3. If no kanban is attached to a product, there should not be any production function carried out.

4. In the event that defective items are produced, they should not be transferred to the subsequent process. This will assist in the elimination of defective parts on the line.

5. It should be assured that only 100% quality parts are placed in the containers available for use. This will prevent line stoppages from becoming a hindrance to the production process.
6. The number of kanbans used in the production flow should be minimized. This will prevent the build-up of inventory.
7. The number of kanbans used in the production process should be reduced over a period of time. This may connect processes and sources of wastes may surface. Thus, the production process can be streamlined further.
8. The use of the kanban can be applied to follow fluctuations which exist in the production process. The kanban can be used to respond to changes in demand by increasing or decreasing the number of units to be produced. Therefore, future changes in demand can be met by levelling the production process as soon as possible to meet these changes. The kanbans accompanying these products will specify the amount of products to be processed in accordance with the changes in demand.

2.5.3 Preparing the plant for the kanban system

The kanban is a control mechanism which links the production activities. Success and proper functioning of the kanban is dependent upon how well the organization prepares the plant for its use. One major area within a plant that must be addressed is the levelling of production.

Smoothing production

The use of the kanban requires that the production process be smoothed. Production smoothing involves minimizing the amount of variation in the

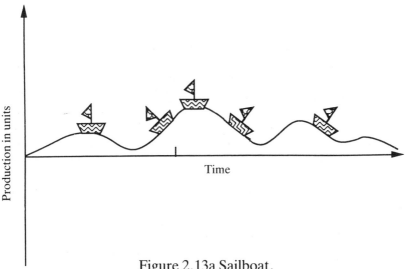

Figure 2.13a Sailboat.

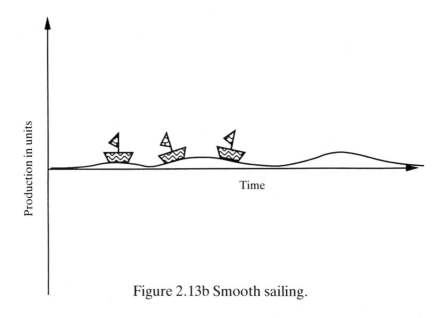

Figure 2.13b Smooth sailing.

withdrawn quantity of each part produced at an assembly. Each part can therefore be produced in a fixed quantity per period of time or at a constant rate. Levelling requires the production function be moderated while ensuring there is enough of a required part produced to meet demand. Smoothing production also involves levelling the scheduling of production processes. Levelled scheduling can reduce parts shortages and increase manufacturing performance. The sales and production departments in an organization would be responsible for determining a fixed level of production and its duration.

Levelling production helps to reduce sudden changes in production to meet changes in demand. This concept is frequently explained with a sailboat analogy, illustrated in Fig. 2.13a and b. Figure 2.13a shows a sailboat upon rough waters. This can be likened to a production schedule which fluctuates to extremes, increasing the difficulties of meeting consumer requirements, while Fig. 2.13b illustrates 'smooth sailing' once production scheduling has been levelled.

To illustrate the use of levelled production, consider the following example. A manufacturing firm is producing 100 units of a product per day in January. The demand profile indicates that the need for the product will increase to 120 units per day in February. In order to avoid this fluctuation in demand which places a greater degree of stress upon the processing functions to meet February demand, production for January could be increased to 107 units per day to assist in levelling the load for February. Thus, levelling smooths out the fluctuations in demand over a period of time. The levelling of production is illustrated in Figs. 2.14a and 2.14b.

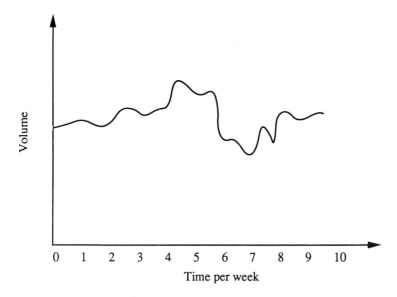

Figure 2.14a Graph of a market demand profile.

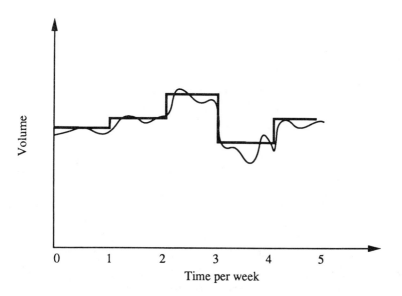

Figure 2.14b Graph of a market demand profile.

Many organizations produce more than one product, therefore, they must engage in mixed production levelling. This involves ensuring there is enough labour, equipment and resources available for use when there is production of more than one product per period.

The idea of cycle time control becomes important in levelling production. Cycle time can best be defined as 'the time between the completion of the last product and completion of the next product' (Suzaki, 1987). Therefore, it involves the rate at which the product flows through the production processes. The use of 'cycle time analysis' can lead to identification of possible activities which can be improved to make the production process more efficient (Hall, 1987). Cycle time analysis involves the following:

- identification of events in the longest cycle time which could be eliminated; and
- identification of events in the shortest cycle time that could be applied or adapted to other cycle times.

Production can be made more efficient by reducing the average cycle time or decreasing the amount of variation within each cycle time. An effective means of observing cycle times is to time ten cycles of an operation while focusing on identifying the events which could be improved upon. Activities to which a cycle time analysis can be applied involve the activities that are carried out in a repeated cycle. These activities commonly include the following:

- material handling;
- cell activities between machines and operators;
- flow of material through the plant;
- maintenance procedures; and
- activities which involve a single operation.

Production of several different products can further be accomplished by specifying the time periods in which production of a particular product will occur. This is carried out by specifying the 'time buckets'. Time buckets are the time durations in which production will occur. They are usually divided into intervals of one or two weeks. Production of one of the products can occur within a time bucket, then the process can be changed over and another product can be processed in another specified time bucket. Use of time buckets ensures that the production process will be smooth and that the organization is effective in meeting its goals.

Cycle time management should ideally be a function of the machine operators. Cycle times can be administered more efficiently through operators assuming a user/supplier role. The key factor in determining efficient cycle times is to develop a fully integrated system where machine operators should view themselves as customers of suppliers and as being responsible for the needs of other specific customers.

Small lot sizing
The use of small lot sizes ensures that production can occur in a constant manner. Small lot sizing is consistent with JIT in terms of producing smaller amounts more frequently. Small lot sizes become especially important when there is mixed production. The work-in-process materials in a lot can be processed through that particular operation and machinery can then be changed over to meet the other goals of production. This is why small lot sizes are required. It should be noted, however, that while small lot sizes are required for JIT production, they should not be so small that the set-up cost of equipment will be spread over very few items, resulting in an increase in the cost per unit of the product.

Other factors
In addition to the smoothed production and small lot sizes, Suzaki (1987) discusses other factors which should be taken into consideration prior to kanban implementation. A synopsis of these points is as follows.
1. The development of levelled production is dependant upon the ability to prepare a schedule for production. This should be accomplished through the co-ordinated effort of sales, production and marketing employees.
2. The kanban should follow the flow of materials. This can be realized by designating locations within the plant. Designating specific locations can reduce any confusion which may arise between the handling of materials and the kanban.
3. There should be small lot sizes and short changeover times to facilitate the levelling of production.
4. The manufacturing of specialized, high value products will have to receive different treatment, with respect to the use of the kanban.
5. The sales and marketing department should give production prior notice if there are sudden fluctuations in demand. This is a fairly common occurrence with products which are in their introductory stage of growth, promotional items or products subject to seasonal fluctuations. Forewarning will allow production sufficient time to adjust manufacturing scheduling to meet demand.
6. Once the kanban is implemented in a plant, it must be updated to conform to changes in sales and those that result from improvement activities. Updating the kanbans should serve to monitor the number and kinds of kanbans used.
7. Gradually, the number of kanbans used in the production process should be reduced. This is another improvement activity that the organization should carry out.

2.5.4 Lead time and cycle time reduction
Lead time reduction in a JIT environment will enable a company to respond quickly to customer needs simply by reducing the time required to make

products and have them available to customers. Manufacturing lead time consists of the following five elements (Bechtel, 1987).

1. *Waiting time*   The time subsequent to the completion of operations. Teardown and inspection times should be included in the assessment of the total waiting time. In many instances, these two activities are included in other elements of lead time. Frequently, time consumed in teardowns and inspection activities is embodied in set-up and run times, respectively.
2. *Moving time*   The duration required to move between machine operations.
3. *Queuing time*   The time prior to the commencement of operations. In many organizations, queue time is responsible for approximately 80–90% of the total manufacturing lead time.
4. *Machine set-up times*   The amount of time required to complete machine changeovers and set-ups.
5. *Running time*   The time required for work-in-process parts to complete a machine operation.

Efficient management of lead time reduction can be achieved through the use of a 'closed loop' system (Schultz, 1987). The closed loop system is capable of adjusting to changes and providing compensations between supply and demand, customers, plants and suppliers. Figure 2.15 gives an example of a closed loop system.

Reducing the cumulative lead time or the sum of lead times for purchasing materials, manufacturing operations and product assembly allows a company to reduce the planning horizon for production. Reducing the planning horizon allows a company to increase the accuracy of its demand predictions. Reducing the inaccuracies of demand prediction diminishes the amount of buffer inventory which would otherwise be required.

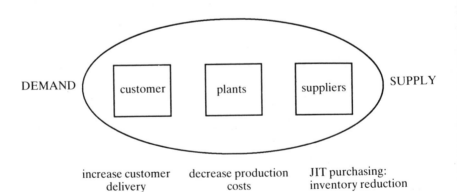

Figure 2.15 The closed loop system (Source: Schultz, 1987).

2.5.5 Implementing the kanban system

Implementing the kanban system provides the organization with several benefits including the reduction of work-in-process inventory, simplification of the product flow, detection of product defects and identification of the cause of defects. An implementation plan must be developed to help management overcome obstacles that arise in embarking upon kanban implementation. Issues to be dealt with include the role of employees, education, implementation procedures and ensuing implementation activities.

Obstacles to implementation

The obstacles to implementation include those factors which increase the risk of incomplete or unsuccessful implementation. Four such factors have been identified. The last three are not obstacles inasmuch as they represent modifications to the ideal procedure of kanban implementation. As the 'real world' encroaches upon the ideal manufacturing environment, several modifications must be performed.

1. Habitual practice of producing continuously, regardless if demand has already been met. Like all bad habits, this one is difficult to break as it involves changing the steadfast beliefs of employees that this is the correct way to manufacture.
2. Modifications in the production schedule and product mix are frequently required; however, in order to adapt the kanban to these, considerable attention must be dedicated to the managing of kanbans. Management activities include extending the number of cards used and tracking these cards throughout the production processes.
3. Extended set-up times are not recognized by traditional kanbans, therefore, the number of active kanbans should be such that they are plentiful enough to withstand demand for the duration of extended set-up times.
4. Unbalanced rates for consumption and production require there be sufficient number of kanbans to compensate for machine, personnel and material handling constraints.

The role of employees

The role of employees in the kanban implementation procedures should result in a sense of ownership in the process, as they are responsible for its functioning and long-term success. Acquainting employees directly with the kanban operations can prevent obstacles from occurring subsequent to implementation.

The role of education

The role of education and training serves to introduce employees to the functioning of the kanban system within their organization. Development of a model for illustrating its application is a requirement of this step.

Implementation procedures
Implementation procedures encompass the selection of a pilot product, establishing procedures and the number of cards to be used with each item in the production flow. The selection criteria of the pilot product include choosing a product with quick set-up times, minimal constraints and a steady production schedule. The rationale for selecting such a product is to ensure initial success, which positively influences the rate of kanban implementation throughout the remaining product mix.

The establishment of procedures includes formalizing which employees are responsible for handling the cards, accuracy, the method of communicating the cards between departments and the appropriate actions to take when kanbans become separated from items.

Determination of the number of cards required for each item in the production process involves consideration of the relationship between product demand, queue time, kanban container size and production variances.

Implementation activities
The activities which should be conducted subsequent to implementation pertain to performance measurement of the pilot project. Actual performance results should be matched against those anticipated. In the areas where performance results fall short of expectations, problems and opportunities should be identified. The greatest opportunities will present themselves in the areas of reducing queue time.

2.5.6 JIT and MRP
The most widespread understanding of the use of JIT and MRP is that the two systems subsume an organizational endeavour exclusive of one another (Helle, 1988). MRP has played a substantial role in the functioning of manufacturing organizations since its advent in the 1960s. The arrival of JIT into the North American manufacturing scene has left many companies with unanswered questions pertaining to which system is preferable. The systems are frequently combined, however in the absence of successful management, this combination can prove to be a costly feature (Spencer, 1990). This discussion will address how MRP can be modified and implemented to achieve success in a JIT environment.

MRP is an expansive computerized system used in an organization to plan and control the materials and resources needed for the production of goods. It can be dichotomized into two systems, namely MRP I (material requirements planning) and MRP II (manufacturing resource planning). The role each plays in this planning and controlling function is complementary. The function of MRP I is to calculate the requirements for material through the application of a bill of material, inventory and a master production schedule. The objective of MRP II is to plan resources for all production activities which include materials, labour and machine usage. The execution of this function is practicable through the application of the bill of materials, master production scheduling and material requirements planning.

MRP I and MRP II

Several strategies have been developed addressing the implementation of MRP II in a JIT environment. The strategies contain commonalties concerning the role of employees, machinery, approaches to planning and strategy development, as well as the specific adjustments necessary to fine tune MRP II with a JIT philosophy.

Combining JIT and MRP II

Two schools of thought which bring forth contrasting ideologies of these two systems are

- JIT applications exceed those of an MRP II system, and
- JIT and MRP II can be integrated to work in harmony, based upon the sharing of a common goal.

The first school of thought presumes that JIT outperforms MRP II in all areas concerning manufacturing planning and control. According to this belief, JIT concepts should receive attention in an organization. These two schools of thought will be addressed separately below.

JIT applications exceed those of an MRP II system

The goals of MRP II are to improve upon an organization's ability to satisfy customers, increase productivity, reduce production and inventory costs; these goals are also reflected in the philosophies embedded in JIT. However, the ability of MRP II to achieve these goals is dependent upon a number of factors. Organizations operating at a level consistent with Class A performance place themselves in a position to receive the maximum benefits of such a system. Class A performance is a standard measurement in which all elements of a system operate at a performance level between 90 and 100% (Buker, 1987). Those organizations unable to achieve a Class A level of performance will be operating less than their potential permits and will fall short of meeting the above goals.

Although many organizations are able to achieve Class A performance standards, the ingredients which determine successful MRP II arrest the manufacturing environment's capacity to perform at levels which become evident with JIT. One such ingredient concerns the rate of inventory movement. MRP II requires a slow rate of inventory movement. Many of the advantages of MRP II can be realized through smoothing production and rearranging the plant for efficient layout. These are activities inherent in the functioning of JIT.

JIT has been viewed as a superior system for numerous reasons such as increasingly efficient flow of materials, improved ability to meet customer demands and reduce costs. Visibility is enhanced through JIT and this enables problems to surface. Product routeings become simplified and in many instances reduced. Inventory accuracy is strengthened due to reduced levels. JIT also affects the 'Master Schedule' with respect to flexibility and reliability. Lead times are reduced which intensifies the organization's ability to respond to customer requirements.

One element of singular importance in determining the success of any system concerns the scope of which people are actively involved in a system. JIT makes particular use of this as it is in itself a people system. Additional benefits received from the use of JIT include the reduction of work-in-process inventory, set-up time, direct and indirect labour, occupied floor space, inventory and capacity reduction.

Integrating JIT with MRP II

The second school of thought assumes JIT and MRP II can be integrated to fulfill the common goal of 'becoming and remaining a world class competitor' (Brooks, 1987). Integration entails modifying elements of MRP II to construct a design which enables an organization to reap the benefits of both systems. Organizations which currently operate in an MRP II environment and are embarking upon JIT implementation will benefit greatly from this discussion. The benefits of using the two systems simultaneously are twofold (Helle, 1988): first, the underlying concepts of JIT preserve the simplicity of MRP II design amid implementation; and second, JIT concepts permit the benefits of MRP II to be realized quicker than the benefits received from an MRP II system operating exclusively on its own.

Several integration approaches have been suggested which embrace the concept of applying JIT to MRP II. These will be discussed in the following.

Integrating JIT with MRP II – first approach

The first approach addresses the functioning of the two systems in varying manufacturing environments of job–shop processing and repetitive manufacturing (Fuller and Brown 1987). Given the nature of product flow under both job–shop and repetitive manufacturing, where operations require distinctive scheduling, processing, reporting and inspecting, it becomes necessary to develop an integrative design where the requirements of both can be satisfied. Such an approach commands flexibility as manufacturing processes change from push or job processing to pull systems or repetitive manufacturing.

An additional requirement to flexibility of design includes planning for the systems. Planning requirements will be modified to include timeliness, the bill of materials, preventive maintenance, inventory integrity and efficient processing and communication of information. The use of JIT with MRP II demands planning for short time periods such as to the day or even the hour as compared to planning requirements for a week or a month. The bill of materials must be modified to link the usage of material to actual operations. Planning for preventive maintenance will be conducted to validate capacity requirements. The use of JIT with MRP II necessitates complete and accurate inventory records to abate the risk of stockouts with the elimination of safety stocks. Communication of inventory status is facilitated through the use of computerized systems. This information must be relayed to the work cells, final assembly, customers and suppliers. The application of kanbans and SPC (statistical process control) is also a requirement to integrate the two systems.

Integrating JIT with MRP II – second approach

The second approach addresses how specific JIT concepts can be applied to various elements of an MRP II system including master production scheduling, implementing MRP I, shop floor control, purchasing and engineering (Helle, 1988).

Master production scheduling (MPS) should be implemented with five JIT concepts in mind. First, all employees in the MPS department should be included in the planning and problem-solving activities which impede goal achievement. Goals should address the function of extended set-up times, the reasons for scrap and rework, maximizing production output and executing a preventive maintenance program. Second, MPS should address the functioning of critical work centres. Third, it should attempt to establish product flow which prevents bottlenecks from occurring. Fourth, the MPS should be capable of delivering information with respect to the limitations of bottlenecked work sites. Fifth, the dynamics of MPS should be fully understood and applied to perform those functions in their entirety.

The application of JIT concepts to the implementation of MRP I addresses the reduction of lead times, movement of material and work-in-process inventory through the simplifying of the bill of material. Lead times assume a main role with respect to this element. For example, many activities will focus upon establishing causes and actions appropriate to reduce long lead times. The cause of extended lead times may rest in the process or the product.

JIT concepts, as they relate to shop floor control, generally address a broad area in the plant, ranging from quality control to scheduling. TQC programs should be organized commencing with the products which possess the highest level of defects. Process flow should be evaluated to establish optimal locations for work cells and furnish employees with training to perform the functions in the cells. Preventive maintenance and set-up reduction programs should be developed and the scheduling of products should be consistent with the pull concept.

Purchasing should be administered with concern for quality being of central focus. Ensuring the quality of the final product commences with supplier's ability to meet customer requirements. An organization should work with suppliers to establish TQC programs. Supplier performance should be monitored based upon three criteria of quality, delivery and price. Areas of concern should be extended to include expeditious deliveries and the elimination of incoming inspection.

JIT concepts applied to product engineering address the manufacturability and lead time reduction of product design. Products should be designed with ease of manufacturing in mind. A product which is designed in this manner will reduce the manufacturing lead times associated with its production. Reducing the amount of time required to design a product can further assist in improving customer delivery.

Integrating JIT with MRP II – third approach

The third approach focuses upon the impact JIT improvements have upon an MRP II system (Sipes, 1987). Attention is directed toward work cells, standardization of products, reduced set-up times, lot sizes and reduced overhead activities.

Two benefits received from the application of work cells are reduced work-in-process inventory and queue time. The effect these have upon an MRP II system is simplification of routeings and reduced number of work centres. Where the transportation of each product is reduced as a result of efficient plant layout, the gathering of cost data is facilitated.

Parts which are similar in physical and functional characteristics can be combined. The effect this has upon systems is to reduce the purchasing, recording and separate stocking of individual items.

The primary JIT benefit received from reduced lead times and lot sizes is the reduction of inventory and increased visibility. Decreasing inventory levels allows hidden problems to surface. The impact upon systems affects the manufacturing lead times, set-up time and planning systems.

The JIT impact upon the system stems from the value added concept – only the activities which add value to the product should be performed, all others should be eliminated. The method of documenting costs should be evaluated.

The dual functioning of JIT and MRP II has the potential to provide a number of benefits as JIT impacts upon existing systems. The third approach provides an outline of implementation activities to perform in three distinct phases, to successfully combine JIT and MRP II. These phases are presented in Table 2.8.

To illuminate further the dynamics of the dual system, where certain manufacturing elements are controlled through JIT and others through the use of MRP II, reconciliation of the 'pull' and 'push' systems is possible through an integration procedure. This procedure commands the customer orders to be verified *vis-à-vis* a 'distributor function' (Edwards, 1987). The underlying purpose of this verification is to determine which system, JIT or MRP II controls various items. MRP II items are additionally categorized into Master Schedule or MRP controlled. This integration procedure wields a substantial effect upon the planning and control elements of the two systems.

The success of combining JIT and MRP II is dependent upon the co-ordinated effort of individuals in an organization. The unifying activities

Table 2.8 Comparative analyses of JIT and MRP II (Source: Raeker, 1987)

Function	MRP II	JIT
Business planning	Establish strategies	Establish strategies
Production planning	Define production rates	Define production rates
Resource requirements	Establish resources, focus on total resources	Focus on rate achievement capability
Master production schedule	Manufacture schedule by product	Manufacture rate by product group
Final assembly schedules	Assemble product per module assembly	Assemble product through pull system
MRP I	Plan for material and production	Plan for sub-assembly rates
CRP	Resources per work centre	Co-ordinate the line with the need rate
Manufacturing	Routeings per item	Routeings per work cell
Plant floor control	Control through dispatch list	Control through pull system
Managing quality	Inspection	SPC
Cost planning	Standard costs through item bills and routeings	Standard costs through item bills and routeings
Inventory control	Track WIP	Minimize WIP tracking
Purchasing planning	Release of individual purchase orders	Long-term contracts
Purchasing releasing	Release of individual purchase orders	Kanban

of work teams provide the linkage necessary to integrate the two systems. Several work teams have been identified which each perform a dynamic function in this unifying effort (Stelter, 1987). The team activities pertain to the tasks performed during the creation of work centres.

- Cost accounting teams are necessary to verify accuracy and correctness of costs applied to various manufacturing functions, such as labour rates and set-up times.
- A foreman assumes the tasks of controlling the work centre areas and informing all active team members of changes in the functioning of the centres.
- Manufacturing engineering teams are required to accommodate process and physical changes as well as equipment rearrangements and communicate these changes to others.
- Production control groups are necessary to select the software to be used to run systems, to remain up to date on product mix changes and convey these changes to others, maintain machines and an efficient labour force.
- Operations management teams obtain needed information from systems.
- Data processing groups fulfill the functions of assessing programs and providing the manufacturing personnel with the necessary resources.

3.

Just-in-time logistics

3.1 JIT purchasing

The purchasing function in a JIT environment transgresses the traditional approaches employed in the past. JIT purchasing differs from the traditional approach in the nature of the relationship between the organization and the supplier, the frequency of deliveries and the number of suppliers a firm typically maintains. The element of purchasing which has been subject to the greatest impact is the quality of the supplier's products. Quality has superseded price to become the primary consideration in the selection of suppliers. The following discussion will examine the changing role of suppliers in a JIT environment.

3.1.1 Contrasts between JIT and traditional purchasing
The function of purchasing in an organization has manifested itself in the past as primarily concerned with obtaining the required parts at the lowest price. The shifting of focus towards quality represents but one change in the role purchasing plays in a JIT environment. Table 3.1 presents a summary of these differences (Voss, 1987).

The JIT literature emphasizes the benefits of JIT purchasing and has identified these benefits as reduced administration costs, inventory levels and storage space, increases in product quality, and identification and determination of quality problems (Giunipero and O'Neal, 1988). Despite the potential to gain these benefits, many supplier organizations are reluctant to enter into a JIT relationship with their customers. Such a relationship requires the supplier to alter its practice and to adopt those commensurate with the JIT philosophy. The full scope of these new techniques require alterations extending beyond merely the purchasing department. Six categories of supplier resistance have been identified (Giunipero and O'Neal, 1988).

1. The supplier deems its purchasing function as incompatible under a JIT environment. Generally, this statement applies to the differences in manufacturing approaches. A supplier may operate under a job–shop manufacturing environment whereas JIT, to a large extent, requires a repetitive flow operation. This perceived incompatibility may induce suppliers to believe that JIT purchasing is strictly appropriate in a

Table 3.1 Purchasing practices

Activity	JIT	Traditional
Purchase size	• small lots • frequent deliveries	• large batches • few deliveries
Supplier selection	• long term • single source supply	• short term • multiple source supply
Supplier evaluation	• criteria include quality delivery, price • no rejects acceptable	• quality, delivery, price • 2% rejects accepted
Inspection	• initial reduction • eventually eliminated	• activities include receiving, counting and inspecting
Negotiations	• long term, quality and reasonable price	• obtain lowest price
Transportation	• on-time delivery • concern for inbound/outbound freight • buyer has schedule	• outbound freight • lower costs • supplier has schedule responsibility
Product specs.	• supplier innovation • emphasis on performance loose specs.	• buyers concern for design specs. • suppliers are not innovative
Paperwork	• less paperwork • ability to change delivery time and quantity	• large volume of paperwork • purchase orders needed to change delivery time and quantity
Packaging	• small, standardized containers which hold exact quantity	• regular packaging • no clear specs.

repetitive flow environment. Practically speaking, however, JIT purchasing can be applied to most manufacturing environments.

2. Many firms regard the success of other firms as irrelevant to them. This is chiefly the result of failing to examine thoroughly the purchasing operations of the successful organizations.

3. Geographical distance from customers may be viewed as an obstacle to JIT purchasing as the frequency of deliveries may increase from monthly to weekly and very often daily deliveries. Many organizations regard fulfilling this requirement as next to impossible. Granted, short distances between supplier and customer facilitate JIT purchasing, however, success need not be limited to the geographically accordant organizations. Careful and logical planning and scheduling can overcome any obstacles related to distance. Geographical desirability represents a subjective preference of any organization. Certain organizations, such as those requiring delivery on a weekly or daily basis, may be flexible about geographical distance. However, the organizations requiring deliveries several times daily, geographical desirability may play a central role in supplier selection.

4. Changing production schedules due to shortages, constraints on materials, engineering changes or customer requirements are viewed by suppliers as potential obstacles. The effect of changes can be minimized through carefully planning and preventing the need for these changes. Several means of preventing these alterations are intrinsically tied to the functioning of JIT. For example, the co-ordinated processes in a JIT environment will eliminate material constraints and shortages. Overcoming the remaining obstacles can be achieved through planning the design of a product based on the contribution of both the customer and the supplier. Correctly determining customer requirements can be achieved through market analyses.

5. Selection of the supplier based upon the lowest bid may motivate the supplier to calculate bids based upon purchase price variances. This method carries with it hidden costs as it is frequently believed that the lowest bid is composed of the lowest material costs. However, this sentiment fails to take into consideration the cost of quality, which can include scrap and rework costs, high warranty expense and inspection requirements. Other costs which are discounted include coping with poor delivery performance. Selection on the basis of the lowest bid can be deceptive as the lowest initial cost may actually be the most costly in the long run. A successful customer–supplier relationship depends on factors other than price alone.

6. The final category regarding supplier reluctance is threefold. The first obstacle to supplier adoption of JIT purchasing practices includes the need to stock extra material. This necessity may arise out of customers reducing their inventory levels. Preventing the need for

this is realizable through the supplier modifying its organization to follow the JIT practices.

The second obstacle relates to concern of the suppliers for the benefits which will accrue to them. The benefits which have been identified include a steady and long-term customer, certainty of demand, larger volume of sales as the customer operating according to JIT principles is likely to rely solely on one supplier, and the ability to develop long-term customer programs.

The third obstacle regards the supplier discontinuing business. A customer can skillfully avoid establishing a long-term relationship with a supplier who is likely to go out of business through careful evaluation of the supplier. This evaluation commonly entails determining how successful the supplier will be in meeting customer requirements over an extended period of time, as well as an analysis of the financial stability and growth of the company. Other supplier selection criteria will be unique to the individual company. This is discussed in a further section of this chapter.

The nature of the relationship between supplier and customer is an important determinant of success.   Three types of relationships have been identified and each can be regarded as part of a broad spectrum (Reeds, 1988).

1. *The adversary relationship*   The underlying mentality and attitude which exist between the supplier and the customer is one of 'us versus them'.   Short-term contracts are established on the basis of the lowest price, with other factors fundamental to achieving quality products such as quality costs and supplier delivery totally disregarded. The nature of this relationship fails to take into consideration the ongoing changing needs of the customer.

2. *The contractual or legal relationship*   The type of relationship developed using this approach represents one step up from the adversary relationship. However, all issues and terms are clearly documented, more often than not leading to extremes in tedium. The supplier and customer exhibit distrust and an inability to resolve differences in the absence of a formal mechanism, such as through legal or quasi-judicial instruments. Parties to such a relationship are governed by the strict terms in the contract and problem resolution frequently results in an inflexible, formidable task.

3. *The partnership*   This relationship is one required for JIT success. The supplier and customer approach it with a 'win–win' strategy, one that makes all aspects of the relationship favorable to both. Such a relationship is characterized by long-term agreements and formal documentation does not necessarily become perdurable law. Communication between the two parties assumes a new importance as information pertaining to changes in products and scheduling is shared. The supplier may possess

relevant information regarding markets and thus be in a position to offer suggestions concerning possible purchasing improvements which can benefit the customer (Deakin, 1988). Goddard (1986) identifies three terms which are essential to the JIT supplier–customer relationship. These include trust, continuity and consistency. Achieving a successful win–win relationship is facilitated through involving suppliers as early as possible in the establishment of JIT purchasing. Advantages of establishing a win–win relationship include the following.

- *Customer advantages*
  - increased control over purchasing activities;
  - purchase requirements will be satisfied and assured through the development of long-term, trusting contracts; and
  - elimination of incoming inspection activities.
- *Supplier advantages*
  - increased volume or share of business;
  - increased schedule stability – the creation of long-term contracts allows a supplier to plan effectively for future needs;
  - a successful customer increases the success of the supplier; and
  - provision of quality products made available under a JIT approach will improve the supplier's ability to compete.

In summary, the establishment of a partnership between customer and supplier is a viable means of allowing the goals of JIT purchasing to be achieved. The efforts of those involved in the partnership should work toward the following goals (Reeds, 1988):

- shrinking the supplier base;
- establishing long-term relationships;
- relying on a single source and eliminating the securing of materials from others as a buffer;
- reducing frequency of order scheduling;
- improving pricing;
- eliminating counting, unpacking and inspection of incoming materials;
- streamlining receiving and payable systems;
- eliminating bulk breaking;
- reducing inventory levels;
- eliminating material spoilage and loss; and
- increasing involvement of the customer and supplier in the design and introductory stages of product development.

3.1.2 Supplier selection

Supplier selection is a multi-functional task with organization-wide implications. One of the main contrasts between traditional purchasing and JIT is the elimination of multiple source suppliers. In JIT production, single source supply is emphasized. This carries with it an added importance to selecting the supplier who is best suited to meet the customer's requirements over an extended period of time.

Advantages of both multiple and single sourcing have been identified in the literature. Supporters of multiple sourcing contend that certain advantages accrue to the customer (Voss, 1987). These normally include the provision of a more extensive technical base, safeguards against possible shortages and promotion of competition among suppliers. Proponents of single source supply maintain that the following benefits are derived by customers (Voss, 1987) and suppliers (Nelson, 1990).

- *Customer benefits*
  - consistency in product quality;
  - resource preservation through minimizing investment and buying activities such as time and travel expenses;
  - lowered costs made possible through purchasing higher volumes of materials and parts;
  - single buyer may constitute a relatively large portion of the supplier's business, therefore, the supplier's motivation to maintain a customer may include special concern for meeting customer requirements above and beyond those typically specified;
  - minimizing tooling expenses; and
  - the development and maintenance of long-term relationships – this is of particular relevance as trust and loyalty are frequent outcomes of such a relationship.
- *Supplier benefits*
  - suppliers are better equipped to plan their own schedules in accordance with their customers' needs;
  - the customer may assist the supplier with the implementation of improvement programs which will benefit both parties in the long run; and
  - reduced amount of paperwork and formal documentation – this frees up time to focus on other activities.

Many suppliers are reluctant to become part of a single source supply relationship with customers. Reluctance manifests itself with supplier dependency and the disclosure of costing data to customers (Nelson, 1990). The issue of dependency surrounds itself with the supplier's eventual assimilation into the customer company. It is recommended that a supplier not enter a relationship in which the customer would control in excess of 20% of the business. The disclosure of costing data is often required; however, the data which must be made available to the customer, should concern only the costs which are relevant to the product being purchased. The supplier should remember that such a relationship exists to serve both parties.

Supplier reluctance to single sourcing also arises in response to the supplier being regarded as a means of storing inventory. Many attempts by organizations to implement JIT have begun with inventory reduction programs. Thus, the cost of storing inventory, which was previously borne by the customer, is shifted onto the supplier. The customer should be aware that the supplier function is not to act as a storage facility.

Selection criteria

Hale and Karney (1987) have outlined a method of selecting suppliers, based on the concept of 'professional qualification' which is defined as 'a process that leads to certain suppliers being designated as "qualified" or "preferred". The process consists of specific steps performed in sequence, and is based primarily on facts and objective analysis. A second facet of the professional qualification process is that companies using it must consistently refuse to purchase components from unqualified suppliers.'

The qualification process consists of the following steps.

1. *Obtaining management support* This represents a difficult task as the process requires changing attitudes and incurring substantial costs to receive benefits which are not necessarily realized in the short run. A method for obtaining support is to develop a clear, operational plan addressing the needs of internal customers, estimating costs of poor quality, acquiring the support of an immediate boss or supervisor, fostering employee ownership of the plan, and finally, selling the plan to internal customers.

2. *Selecting the components to initialize the process* Selection of where an organization will commence the process depends on what is regarded as germane. To illustrate, process initiation can include the areas where substantial cost savings can be realized, or areas where inadequate supplier management prevails. A rule of thumb to follow is not to begin the process with components which comprise 25% or more of the total supplier base.

3. *Selecting a cross-skilled team* Teams are the preferred choice for implementation. The team should be guided by the efforts of the purchasing department, however, members should consist of employees from all relevant areas in the organization. Team member selection should focus on including individuals who are capable of remaining objective and avoiding those who wear the label of 'token team member'.

4. *Selection criteria for supplier evaluation* The criteria chosen to evaluate suppliers must be key to the success of the potential relationship. Criteria will vary from organization to organization. However, common elements have been identified which find their place in many organizations, and include delivery performance, quality, reliability, price, responsiveness, location, financial stability and technical capability.

The establishment of selection criteria involves two tasks: the determination of the criteria and the development of weighting factors. To ensure that an organization will select a supplier capable of meeting its requirements and one which possesses the potential to lead an organization into world-class competitiveness, it is suggested that supplier performance weighting be compared with organizations already considered world-class.

5. *Collection and analysis of data*   The first requirement of this step is to establish an efficient means of collecting and gathering data from various suppliers, if such a system does not already exist in an organization. Once a data collecting system is formalized, the team can gather the necessary information from the suppliers. These activities commonly include visiting suppliers and observing their processes as they actually occur in their organizations.

Collection of material does not often present itself as an easy task to fulfill. The main obstacle to information procurement includes supplier's reluctance to disclose information which they deem to be confidential. Team members who visit supplier's plants should be capable of assessing the supplier's technical and process capability to meet their requirements for quality. Overlooking this assessment could lead a company into accepting poor quality material from a supplier.

6. *'First pass' supplier qualification*   The objective of a 'first pass' qualification is to eliminate the suppliers who are incapable of meeting an organization's absolutely essential requirements. The three main criteria with which this elimination procedure occurs are the supplier's delivery performance, financial stability and technical profile. The level of performance sought by a customer is termed 'quality delivery', which is defined as 'delivering the agreed-upon quantity of acceptable product on time, neither before nor after the agreed-upon date'. This is a strict definition which many companies choose to relax by allowing suppliers to deliver materials a few days early; however, never late. A further aspect of delivery includes lead times (Lancendorfer and Siegel, 1988). The supplier capable of delivering material with short lead time ties into customer responsiveness. Meeting customer requirements in short periods of time leads to the fulfillment of the final customer's needs. Service is also an important element of this criterion which commonly includes such areas as factory and field support, responsiveness, supplier history, and flexibility, to mention a few.

The second criterion, financial stability, involves establishing whether a supplier is capable of meeting long-term obligations, or a measure of supplier solvency. Financial stability can be determined through analysing the supplier company's financial statements or annual report and by conducting ratio analyses. Ratios can be compared to industry averages to determine how well a single supplier fares in its industry.

The third criterion pertains to the supplier's technical profile. A technical profile includes elements which address the supplier's technical and mechanical capabilities as well as their process quality. Elements of assessment include the supplier's use of SPC charts and TQC, the number of engineers employed, level of process quality and automation.

Organizations which currently include suppliers who do not meet the initial requirements but are included in the supply base should establish other means of obtaining the required material. Contracts with suppliers who cannot measure up to a customer's requirements should eventually be cancelled.

7. *Final supplier qualification*   Final supplier qualification entails the ranking of suppliers relative to one another who succeeded the initial qualifications. This is the final step included in professional qualification and frequently leads customers to believe that this process need not be followed in a strict manner. In certain circumstances it may not be necessary to employ this process at all times to select the best supplier. However, the prudent manager should remember two things about such a process. First, the professional qualification process will assist in identifying problems which may otherwise lead to substantial expenditures on the part of the customer further along in the relationship. Second, weighting factors may not consistently reflect the customer's values. A common scenario illustrating this is when weighting factors reflect what should be, rather than what actually is. Under these circumstances, weighting factors should be adjusted.

An overview of the benefits which accrue to the customer and the supplier through the establishment of a single source relationship are shared by many organizations which operate in a JIT environment. The supplier screening function lends itself to universally shared criteria, however, with certain modifications depending upon the goals unique to specific organizations. Characteristics which one organization perceives to be of primary importance may not carry the same weight in another organization. Organizations are subject to determine the supplier qualities in line with their goals.

The supplier screening function is most effectively carried out through a team approach (Burt, 1989). The rationale for a team effort surpasses the colloquial 'two heads are better than one'. A team composed of individuals from various departments in an organization is equipped to select a supplier which is capable of meeting the organization-wide requirements. A typical selection team consists of employees from purchasing, engineering, finance, quality, product planning and manufacturing.

The screening of suppliers frequently results in a time-consuming task and, for this reason, has spurred many organizations to develop a standardized method for carrying out the supplier screening function. Factors which determine the selection of a supplier extend beyond that of price into the following areas (Deakin, 1988).

- The provision of back-up and production control systems to meet production schedules. This is deemed to be the most important criterion as efficient use of control systems places the supplier in a superior position to meet production schedules with products produced according to specifications.
- Supplier's control over subcontract work, i.e. receiving products in time to fulfill customer schedules.
- The supplier's ability to deliver quality products in a consistent manner. The elements which the customer regards of particular importance to quality is the supplier's use of process control equipment to insure products are made according to pre-established specifications.
- Supplier capability to identify potential problems which may cause delays in product delivery to the customer.
- The supplier's co-operation with the customer in keeping them informed of their ongoing business activities and delivery conditions.

The initial selection of suppliers does not terminate the evaluation procedures. An audit should be conducted to measure the performance of the supplier (Deakin, 1988). Critical questions which should be answered through the audit regarding whether or not the supplier is performing as expected (e.g. on-time deliveries of quality products) and identifying the areas which could be improved upon further to meet customer's requirements. For example, the customer and the supplier should be able to work together to improve processes for increasing quality levels. Over the long run, quality levels should be such that the customer can eliminate any and all forms of incoming inspection activities. The supplier's inability to meet customer requirements should result in the selection of another supplier.

A case study of supplier evaluation at GM

The system GM has developed for evaluating suppliers focuses upon building a relationship between customer and supplier, enables both to express desires and facilitate the attainment of goals (Pallas, 1989). A critical element for GM is obtaining information from the supplier without placing it in a tenable position. One method of establishing this two-way relationship is to assist the supplier with improving their operations.

The evaluation procedure is performed in three distinct steps. The first step is initiated by suppliers answering a standardized questionnaire regarding operations, business systems, R&D, costs and financial status. The second step encompasses visiting the suppliers to evaluate their operations and systems. The five critical areas which are assessed include 'organizational effectiveness and commitment, planning systems and documentation, cost awareness, monitoring and development, scheduling and delivery compliance, technology capabilities and R&D' (Pallas, 1989). All of GM's assessments are shared with the suppliers to offer feedback on strengths and weaknesses of the company. The supplier companies which require improvements will be assisted by GM. The third stage of the evaluation entails the sharing of information from suppliers pertaining to GM's performance.

3.1.3 Supplier education
The completion of the supplier audit should set the stage for education of suppliers. The goal of education is to provide the supplier with insight into the company's needs and assist them in further developing their systems and processes to improve the quality of their products. A 'supplier quality training plan' was developed to assist the supplier in improving product quality and ensuring on-time delivery (Peters, 1990). Supplier quality training serves to identify the requirements of both the customer and the supplier to meet the manufacturing needs.

3.1.4 Supplier commitment and customer dependency
The development of commitment from employees and management involves the use of open communication, trust, training and support. The availability of necessary funds required for the changeover is also fundamental to committing the company to JIT. In addition, sharing the power to make decisions which extend beyond the traditional managerial functions to include employees may also be necessary.

External commitment with the suppliers may be more difficult to achieve than commitment from employees and managers. The need for this arises primarily out of constrained monetary resources. In order to achieve the type of relationship with suppliers that is required for JIT, the supplier in a sense becomes an extension of the organization. In many instances, the use of an outside supplier is not necessary as many companies have become vertically integrated. However, this would be particularly relevant in the past, while the present economic conditions and increased level of technology of component parts requires the use of a supplier. The role of a supplier has increased in importance as many companies cannot afford to become vertically integrated The main reason for this lies in the increased level of technological requirements for products. This calls for specialization of labour and original equipment. Most companies lack the financial resources necessary to acquire equipment used in the production of component parts and materials. Therefore, they turn to the assistance of a supplier.

The customer–supplier relationship
There are issues which the supplier and the company will look toward fulfilling in the relationship. The issues for the supplier will involve customer commitment, job security and contracts. It should be noted that there is a great deal of difference between a relationship and a contract which the customer and supplier develop. A contract is simply a legal document which

is used to spell out the terms of the agreement. If one party fails to adhere to the terms of the contract then the other party can seek redress. A relationship which develops between the two parties transcends that of a contract. The establishment of a relationship involves the components of trust and fulfillment of common goals. The shared concerns include the development of a relationship which provide for profit and growth.

Components of a mutually beneficial contract consist of the following.

- The commitment which is developed between the supplier and the company. The company's commitment to the supplier reaffirms the supplier's concern for job security and vice versa. A successful partnership can reduce the built-in protectors that many North American companies have come to use. These safeguards include the use of holding safety stock and inspecting incoming shipments.
- The development of trust is crucial for success. Without trust, the relationship is not functional. The components of trust include consistency of behaviour, respect for the other company, openness in communication and honesty. In the absence of a trusting relationship, both the supplier and customer will hesitate to carry out the terms of the contract.
- The relationship developed should aim for long-term results. Success will be realized in the long run, therefore the customer should not focus on short-run results. This is an important fact to realize as the development of suppliers is costly in terms of time and financial expense.

Several ways of developing these components of the customer–supplier relationship have been suggested (Lubben, 1988). These methods focus upon developing supplier capability to meet customer requirements.

1. *The use of programs extended through the customer* Providing workshops and conventions to assist in supplier training serves two purposes: to create an awareness of what is required to fulfill the customer's needs and to substantiate the customer's commitment to the supplier. Programs can also be used to improve communications between the two parties.
2. *Linearity of production* This involves the levelling of the supplier's production schedule. The ability to meet demands depends upon the supplier's effectiveness in reducing lead times. Lead time reduction will require the supplier to reduce set-up time for machinery and equipment, balance the production system and identify bottlenecks. Production must also occur in smaller, more frequent lot sizes. In effect, the use of JIT by a customer very often requires the supplier to adopt the JIT method of production in order to fulfill its contract obligations.
3. *The changeover procedure* The changeover which occurs on the supplier's production floor is gradual and, therefore, allowing time for change will assist in the supplier's ability to meet demands. The most likely changes which will occur will include changes in equipment used

for production, training labour for multiple skills, changes in work shifts and the methods the supplier uses to purchase materials. The changes in equipment may involve any additions necessary to complete the parts. Work shifts may change in response to producing more frequent and smaller lot sizes and employees will not necessarily be utilized at all times. The company implementing JIT may be able to assist the supplier in the changeover by providing information about estimated demand for its product.

A case study of JIT purchasing
This case study presents an example of General Electric Company's Transportation Systems Business Operations (TSBO) endeavours toward implementing JIT purchasing (Schonberger, 1987). The issues addressed involve the conflicts between the goals of the company established under the traditional methods of purchasing and those of JIT purchasing, reducing the number of suppliers, measuring performance in the purchasing function, establishing and maintaining relationships with suppliers and the use of pilot products to commence the JIT purchasing function. The critical activities and events which transformed the organization's purchasing department to pursue JIT production, as well as the benefits received from such a transformation, are addressed.

The products of the firm involve the manufacture of locomotives to meet the customer's needs. The objectives of the firm include expanding JIT purchasing effort plant-wide and diminishing the supplier base in accordance with JIT principles. The latter objective presented the firm with a substantial venture as the pre-established and well-practised policies of the company were to aim at reducing costs through multiple competing sources.

The critical business conditions affecting the company during the 1970–76 period presented one of business decline, where the product was largely regarded as of poor quality and high cost. The company's product was purchased as a means of second source of supply or to provide buffers in the event the preferred supplier was unable to deliver.

The year of 1977 saw the appointment of a new general manager, who, with the backing of other management in the plant, was successful in convincing corporate management that the plant could be salvaged. With this in mind, the company initiated improvement activities to increase productivity, cost reduction and product quality. The procedures commenced with the introduction of automated and numerically controlled equipment in welding and fabricating shops.

Programs for improving productivity and reducing costs were extended into the materials management areas of the firm. The purchasing function prior to 1978 included 6 000 suppliers, 40 buyers and 40 expediters handling purchasing of 50 000 parts. The purchasing function was segmented into four parts operating independently of one another. These included locomotive and diesel, propulsion, control and transit cars. Two problems with purchasing became evident: extremely short lead times and tight deadlines.

The problems apparent in the materials management function included inadequate sales forecasts and capacity planning, delays in product introductions, inability to adjust to scheduling changes, lack of support for MRP systems, departmentalized goals which were in conflict with organization-wide goals and lack of planning.

By 1979, the company was successful in obtaining the support of the employees to establish a working MRP system. The development of a total systems plan, MRP education, inventory reduction and integrity, and cycle analyses were accomplished. The cycle analyses were conducted by study teams who addressed such issues as reducing cycle times and inventory levels for each product. Toward the end of 1979, the company had obtained the support of employees, an operating MRP system, improvements in the functioning of materials management. These improvements were supported by specific data such as a 25% increase in material availability and inventory integrity improvements of 10%.

The activities during the period of 1980–81 focused on advancing improvements in the purchasing and materials areas of the company. For example, in the purchasing function, integration of three of the four independent operations occurred, with the transit car operation being eliminated. The number of buyers required was reduced to only one, which significantly reduced the level of the purchasing labour force. This re-organization established the newly found importance of the purchasing function. In keeping with this newly found importance, three programs were developed to address cost reduction and quality improvements of the purchasing function. The three programs were known as PACE (product application and cost evaluation), SOS (supplier originated savings) and DSS (dual source savings).

The objectives of the PACE program were to solidify the relationships between the TSBO and their suppliers as well as increasing the productivity and effectiveness of the high dollar volume suppliers. These objectives were accomplished through bringing in the supplier to observe the functioning of the company's operations, identifying areas of improvement in the supplier company's operations and sharing the TSBO's concerns and problems with suppliers.

The success of the PACE program was contributed to top management commitment and to the company's critically evaluating suppliers' suggestions. It involved over 90 suppliers which constituted in excess of 60% of dollar volume of purchased parts. The savings associated with the functioning of the PACE program were estimated at $4 million.

The SOS program was designed to include the remaining suppliers who constituted the low dollar volume supplies. The objective of SOS was to reduce purchasing costs by 6%. The savings associated with the functioning of this program were approximately $1 million. The program functioned to solicit suggestions from suppliers through the offering of incentives such as prizes and rewards. The program was introduced by sending the suppliers within the low volume categories brochures indicating the objectives of the TSBO. These operational objectives primarily included reducing costs, improving quality and improving customer service. Communication with the suppliers was not as concentrated as that with the high dollar volume suppliers.

The third supplier program is the DSS and its objective was compatible with the traditional purchasing methods: to reduce purchasing costs through increasing the level of competition between single source supplied parts. The company sought to increase the level of competition among suppliers through requesting bids from and placing orders with other suppliers. Approximately half the parts were supplied by a single source. Single sourcing existed under the plant conditions throughout the 1980–82 period as a result of strict engineering specifications and limitations in supplier tooling.

Teams were established which measured the performance of purchasing and developed supplier evaluation criteria and budgets. The DSS was a slow to warm-up program with few initial cost reductions. Substantial cost savings were not realized until the third year of operations. The results increased supplier competition and supplier-by-supplier price reductions. The savings were approximated at $3 million.

The previously outlined periods represented an era of the TSBO's concerns for stabilizing the operations of the company and regaining lost ground from competitors. Throughout 1982 and the ongoing period, the TSBO's activities encompassed an investigation of the JIT concepts as they apply to purchasing. The company originally devoted JIT as a method of reducing inventory. Extending JIT into the other areas of the plant was stipulated as an eventual goal, however, this was highly dependent upon the company improving the timeliness of deliveries.

The inquiry into the JIT concepts commenced with visits to Japanese manufacturing plants. Observing the Japanese purchasing functions revealed that the flow of work-in-process parts not needed at a particular point in time on the production line would have to be sent back to its original source. The implications of pushing back WIP would mean that all parts not required would be returned to various inventory points. The ultimate destination of pushed back WIP would be on the supplier. All safety stock would be eventually eliminated and delivery sizes reduced under the JIT method. This led to the concern for the provision of quality products, although it was felt by increasing the efforts of the PACE and SOS supplier programs, the required level of quality could be obtained.

The concerns of employees in the TSBO focused upon the possible lack of work for their current employees, modifying the existing MRP system to accommodate daily rather than weekly deliveries, improving the accuracy of scheduling and their ability to correct problems in a shorter time span. Furthermore, many managers attributed the Japanese JIT success to an element unique to their environment, a success believed not to be obtainable within the TSBO.

Ultimately, JIT purchasing was pursued with great effort, despite the above problems and concerns. The pilot product selected to initiate JIT purchasing was the diesel engines. The functioning of JIT purchasing in the test case was subject to intense study by various teams, who concentrated their effort on shortening the delivery times of certain engines. This was determined based upon evaluating the criteria of geographical proximity, size, weight and mode of delivery.

The study teams at the TSBO established the criteria of Japanese success as the development of close relationships with their suppliers, or the idea of 'codestiny', where the supplier becomes an extension of the firm. Simply increasing the frequency of deliveries will not ensure purchasing success. Success stems from the closeness the customer and supplier can achieve, where reliability and quality are an integral part of the relationship. This success is championed through the reduction of the supplier base, or the pursuit of single supplier sourcing. This realization in TSBO represents a turning point for the organization, as their goal of reducing costs through increasing supplier competition, the objective of the DSS supplier program, runs counter to this ultimate method of cost reduction.

Single sourcing was initiated through the selection of a supplier who was capable of meeting the TSBO's requirements. Criteria for selection included supplier past performance, reliability and quality. The chosen supplier was supportive of becoming a single source as they perceived the following benefits would accrue to them: long-term contracts and ability to plan investments.

Single sourcing for the TSBO represented a substantial leap into JIT away from the traditional purchasing practices. The transition carried with it several concerns of the TSBO, such as completely relying on one supplier and thus subject to any changes which could put them in a less than desirable position. Other concerns for both the TSBO and the supplier addressed the terms of the contract, pricing, the reassurance of risk-free quality products being delivered when required, reducing early deliveries and further improving the quality of supplier's products.

The activities of the TSBO reflected the ideal concepts presented in many JIT textbooks. Evolution of the traditional purchasing practices gradually came to reflect those of JIT. Transformation of purchasing practices represents a substantial change to an organization and the concerns of the TSBO reflected this change.

3.2 JIT delivery

JIT customer delivery strives to exceed the traditional means of meeting the customer's needs. The two avenues available for achieving superior customer delivery include external and internal methods. External methods focus on determining the customer's needs, while the internal methods aim at improving the productivity and efficiency standards of the production processes in an organization, separate and distinct from the customer profile. These two avenues gradually integrate to become one, as meeting customer's requirements becomes the goal of the firm. The JIT perspective challenges the firm to fulfill its production requirements, as defined by the customer, for the customer. It is a highly customer-oriented approach.

The discussion of customer delivery will be addressed in three categories, namely production elements, problem identification and resolution, and forecasting demand. Production facets include the internal activities which an organization can embark upon to improve delivery. These commonly include reducing cycle time, informal and formal organizational systems and operation sequencing. Increasing customer delivery through the identification and resolution of problems which may exist with an organization's prevailing approach to customer delivery represents another internal activity of the firm. The external activities typically surround methods of determining the customer's level of demand and product requirements. It also addresses the application of 'distribution requirements planning' (DRP), a system which complements JIT. Figure 3.1 presents a summary of the internal and external elements of JIT delivery.

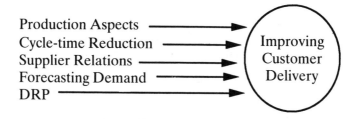

Figure 3.1 JIT delivery.

JIT delivery seeks to fulfill customer requirements through the production of 100% quality goods, reducing lead times, elimination of waste, increasing productivity and continuous improvement (Ford, 1987). The following discussion of customer delivery addresses several approaches to meeting consumer needs through improvement upon the above means.

3.2.1 Increasing delivery frequency through production related elements

A method which is successful in reducing the time required of the manufacturer to prepare and deliver the product to the customer is known as 'cycle time reduction' or 'increasing customer responsiveness', already discussed in an earlier section of this book. Kidd and Reinbolt (1990) present a case study of a cycle time reduction program established in a firm which results in an increase of delivery frequency by 50%. Reducing cycle time, administrative and transit time were addressed through the use of a team approach. According to Kidd and Reinbolt, methods for reducing the time absorbed in each of these activities can be developed through the following.

- *Analysing the seven wastes of manufacturing*   These wastes include waste from waiting, over-production, motion, transportation, holding excessive inventory, defective products, and processing wastes. An assessment of the wastes will allow an organization to identify and eliminate activities which do not add value to the product.
- *Developing process flow charts*   Viewing flow charts will present the company with a visual picture of the flow of goods throughout the plant. This may provide the opportunity to trim down the path, thus reducing overall flow time.
- *Assessing the amount of time required for changeovers*   Inefficient methods of changeovers leading to long set-up times can be eliminated through converting the internal set-up activities to external set-up activities, and providing the necessary tools and training to workers.
- *Reviewing total productive maintenance*   The employment of an organization's complete workforce to improving productive maintenance activities will ensure the continual and flawless operation of equipment and systems.
- *Workplace organization*   Upgrading the plant conditions through clearing and simplifying and removing all unused material can assist in increasing the efficiency of the manufacturing processes and ultimately reducing the time required to deliver products to customers.
- *The implementation of group technology or cellular manufacturing*   The use of work cells to manufacture products can improve the overall flow and production of goods.
- *Reviewing the time required to perform all administrative tasks*   This represents an important and frequently ignored function. Its significance is derived from the vast amount of time organizations spend in conducting

these activities. Much time can be saved through the elimination of redundant order processing activities.

- *Analysing systems of measurement* Data accuracy and integrity are critical to eliminating unnecessary delays in production. For example, accurate measurement systems can inform management of possible shortages in supplies.

Increasing customer responsiveness through internal or production activities by virtue of operations sequencing, or linking planning and executing activities represents another method of improving delivery (Bruun, 1987). Alternative names for the planning and executing activities are formal and informal systems, respectively. Formal systems include MRP or the formulation of the production plan, while informal systems are used to execute the plan.

The function of operations sequencing includes carrying out a series of steps which commence with the MRP generated production plan and terminate with work order completions. The steps, in sequence, include the following:

- receipt of the MRP developed production plan;
- prioritization of work order;
- development of capacity profiles;
- rearrangement of due requirements;
- alignment of work orders to available capacity;
- development of daily work lists; and
- planning for work order completions.

Although operations sequencing can improve customer delivery by providing daily work lists and projecting work order completions, several limitations do exist. The formal or MRP system must be intact, daily production schedules should be timely and indicate current labour status, and finally, in order to be effective, operation sequencing should be performed on a daily basis.

The overall approach to customer delivery espoused by JIT is to become closely acquainted with the customers and their needs. Most distribution systems habitually involve several parties which make up the channel. The longer and more detailed the channel, the longer the delivery times. To satisfy customer needs by having the right product available in the right quantity at the right time demands the channel to operate effectively and efficiently on a continual basis. This presents an ideal view of how the channel should operate. According to Andrew (1987), JIT delivery applies the concepts of waste reduction to the distribution functions of the firm, in addition to the manufacturing functions. Reliability should become the goal of the marketing department as well as the manufacturing department. This can be accomplished through the removal of stock points from the distribution system.

Methods for reducing the length of the channel to facilitate the flow of goods should commence with the removal of various waste-producing stock points. The following methods can be used (Andrew, 1987):

- shipping direct from factory to customer;
- scaling down the levels of warehouses in the channel;
- eliminating products with low profit margins and concentrating on improving the distribution of the high profit margin products;
- developing product designs which are relatively easy to customize through assortment or add-ons;
- using packaging which can be shipped from manufacturing to sale;
- developing products with a modular design and ease of assembly to allow the customer to perform final assembly; and
- engaging in mixed model production to allow for assortment to be shipped to customers.

3.2.2 Improving customer delivery through problem identification and resolution

Attempts to improve customer delivery can be drawn on from a variety of sources. Problem identification and resolution are aimed at meeting customer delivery promises 100% of the time. Failure to do this would result in the company extending a 10% discount to customers for late shipments (Aus, 1987). The establishment of such a policy can motivate employees to develop a method of 100% delivery by emphasizing the lost revenue associated with the firm's opportunity cost.

The application of brainstorming techniques is effective in identifying the problems which may exist in a company's established course of delivery. Examples of common problems which pose barriers to the operation of an effective delivery system are discussed below. It should be noted that many problems will arise out of a company's method of delivery and unique circumstances. Thus the following problems may or may not be relevant to all companies. These problems in turn can be used to initialize the identification process in various companies.

1. *The creation of excess forecasts on products which have a reputation for being difficult to deliver* This creates a chain reaction which impacts upon the master production schedule, inventory build-up, and causes other products to further be delayed. To resolve this problem, all employees should follow the forecasted plan directly as stated.

2. *Products with low reliability are questioned by master schedulers, often incorrectly* To deal with this problem, bi-weekly master production schedule meetings can be held to review potential problems and reach a consensus on a plan of action. Participants of the meetings should include employees from marketing, production planning, purchasing and manufacturing.

3. *The production plan becomes ineffective when demand from foreign branches is not forecasted* This problem can be solved by establishing freight forwarders in the foreign branch territory to improve delivery.

4. *Certain product lead times are equal or longer than the forecast horizon* To overcome this problem, forecasts for products requiring long lead times can be extended beyond the original forecast horizon. Suppliers should be informed of the changes to provide them with visibility and the necessary time to respond to changes.

5. *Ineffective supplier relations may cause a firm unnecessary delays in its production schedule* Thus, lack of supplies means further delays in satisfying consumer requirements. To settle this problem, suppliers should be informed of the changes in a firm's customer delivery policies to allow them time to make necessary changes to meet their customer's new demand requirements. Suppliers' input should be sought to further improve the process.

6. *Products which are costly and demand large inventory space for storage* This problem can be solved by assessing levels necessary to support demand, without increasing inventory levels for the products which require long lead times or are subject to capacity constraints.

7. *Communicating new delivery policies to all employees within a company* Support for new ideas may be difficult to secure as new policies require a change in the well-practised activities of many employees. To deal with this problem, the company should explain the purpose of the policy, the new role of each employee and the potential benefits of the change to all employees.

8. *Companies which are subject to seasonal sales may experience fluctuations in demand requirements* Juggling of the production schedule is frequently the response. The key to solving this problem is to become flexible by cross-training workers to develop a flexible workforce. The company embarking upon change should also adapt to a flexible work schedule to accommodate rapid changes in demand. If necessary, extra work shifts should be added to the schedule.

The process of identifying problems and their solutions can improve the overall performance of an organization. Numerous benefits have been observed which include the following:

- enhancing existing customer satisfaction as well as increasing customer base through improved ability to meet customer's requirements – a company may develop a reputation which communicates their ability to satisfy the customer above and beyond their competitors' ability;
- consolidating work effort through the development of teams and overall improved employee relations – employees may work more effectively with one another;

- improving supplier relations–customer delivery improvement programs may establish a base for the development of a supplier relationship;
- analysing the company's inventory levels may lead to identifying opportunities for cost reduction;
- keeping the same levels of work-in-process and finished goods inventory – in some instances they can be diminished as such a policy requires a thorough analysis of the demand profile, inventory levels and the production schedule;
- reducing the amount of time consumed in administrative tasks through decreasing the level of required paperwork; and
- applying the learning experience of one attempt at improving to other areas of the firm.

3.2.3 Improving customer delivery through forecasting and DRP

The last category of improving customer delivery addresses what the firm can do to improve delivery though the customer profile. This can be attacked through several approaches. One approach has been identified as customer networking and its meaning is aptly described as 'taking a proactive approach to bring your customers into your JIT plans and goals. It is taking JIT to the customer with the objective of managing how and when they order and it is working with them to eliminate all unnecessary fluctuations in demand before it reaches your plant. It is establishing a partnership with these customers that offers: trust, stability, inventory reduction and cost savings opportunities to both parties.' (Burns, 1987).

The objectives of sales planning and forecasting are to establish a balance between supply and demand and to substantiate the level of future demand for the firm (Artes, 1987). They involve the task of determining the future needs of customers and preparing the production plan accordingly. These two functions are executed on a regular basis within many organizations. Artes (1987) has identified 12 steps which can be performed to improve upon the effectiveness of these two tasks.

1. Promoting understanding through education.
2. Determining company, product, market characteristics and determine how they will impact the sales planning and forecasting functions in the company.
3. Facilitating the sales planning and forecasting functions through determining rational categories of the company's products and markets.
4. Establishing systems in the company which support all organizational requirements.
5. Selecting a statistical model which most suitably meets the product and market characteristics of the firm. Selection should be based upon the completion of an analysis of historical demands and one which has the lowest expected error between forecasted and actual demand.

6. Generating forecasts by the application of a statistical model should be used as a foundation for future adjustments.
7. Establishing operational plans to meet the goals of the company sales business plan.
8. Determining the external environmental factors which could impact upon the operations of the firm. Several of these factors may include economic, technological, and competitive factors.
9. Establishing a forecast which is composed of the results of the statistical forecast and any adjustments.
10. Undertaking monthly reviews of the sales forecast and sales plan to verify their accuracy.
11. Taking corrective action to revise the plan and forecast should variances occur.
12. Striving to create an environment which promotes accountability of action, provides the necessary tools to perform the development of sales plans and forecasts, and strives to meet established goals and objectives.

Distribution requirements planning plans the movement of material in a distribution system. It has been regarded as the most crucial element required to establish JIT delivery systems in an organization (Ford, 1987). DRP assists in determining the level of materials required for a fluctuating level of demand. Its functions include forecasting, monitoring, shipment and allocation planning, and interfacing to other established systems in an organization.

An effective DRP system demands the support of the various channel parties, including manufacturers, wholesalers and distributors. Each group of channel parties will be required to perform a distinct role as DRP applies to them. Martin and Sandras (1990) define the varying roles of each channel party.

- The role of the *manufacturer* is to establish an efficient means of information and material flow throughout their plant. Prerequisites include the implementation of MRP II and TQC, as well as electronic data interchange (EDI) systems.
- The role of the *wholesalers and distributors* is to respond quickly to demand from retailers. Their role in the channel is to facilitate the flow of goods from the manufacturer to the retailer. This task is enhanced indirectly through improvements in the manufacturer's delivery system including shortened lead times.
- The role of *retailers* in the integration of DRP is to reduce and balance inventory levels. They receive the benefits of cost reduction due to less inventory holding.

The overall benefits identified with the implementation of DRP can be experienced by all parties of the channel to a varying degree. Ford (1987) identifies the benefits as follows.

- Reduced inventory levels up to 80%.
- Increased levels of customer service, these may reach into the 90% range.
- Increases in management's control.
- Diminishing transportation expenditures.
- Reduced overhead, labour and storage costs.
- Manufacturing at the source.
- Improvements in the balance and mix of inventory at various stock points.

Many organizations may currently be in the process of considering the use of JIT delivery. The impetus for implementing JIT in an organization is to receive the many cost advantages and benefits associated with its use. Despite these advantages and benefits, many organizations may question whether implementation of JIT delivery is required of them at this point in time. Several industry trends already exist which will eventually require a firm to change its existing practices in order to remain competitive. These trends include the following (Novitsky, 1988).

- A market characterized with short product life cycles and response times.
- Reduced sales forecast accuracy.
- A highly competitive industry, undergoing rapid change.
- Increasingly demanding customers with requirements for improved service, frequent deliveries and improved product quality.
- Product design, development and distribution are allowed a diminished amount of time to get the final product to market.

4.

Total quality management

Total quality management (TQM), in its simplest form, encompasses all actions, values and beliefs of an organization which aim to improve and maintain quality standards. It is 'a systematic approach to education, management and operation designed to focus and co-ordinate the efforts of all employees in an organization,' (Bently, 1987). Improving quality is made possible through TQM. Employees in organizations which espouse the principles of TQM are required to possess a full understanding of job requirements, prevent quality problems, understand the impact of quality costs and seek to reduce or eliminate the costs of poor quality.

Maintaining and improving quality is an integral part of JIT. It is difficult to speak about one without mention of the other. Many methods of maintaining and improving quality standards are used to varying degrees within different organizations. This chapter examines some of these methods, which aim to prevent problems and build in quality.

Many of the quality principles which we associate with the Japanese can be attributed to W. Edwards Deming. Deming has developed a philosophy of management, 'the Fourteen Points', which provides the foundation for the practices of JIT, and signifies these quality principles. The fourteen points, listed below, are the basic principles developed for an organization to adopt into its practices and, when fully incorporated into an organization, promote success. (Walton, 1986).

1. Create constancy of purpose for improvement of product and service. The organization's purpose should focus on innovation, maintenance and improvement.
2. Adopt the new philosophy. The acceptance of mistakes and negative attitudes should no longer be permitted.
3. Cease dependence on mass inspection. The organization should seek to constantly improve processes and build quality into products or services.
4. End the practice of awarding business on price tag alone. The organization should focus on developing supplier relationships and product quality, and set its priorities to emphasize quality, not price.
5. Improve constantly and forever the system of production and service. The concept of continuous improvement should become an ongoing practice of the organization.

6. Institute training. Train employees to do the job right the first time.
7. Institute leadership. Leadership is required to assist people to perform their jobs better and facilitate employee learning.
8. Drive out fear. Create a working environment in which employees are free to offer suggestions and ask questions.
9. Break down barriers between staff areas. Eliminate the conflicts and competing goals which exist between separate departments. Competing goals can work against organization-wide efforts.
10. Eliminate slogans, exhortations, and targets for the workforce. Employees should become part of the process.
11. Eliminate numerical quotas. Quotas should be eliminated as they only consider numbers, while ignoring quality and procedures.
12. Remove barriers to pride of workmanship. Eliminate the barriers such as malfunctioning equipment, defective materials and other hindrances which exist to frustrate employees.
13. Institute a rigorous program of education and retraining. Education and training of new procedures should be directed toward management and the workforce.
14. Take action to accomplish the transformation. The team approach should be applied to direct implementation efforts. Managers and workers must combine their effort and work together to accomplish goals.

Employees, both managers and workers alike, should understand, remember and institute the 'Fourteen Points' into their work practices and make them the company philosophy.

4.1 Quality and quality costs

The success of quality programs depends on how well an organization is able to identify customer needs. The question 'What is quality?' is perhaps the most important question an organization should ask itself prior to embarking upon quality improvement. Quality is a subjective term, deficient of an exact meaning, where the customer's perception is highly significant.

Defining quality involves two components which include product/service requirements and customer expectations. Quality requirements relate to the essentials of a product or service which the customer cannot do without. Requirements include meeting the basic standards established by an organization or an external regulatory body. Customer expectations involves the degree to which the customer will be satisfied with the product or service. It is this second component which injects subjectivity into the quality definition. The growing trend of consumers seeking high quality products and services presents organizations with a challenge to increase and meet quality standards; this must be achieved successfully in order to remain competitive.

4.1.1 Quality: a systems perspective

The absence of a precise definition of quality illustrates the importance of the customer to an organization. The basic long-term objectives of an organization are to satisfy its shareholders and ensure its continuation. These objectives can be achieved through maximizing consumer satisfaction. First, it must be realized that quality improvements are possible through focusing on all elements which give rise to the product or service: people, plants and systems, as identified by Goddard (1986). These elements operate interdependently within any organization regardless of the product or service being offered. Thus, a systems perspective will allow an organization to identify and manage all factors which affect quality. Each element within the systems perspective and its impact upon quality will be discussed in subsequent paragraphs.

The initial step toward quality improvement begins with the people who embody the organization. Questions such as the following should be asked by each employee:

- What is my role within the organization?
- How well do I understand the organization's product or service?
- Am I able to identify the customer's expectations of the product or service?
- What are the current quality requirements?
- How can I improve my work performance to increase customer satisfaction?

These questions function as a means of identifying how individual performance can be improved to enhance customer satisfaction. The organizational level of quality improvement is made possible through the following steps:

1. Identifying the customer's expectations is possible through the development of questionnaires or a customer profile, which are sent to the established and potential customers of the organization. The questionnaire should focus on determining how well the customers needs are currently being satisfied, seeking customer input concerning how the product, service or other related elements of the product/service such as delivery or after sales service can be improved upon.
2. Assessing organizational capability. Organizational assessment is a prerequisite to establishing overall quality standards, the capability of employees, equipment and systems to meet higher quality standards, the compatibility of organizational culture and beliefs in achieving the new quality standards. In effect, the assessment should present a snapshot view of the current organizational conditions.

   Frequently, the assessment will reveal requirements for increased training and purchases of new equipment. Perhaps the most difficult aspect of striving to achieve increases in quality is changing a culture which does not support such an endeavour. An organization's culture is pervasive and practised by all employees. Companies which focus on achieving quick results and high output may be faced with a formidable task of trying to improve quality. Quality is as much a part of performance as it is attitude. Acceptance of new ideas and willingness to work toward their successful implementation represent some of the attitude changes which must occur before any quality improvements will be realized.

3. Relating current quality standards with quality goals. The discrepancy which exists between current quality levels and the goals an organization strives to achieve is known as the 'quality gap'. The quality gap exists wherever the performance of one of the elements of the system is unable to meet new quality standards. Examples include failure of the shipping department to deliver a product on time, lack of qualified machine operators, equipment which operates outside specified tolerances or systems which fail to co-ordinate the flow of work-in-process inventories.

4. Bridging the quality gap. The goal of the organization at this point is to reduce and eventually eliminate the quality gap. The process should commence with the elements identified in the organizational assessment, i.e. what can be done to improve performance and processes to meet the new quality standards? Many of these deficiencies can be eliminated through increasing the level of training, improving communication between employees, e.g. through employee involvement programs and increasing the level of visibility through workplace improvement, and seeking commitment from top managers and all employees. To ensure the desired behaviour is continued, performance which is compatible with a culture supportive of improvement should be recognized.

Several factors which contribute to the quality gap are frequently shared by many organizations, whereas others will be unique. Formulation of effective methods to reduce the quality gap depends upon how successful employees are at correctly identifying the causes of quality problems. Various methods of problem identification and solution generation will be discussed in section 4.5.

5. Implementing the quality improvement system. Table 4.1 presents an example of the quality improvement system applying to people, plants and systems.

Resistance to change, as discussed in Chapter 1, is impossible to avoid; however, it is not impossible to overcome. While top management is responsible for initiating the organizational change, all employees should become an immediate part of the process in order to realize success. Employees should be involved in identifying the discrepancies which constitute the quality gap. Attitude changes should stem from the top down: a difficult lesson learned by many JIT enthusiasts. Failure of many managers to demonstrate commitment to JIT quality improvement and support of employees has resulted in abandoning the effort.

4.1.2 The cost of quality

The cost of quality is essentially broken down into two components, which at first seem to be at odds with one another. The first component includes the cost of producing a product or service which fails to meet established requirements and customer expectations. The firm's failure to supply an acceptable product will result in other costs such as the cost of returns, lost customers, poor advertising, warranty and service expenses. The second component includes the organizational cost of achieving established quality standards. These two broad components of the cost of quality include the cost of nonconformance and the cost of conformance, respectively. In short, the cost of quality includes 'all expenses incurred to control and assess quality and to pay the consequences of inferior quality' (Broh, 1982).

Broh groups the costs of quality into three broad categories which encompass the following.

1. The cost of product/service appraisal includes the costs incurred to assess the quality of the firm's products and services. Appraisal costs fluctuate with the nature of each product.
2. The cost of failure includes the expenses incurred as a result of production of a less than satisfactory product or service. Common costs which constitute this broad category include scrap, rework, warranty and litigation expenses. Perhaps one of the most significant of the costs of failure is the loss of existing and potential customers. Loss of customers can have a severe impact upon an organization in terms of creating a reputation where the firm will be associated with producing shoddy products.
3. The cost of prevention includes the cost of methods employed to reduce or eliminate the cost of appraisal and failure. The adage 'an ounce of prevention is worth a pound of cure' holds true in this application.

The concept of value added plays an important role in reducing the cost of quality. Activities which are commonly carried out but fail to add value to the product or service should be eliminated. For example, final product inspection does little to prevent the production of a defective lot of products. Operating within a JIT environment assists in eliminating many of these costs through the establishment of effective methods of production, employee utilization and other organizational resources.

Figure 4.1 presents an illustration of the cost of quality 'iceberg' analogy (Lucht, 1988). Avoidable costs of nonconformance contribute the greatest to reducing quality costs.

4.1.3 A general guideline to quality improvement

The approach to quality improvement is a unique endeavour in itself as an organization strives to meet newly defined quality goals. Townsend and Gebhardt (1986) have identified four elements which act as a general guideline for directing organizational actions toward quality improvement.

Table 4.1 Quality improvement system summary

Identification	1 Identifying Customer Expectations	• development of questionnaire • 'How can the product/service be improved?'
	2 Organizational Assessment	• strengths and weaknesses of people, plants and systems

Analysis and Measurement	3 Identify the Quality Gap	• determine the quality gap factors
		• fundamental quality gap factors include the following:
		  • lack of total commitment
		  • poor organizing and co-ordinating effort
		  • ineffective communication
		  • disregard of customer expectations
		  • lack of employee motivation
		  • no employee ownership
		  • poor relationship with suppliers
		  • poor housekeeping habits
		  • lack of worker visibility
		  • ineffective arrangement of equipment
		  • defective equipment
		  • insufficient training programs

Solution	4 Bridging the Quality Gap	• generating solutions to problems, subject to organizational constraints

| Execution | 5 Implementation of Solutions | <ul><li>formulate the quality improvement plan</li><li>establish well-defined goals</li><li>develop operational goals</li><li>assign roles to key teams and individuals</li><li>allocate organizational resources</li><li>develop contingency plans</li></ul> |
| Follow-up | 6 Monitoring and Measuring Performance | <ul><li>relate performance to operational goals, compare on the basis of:<ul><li>timeliness</li><li>availability of resources</li><li>additional problems encountered?</li><li>resort to contingency plans</li><li>need to establish additional plans?</li></ul></li><li>seek employee opinion and involvement continuously</li></ul> |

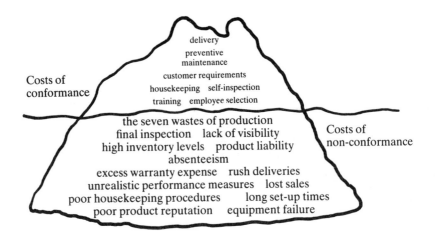

Figure 4.1 The cost of quality.

Each element as discussed below serves a purpose in leading an organization one step further to realizing their quality goals.

1. *Clearly identifying the customer*   Possessing a concrete knowledge of customers and an understanding of their needs provides the motivation necessary to begin quality improvement. 'Customers' in this sense include internal and external customers. Employees have the most control over the internal customer. Through determining what the downstream process desires from the product, each employee can work toward individual improvement. Communication and sharing of expectations assists in flushing out unnecessary actions, wasted effort and resources (i.e. eliminating non-value-adding activities) and developing a process which is capable of producing the desired product.

2. *Publicizing the quality improvement effort*   Publicity is made possible through memos, meetings and inclusion of quality improvement efforts in company philosophy. Publication material should be directed toward all company employees in order to secure their involvement in the effort. Many organizations have developed 'close' relationships with suppliers and customers, rendering their involvement necessary.

3. *Seeking the assistance of external organizations*   Pursuing the assistance of an independent consultant can serve to assist the company in correctly identifying quality problems, in providing the necessary training and, most importantly, in obtaining an objective opinion. Correctly identifying the true causes of quality problems is essential to their rectification. Although problem identification ideally should not be a 'placing blame

process', it 'can assume this role. In the event this occurs, problem identification becomes obscured as effort is directed away from objective analysis toward concealing errors, rendering the process ineffective.

4. *Establishing specific, operational goals* Developing workable goals, subsequent to the formulation of the overall organizational objectives, is required to carry out the 'how' of the quality improvement process. The activities which should occur are planning, monitoring and measuring progress.

The essential ingredients of success, according to Townsend are fourfold: first, quality improvement efforts must be fully supported by top management; second, quality teams should be established with well-defined and congruous goals; third, a general framework must be developed and followed; and fourth, a team must be set up to guide the pursuit of operational goals.

4.1.4 Defining employee roles in the quality improvement process
The emphasis on quality improvement as a systems approach will lead one to the understanding that quality is not the result of an individual, fragmented effort. Although each member of an organization assumes a unique role and effort in the quality improvement process, the most successful approach constitutes a team effort.

The team approach to quality improvement requires each employee on the team to have an understanding of his role and responsibilities. Bently (1987) identifies seven groups within the organization and their roles.

Management
Managers within organizations are largely seen as directors, leaders and overseers: those who provide guidance and support and are able to inspire the workforce. Management's role is fundamental to the quality improvement process. Thus, as quality successes are attributed to the actions of management, so too should the emergence of quality problems. Oversmith (1987) identifies six actions by management which are responsible for poor quality:

- failure to communicate the organization's quality expectations to all employees;
- failure to establish accurate and consistent quality standards;
- planning activities under the assumption that inconsistent quality performance is inevitable;
- operating under the assumption that quality improvement will be a costly process;
- failure to remain objective in determining the causes of quality problems; and
- failure to provide positive role models to employees.

Product development

The group of individuals responsible for new product development will be required to possess a thorough understanding of their customer. Knowledge of what the customer expects from a product is a prerequisite to the design of the product. Product design should consider manufacturability, reliability, product life, service and warranty, part interchangeability and the length of time required to complete development of the product. Quality of design is the topic of a later section.

Marketing and sales

The necessary contribution to quality improvement and the day-to-day functioning of a JIT system requires sales and marketing to communicate the changes in sales forecasts, establish shipping dates in accordance with product lead time and establish the priority of customer needs.

Production

Employees who constitute the production function of the organization must assume new roles compatible with the new quality policy. The most significant of these roles is the willingness to perform self-inspection and inject a new level of consciousness into their work. New standards set for product characteristics such as durability and reliability, as well as aesthetics will require all elements of the production process to perform without accepting mistakes and justifying their occurrence.

Manufacturing engineering

Quality improvement is supported by the actions of manufacturing engineering through process improvement activities. The role of manufacturing engineering serves to increase productivity, lower cost and reduce product defects.

Materials management

Employees responsible for materials management perhaps assume a role which embodies the true essence of JIT: 'providing the right quantity of quality material to be used at the right place and time.' Materials management is responsible for linking the receipt of goods with the material requirements of production.

Quality assurance

The role of quality assurance is to facilitate, educate, track and evaluate the performance and progress of the quality improvement process. The function of education and training for TQM cannot be over-emphasized. TQM for many companies represents a significant break away from traditional attitudes about quality.

In subsequent chapters we present the advantages of using a task team or team approach to plan and implement the JIT concepts with regard to production. The team approach should also be employed in the implementation of TQM. Such an approach shares similar advantages as those mentioned previously. Bently identifies three specific teams each of which performs a separate function in implementing TQM.

1. *The executive steering committee*   It is generally composed of senior managers with responsibilities for planning the implementation, securing commitment and maintaining a constant level of momentum. Specifically, this team functions to perform the following activities:
   - directing the TQM implementation efforts;
   - substantiating organizational commitment to TQM;
   - securing management concern in areas of improving quality and productivity;
   - establishing organizational policies consistent with improving quality and productivity; and
   - allocating organizational resources to cost reduction and prevention of quality problems.
2. *Quality management teams*   These are composed of middle level managers whose responsibilities address implementation rather than planning aspects. Functions include:
   - establishing task teams;
   - developing relationships between internal and external customers and suppliers;
   - implementing a system for quality problem prevention; and
   - ensuring operational goals are realized through assigning responsibilities to individual employees.
3. *The task team*   It is composed of groups who perform activities which are highly action oriented. They include:
   - reducing the costs of quality through corrective action steps;
   - monitoring the costs of quality;
   - identifying and reducing wasted production time and time consumed in set-ups; and
   - identifying the customer/supplier requirements.

4.1.5 Quality improvement through employee ownership
Traditional approaches to manufacturing have ingrained pictures in our minds of employees who complete their tasks, go home at the end of the day and rarely see the final outcome of the product which flows through their workstation as work-in-process. Today, the concept of ownership has arisen and found a new place in many organizations. Ownership has proven to be successful in building in product quality. However, unless management is fully committed and supportive of the concept, ownership will remain simply a romantic idea.

Employee ownership is the art of instilling in employees a sense of responsibility, control and ability to affect the final product. The ownership process should result in employees recognizing how their input can lead to quality improvements in the product. A true sense of employee ownership provides a recognizable link between employee actions and their future within the organization.

Employee ownership is an evolutionary process: it begins small but the process gains momentum. For example, the ownership process may commence with the development of a simple suggestion system. Employees may be encouraged to submit suggestions on how to improve quality. Suggestions are then evaluated and may be implemented. According to Werther *et al.* (1990), suggestion systems must contain three elements critical to success: idea generation, evaluation and implementation. The absence of one or more of the elements will result in failure. Management commitment to suggestion systems is evident with the feedback they offer employees. Continual refusal to accept and implement employee suggestions in the absence of constructive feedback will only serve to discourage employees and negate past efforts. Employees may eventually 'outgrow' the simple suggestion system. The emergence of this stage should signal management that employees require greater flexibility and control over their working environment.

Attempts at creating employee ownership need not be limited to the product. The ability of employees to affect their immediate work environment is equally important. Employees who operate equipment on a continual basis and work within the same area from day to day understand their environment and are able to recognize how it should be altered to best fulfill their needs. Rearranging the placement of machines, creating visible signs and production schedules can improve the flow of work-in-process. Simplifying and speeding up the flow of WIP can assist quality improvement indirectly through reducing lead time, ensuring the right quantity and quality of goods are available at the right time and identifying problems through improved worker communication.

Successful employee ownership commands consistency and becomes one of the elements which constitute the organizational culture. Oversmith (1988) has developed a comprehensive method of instituting employee ownership. The method addresses implementation from the initial to the final stages. It includes the following:

1. *Development of a formal quality policy* The development and publication of a quality policy provides a standard meaning of 'quality' to which all employees must adhere. The policy also serves to substantiate management commitment to new quality philosophies. The opportunity to view a formal written statement assists in reaffirming employees' belief in the quality improvement process.

   The quality policy should include the following components:
   - a definition of quality;
   - identification of systems for achieving quality (problem prevention);
   - the defined performance standards; and
   - methods to measure performance results.

2. *Providing education and training to all employees* Education and training should serve to relate the quality goals of the organization to each

employee. Knowledge of organization-wide goals assists the employee in identifying what specific actions they can perform to improve quality. Training should also address methods of problem identification through group problem solving.

3. *Providing written requirements* which address set-up procedures, preventive maintenance and acceptable tolerance levels. Established, visible written requirements provide a standard method for carrying out routine procedures. Written requirements should detail the most effective method of executing activities. Adherence to such a procedure will assist in ensuring that productivity and quality levels are consistent.

4. *Assigning responsibility to employees for quality improvement* Quality improvement through individual responsibility can be realized through several methods. Two methods include the following:
   - developing job descriptions which clearly outline the responsibility of employees in quality improvement; and
   - the use of individual or group effort quality projects to achieve quality improvement. The project approach clearly defines responsibilities of group members and provides rewards based upon the contribution of employees to quality improvement.

   Irrespective of the approach used, providing employees with the necessary resources to ensure their quality responsibilities are achieved is essential. Failure to do so will result in frustrated employees who are penalized for top management's mistakes.

5. *Developing a system to identify and eliminate quality problems* The development of a formal problem identification system provides employees with a mechanism for reporting and generating solutions to problems. Formal systems can serve to eliminate ambiguity over whether a problem has been reported or not. The system should also provide a method of relaying feedback to the problem identifier. Employees' responsibility for the system includes correctly identifying the problem; however, a solution need not always be developed. Generating solutions to problems should be made a group effort as problems often extend beyond the scope of the individual's work area and knowledge.

6. *Development of quality corrective action teams* Mandates for such teams should include clearly defined objectives, methods for determining the causes and solutions of quality problems and availability of required resources. Prerequisites to the success of quality corrective action teams include training and rewarding desired results. The development of quality corrective action teams is a dynamic process. Teams arise in response to specific quality problems, thus team composition varies over time.

7. *Establishing teams to direct quality improvement efforts* The direction teams are composed of several employees who are responsible for establishing quality priorities, measuring the extent of quality problems,

relaying activities to other employees and recognizing quality improvement results. The objective of placing the directing function in the hands of other employees is to increase the level of control employees have over quality issues.

8. *The use of reward systems which encourage employee ownership*   Using formal reward systems indicates to the employees that they will be recognized for their efforts in the quality improvement process. Formal reward systems reflect the commitment of management to employees.

4.2 Quality of design

The preceding section focusing on the essence of quality has communicated to the reader the ambiguity of defining quality and its dependance upon the elements of the system: people, plants and systems (Goddard, 1986). This section addresses the very nature of the product: how its design can affect the level of product quality. Traditional approaches to product design have mainly focused on whether the product is manufacturable or not. JIT's focus on quality at the source requires an in-depth view of product design which extends beyond this traditional emphasis. Quality of design, in accordance with a JIT perspective, surveys the components of waste and non-value-adding activity elimination, process design and problem-solving activities which assist in designing a product compatible with the customer's requirements and expectations.

4.2.1 Defining quality of design

Quality of design is most easily understood if viewed as a component of the system perspective identified in the preceding section. It is but one element of many which contributes to the overall system, however, its role is fundamental to the quality process. Quality of design is the first of a series of many inputs, processes and support activities which affect the quality of the final product. A useful analogy in communicating the significance of quality of design to the overall system is to view each element of the system as a building block of a wall, as illustrated in Fig. 4.2. The lower levels of the figure must contain blocks which are strong, durable and securely placed, otherwise, a weak foundation can cause the situation presented in the wall on the right of the diagram.

Kinsey (1990) effectively summarizes the role of product design in the overall quality process: 'The first step in assuring that quality is always present in the product is the design of the product itself. The product's design provides the greatest opportunity for quality improvement, because the design impacts all of the downstream functions required to place a product in the hands of the ultimate user.'

The Building Blocks of JIT Quality

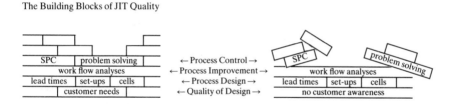

Figure 4.2 Quality of design: the foundation for quality.

4.2.2 Improving the quality of design

The first question one should ask is 'how can quality of design be improved upon?' The customer plays the primary role in determining varying aspects of the product. The fundamental rule to remember is that the company and its products exist because of the customer, and for the customer. Consistent application of this simple rule will most likely lead an organization, regardless of what avenue is pursued, to commence with the customer. The information required from the customer to carry out the design improvement activities can be obtained from the questionnaire or customer profile presented earlier. More specifically, detailed questions regarding functional and aesthetic product characteristics can be added to the existing customer profiles. The design improvement steps should be conducted through the team approach as identified by Bently.

Compilation and evaluation of the customer profile

The completion of collecting customer information related to the product function and characteristics leads to the next logical step: to compile the information and interpret or evaluate its meaning to the organization. The customer profile approach can be applied to new product development or product redesign. The information collected from the profiles can be categorized according to specific aspects of the product. For example, it may be determined that customer requirements and expectations may focus on specific components of the product, the product's flexibility, durability, reliability and time required before the product is ready for market. Other aspects of the profile may indicate a need to improve upon service and support systems of the product.

Interpreting the data is fundamental to the organization in creating an awareness of the prevailing design weaknesses. The frequency of similar customer responses to the profile can assist in pinpointing specific areas for improvement. Therefore, an analysis should entail calculating the ratio of responses directed to specific design areas.

The use of the customer approach will assist the organization with the initial definition of the product. Designing the product right the first time, rather than determining the product is not what the customer wants after the fact, is more likely to occur.

Application of the customer profile to design activities
The completion of this second step requires the organization to apply the new information to the development of design improvement activities. Questions which the organization should answer prior to adjusting or modifying any established activities include the following:

- New product development
  - How can existing design activities be applied to the new product(s)?
  - Does the organization possess the necessary resources to accomplish the required design?
  - Who will be involved in the design process?
- Product redesign
  - What changes are necessary to the established design process?
  - What resources are required for completion?
  - Who will be involved?

Kinsey (1990) suggests the outcome of the customer profile evaluation will result in a sequence of technical specifications for the redesign. Conflicts or competing goals may cause the organization to prioritize the needs of its customers. Specifically, conflicts may originate from the technical specifications being incompatible with market competitiveness for cost, delivery and reliability.

Improvement through identifying critical factors
Identifying critical factors, that is, the components which interfere with the design meeting the customers' requirements and expectations, include factors which contribute to waste (i.e. non-value-adding activities) and those which delay delivery of the product to the market. Correctly identifying these factors will require an analysis of the design process, or the system used to transform an idea into a tangible product. Process design distinctively addresses the manufacturing of an idea which is producible, the selection of the equipment and sequence of operations or work flow.

Process design, departing from the traditional approaches practised by many, will require engineering, or those responsible for the creation of the product blueprint and manufacturing, those responsible to build the product, to become integrated (Plossl, 1987). Integration of these two disciplines is necessary for one main reason: to create a shared awareness of the limits of manufacturing and to develop a product design which is manufacturable and incorporates the customers' requirements and expectations. In short, the integration of these two disciplines can assist in the development of a better product. Strong emphases on the integration of engineering and manufacturing is clearly documented in the literature, however, regard has unequivocally be given to the team approach for product and process design. The team approach requires input into the design process by engineers, machine operators, the customer, manufacturing and supplies.

Eliminating the wastes in product design
Wastes associated with product design and process design will include any aspect, whether it is material or equipment operation that can cause delays in product delivery to the market. Effective product and process design can eliminate many of these wastes through the following six ways.

1. *Designing a product which aims to reduce the level of required inventory* (Waliszewski, 1987). This can be accomplished through standardizing parts, developing part modules, eliminating bill-of-material levels, designing products with reduced final assembly time requirements and designing products which are able to use the capabilities of new technologies.
2. *Simplification of the product design* to reduce work time.
3. *Provision of training* to create an awareness of the functioning of machines, tools and systems as well as information regarding limitations of their application.
4. *Developing a prototype* The prototype should be run through the manufacturing processes to determine possible problems. Problems which occur should be analysed, solutions developed and the design and manufacturing process should be adjusted to eliminate these problems. The prototype process helps to identify and eliminate problems prior to full-scale production and assists in reducing required lead time. Problem-solving techniques are discussed later.
5. *Performing an analysis* of the activities which constitute the design process. Plossl (1987) has developed a rule of thumb for the amount of time which is likely to be consumed in design activities. It is estimated that approximately two-thirds or 67% of the total design time is consumed with conducting office activities such as meetings, research, and coordinating activities. Analysis of all the activities required to conduct product and process design places the organization in a position to identify and eventually eliminate non-value-adding activities.
6. *Use of work cells* or group technology to assist in reducing lead times, inventory levels, eliminating work-in-process queues and transportation of the product throughout the plant.

Continual monitoring and feedback
Improvement activities for product and process design have a beneficial impact upon the organization. The product's design will not only contribute to waste reduction and customer satisfaction, but will also dictate, to some degree, the implementation of JIT. Thus, a clear understanding of the organization's customers is a prerequisite to JIT. Furthermore maintaining a clear understanding of customers' changing needs is a dynamic process: constant communication with customers, the changing marketplace and adjusting process design in accordance with these changes is a necessary element of quality of design. The following provide examples of how product design impacts upon the implementation of JIT.

- The design of production or work cells.
- The training requirements of each cell.
- The work flow and consequently the set-up of machinery.
- The systems used to monitor and measure product quality.
- The lead times associated with various stages of product development.

4.3 Quality of conformance

Quality of conformance specifically refers to how closely the product adheres to pre-established specifications. The main concern of most organizations does not rest with products which conform to specifications, but rather with what happens when nonconformance occurs. Nonconformance presents a problem as it contributes to the cost of quality, especially the cost of appraisal. It serves then that a means of prevention is in order: to prevent nonconformance from occurring is to eliminate costs.

Successfully averting the costs of nonconformance necessitates replacing traditional approaches to quality with those consistent with the JIT philosophy. The idea of 'quality at the source' most completely captures the essence of JIT quality. First, the elements of the traditional approach to quality must be replaced. Identifying these elements requires one to consider the quality continuum presented in Fig. 4.3a, which contains all elements which can impact upon the quality of the final product, commencing with the source of material and parts supply, the production processes, techniques used to monitor and measure quality and ending with the outcome of these elements – the final product.

The traditional approach to quality works well when operating under a number of assumptions:
1. machines and tools will never operate outside of specified tolerance levels;
2. operators will never make mistakes; and
3. it is acceptable to pass on products with defects not identified through acceptance sampling or final inspection to consumers as long as they represent less than a specified percentage.

Unfortunately, machines and operators do make mistakes and consumers pay the price for these mistakes when they purchase defective products. The organization also pays a price for less than 100% quality products: increased scrap and rework expenses, high inventory levels and warranty expenses, product recalls, consumer apathy and reduced competitiveness. Figure 4.3b illustrates the quality control techniques used in the traditional approach, while Fig. 4.3c presents the application of JIT quality principles to the quality continuum.

The JIT quality philosophy requires building quality into the product. Mechanisms must be put into place to prevent quality problems from arising. These methods, working in concert, assist operators in detecting when and where quality problems occur and how to prevent them from reoccurring.

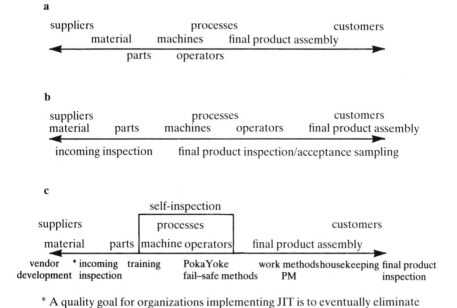

* A quality goal for organizations implementing JIT is to eventually eliminate
  this step through vendor development.

Figure 4.3a. the quality continuum; b. the traditional approach;
and c. built-in quality.

The results in reduced or eliminated scrap and rework expenses, low
inventory requirements and warranty expense, and a satisfied consumer.
The quality techniques of JIT will now be discussed in detail.

The source of materials and parts: incoming inspection

The initial receipt of materials and parts to be used in production represents
the beginning of the quality continuum. Thus, it stands to reason, if
inventory at this stage is of poor quality, it is going to adversely impact upon
the downstream processes. Hamre (1988) identifies three cost categories
associated with nonconforming material. These include the following:

- inventory costs include expenses from rejected parts, replacement parts
  and related carrying costs;
- labour costs of production, material handling and shipping personnel;
  and
- labour costs of support, purchasing, engineering and quality personnel
  when a poor quality part causes problems.

Many organizations currently undergoing JIT implementation conduct
inspections of incoming inventory. However, the goal of JIT is to eliminate

this process eventually. Achievement of this goal is affirmed through eliminating the need to perform incoming inspection. Consideration should be given to why this form of inspection should be eliminated. The answer lies once again in the concept of value added. Inspection does not reduce the number of defects, it does not build in quality. It simply serves as a means of identifying defects the supplier has failed to recognize subsequent to the manufacturing of the product. Thus, inspection does not add value to the product.

Organizations implementing JIT are seeking eventually to eliminate the need for performing incoming inspection activities through a combination of reducing the supplier base, selection through qualification and vendor development as discussed before. Vendor development seeks to assist the supplier who maintains an interest in striving to provide 100% defect-free materials and parts.

Training employees in how to prevent quality problems from occurring
Employees are likely to receive training on how to identify, solve and prevent quality problems from occurring. Training addresses the proper use of SPC, self-inspection, housekeeping and preventive maintenance activities, work methods such as job rotation and 'pokayoke'. Pokayoke is a means of 'mistake proofing' the plant for prevention of quality problems and have many applications (Shingo, 1986). For example, incorporating checklists into operations can serve to eliminate employee mistakes.

Statistical process control (SPC)
This is a method of monitoring and measuring variances in the performance of machines through the interpretation of process charts and is employed to manage in-process quality. Training for SPC should focus on four levels (Duffy, 1987).

1. *Helping employees to understand the need for change* Although SPC is not a new concept, its application in many organizations is. Therefore, success will require helping employees to understand the need for its use. SPC is an effective means of defect prevention and is akin to the quality principles of JIT.
2. *Developing problem-solving skills* Problems identified through SPC necessitate the need for problem-solving skills. Employees, collectively, should be able to identify reasons for machine failure. The most common of the group problem-solving technique is engaging in an activity known as brainstorming, and is discussed in greater detail in a later section.
3. *Understanding and applying the mechanics for charting* SPC is useless unless employees are able to maintain the charts without constant supervision. The use of SPC should be applied to areas where it is deemed to be most effective. The continual success of SPC will require fostering a sense of employee ownership of the process.

4. *Interpreting the charts*   The prevention of quality problems rests with the employee's ability to interpret correctly the process charts. Interpretation of a chart may indicate that something in the process has changed or a pattern or trend is developing. One of the main benefits of SPC is to involve the employee in the process while eliminating inconsistencies which can occur if sensory inspection was chiefly relied upon. Detection of a change in the process or development of a trend leaves three possible courses of action open to the employee: to adjust the process, shut down the machine, or call for assistance. Training should address the appropriateness of each action.

Interpretation of charts is a difficult task. Employees may be faced with situations where determining the appropriate course of action is not evident. The occurrence of such a situation requires employees to seek assistance.

Two errors, known as Type 1 and Type 2 errors are possible and serve to increase difficulty in interpretation. Type 1 errors occur when employees interpret a process to be operating out of control, when in fact it is not. Type 2 errors arise when the process is deemed to be operating within the specified limits, but it is in fact operating out of control. The upper and lower control limits should be chosen to reduce the likelihood of Type 1 and Type 2 errors from occurring.

The types of process charts used to monitor machine performance include the mean (X-bar), range (R) and fraction defective (P) charts. Figure 4.4a illustrates the common features of all process charts. The upper control limit (UCL) and lower control limit (LCL) are the standards set for processes, taking into account the naturally occurring variability of a process. The natural variability found within each process is the result of 'chance causes', or 'random variations naturally inherent in the process when it is working correctly' (Dilworth, 1989). Variability in the process which is due to an 'assignable cause', such as a machine malfunction, requires immediate attention.

The X-bar chart records the average measurement of a process. For example, the X-bar chart may record the 'average' fullness of bottles. The R chart is used in conjunction with X-bar charts to show the range of variability of the process. Both X-bar and R charts as shown in Fig. 4.4b are used to plot continuous variables.

P charts record the fraction defective produced by a process. They differ from X-bar and R charts as they plot discrete variables. The defects per unit chart is appropriate when the number of defects found in a unit is indeterminate. Figure 4.5c provides an example of a fraction defective chart.

Housekeeping

Housekeeping and preventive maintenance activities contribute to quality problem prevention as they function to maintain the working environment

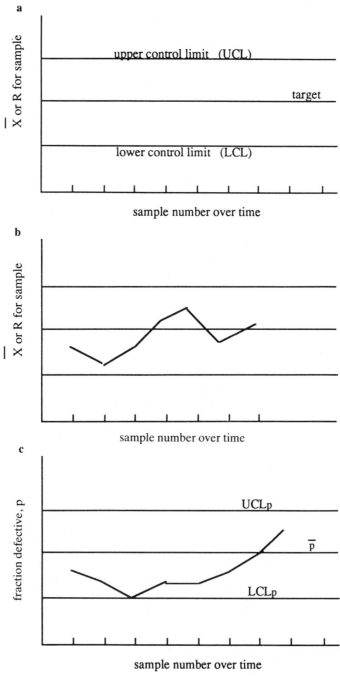

Figure 4.4 SPC control charts: a. common features; b. X̄ or R chart; and c. fraction defective chart.

and correct problems before they adversely affect in-process quality. Housekeeping and preventive maintenance were discussed in Chapter 2.

Work methods

Work methods such as job rotation, as discussed in Chapter 2, assist in the prevention of problems as they provide the workforce with broad exposure to the demands of manufacturing. Job rotation allows employees to remain alert and effective at their jobs. An increased level of employee alertness is more apt to lead to quality problem detection in the early stages of its occurrence.

Fail-safe methods

Fail-safe methods are used to 'mistake proof' the plant from mistakes and mishaps which commonly occur and is an example of a pokayoke system. Fail-safe methods are very effective in bringing problems to machine operators' attention. The use of pokayoke devices can be as simple as installing switches on machines to detect malfunctions. For example, the use of a switch can detect if a bolt has been placed properly. In the event it has not, the machine will automatically shut down. Fail-safe methods for machines are useful and adaptable to quality problem prevention, as are other forms of pokayoke systems. Organizations can be equally successful with other forms of 'mistake proofing' the plant. Enhancing visibility through the provision of checklists and standardizing operations are other examples of pokayoke systems.

Self-inspection

Self-inspection is a form of subjective inspection where employees check their work to ensure it has been completed correctly. Self-inspection, in combination with the internal customer concept, allows employees to ensure that the work they send to the next process is what is required and expected. It allows mistakes to be identified and corrected immediately, rather than in a downstream process where the mistake will have a compounded effect. Self-inspection allows for 100% inspections since every employee must check each piece of work which flows through his or her hands.

Final inspection

Final inspection, or inspection of the product once completed, is an ongoing practice by many organizations. It is often viewed as a 'necessary evil' as it does not add value to the product and is not 100% effective in detecting all defects. Final inspections are conducted through acceptance sampling, i.e. only a percentage of all final products of a lot are chosen for inspection. It should become the goal of the firm operating in a JIT environment to eliminate final product inspections eventually. However, the need for final product inspection can only be eliminated through application of the methods and work practices which serve to build in product quality.

4.4 Quality of services

Managing the quality of services has assumed a new level of importance relative to the growing number of companies operating in a service industry. The shift in industries away from primary and extractive manufacturing to services represents a trend which is expected to continue into the next century. Earlier it was stated that the concepts of JIT are being adapted to managing services. The following discussion addresses how JIT can be applied to managing the quality of services.

The meaning of service is difficult to define as a 'service' constitutes a large number of activities. To simplify the definition of service, these activities can be grouped into three categories.

1. Services provided directly to a customer in exchange for payment. Activities such as personal services from a doctor, dentist or hairstylist are included in this category.
2. Services offered in support of a product, such as warranty, delivery of the product, and other after sales support activities.
3. Services provided to a product, such as overhauls and repair work for heavy equipment, or products supplied by original equipment manufacturers (OEMs).

Managing the quality of service, as it applies to the last two categories, will be the focus of the following discussion. The quality of services provided is composed of several characteristics. Variability of the characteristics affects the degree to which a customer is satisfied with the service provided. The service quality characteristics include (Juran, 1988):

- *psychological* or the comfort of surroundings and recognition of regular customers;
- *time oriented* or the time required to repair an item or queuing time;
- *contractual* or the guarantee of service;
- *ethical* or the conduct of service personnel, honesty, integrity and reliability; and
- *technological* or the degree to which the customer is satisfied with the service work, e.g. the repair work.

The idea of preventing quality problems is also applied to managing the quality of services. To accomplish this, the service must be broken down into its constituent characteristics, and each be subjected to analysis. The quality improvement system, as it relates to the prevention of service quality problems, is as follows.

- The customer profile
  - defining the costs of service quality; and
  - determining customer service requirements and expectations.
- The organizational assessment
  - identifying the factors which contribute to variability; and
  - instituting measures to prevent variability.
- Implementation of ideas

- formulating the service quality plan.

Defining the costs of service quality
The costs of quality, as applied to a product or manufacturing company, are grouped into the cost of product appraisal, failure costs and preventive costs. Similarly, Broh (1982) groups the costs of service quality into four broad categories.

1. Appraisal costs for services, which include the costs for monitoring service quality and its components.
2. Internal failure costs, which can result when an organization eliminates a potential or real quality problem prior to customer delivery; or when a quality problem arises obstructing the completion of the service to the customer. Examples include disposal of a faulty piece of equipment or tooling prior to its use, and an untrained machine operator misusing equipment which interferes with the delivery of a service.
3. Market failure costs address the delivery of a service to the customer which is less than satisfactory; or failure to deliver the service when demanded by the customer. Examples of market failure costs include the delivery of an engine which has not been adequately repaired to the customer's expectations and the inability to repair an engine when needed by the customer.
4. Preventive costs include all costs of quality which are directed toward reducing the costs of appraisal. Thus, this cost will entail all costs an organization incurs to prevent quality problems from arising.

Preventing service quality problems is an important function of an organization and impact of their occurrence becomes evident when one considers the costs of service quality. Although preventive costs constitute a cost of quality, their realization is far less costly to the organization when one considers the costs of lost customers, litigation, etc. Similarly, the internal failure cost of eliminating or disposing of a faulty piece of equipment is a step taken to avoid potential problems and is beneficial to the organization. An effective approach is to imagine all the potential costs which could have arisen if the preventive steps were not taken.

Determining customer needs and requirements
Determining customer needs and expectations is the first step taken to reduce the appraisal, internal and market failure costs of quality. Hensel (1990) effectively summarizes the relationship between quality problems and a customer-oriented approach:

> Imprecise definition and/or misjudgement of the relative importance of customer service quality expectations can be a serious barrier to the delivery of acceptable levels of perceived service quality . . . service quality problems related to management not understanding consumer expectations is a function of the extent to which a company recognizes the importance of consumer input, receives accurate communications

about consumer needs, and places barriers between customer contact personnel and top management.

Establishing customer needs and expectations need not be a difficult process. Whittle and Foster (1989) have developed a customer profile model to assist in developing an understanding of the customer, effectively utilizing five characteristics which contribute to functional models in terms of identifying who the customer is and their needs and expectations. The model allows an organization to identify these needs and expectations from the customer's point of view, as well as from the employee's perspective. The five characteristics which constitute effective models follow.

1. The service provider/customer relationship should be recognized as a dynamic process. Customer's needs and expectations are constantly changing and the methods used to identify customer needs and expectations must reflect these changes.
2. The service provided to the customer should be regarded as a 'total service experience'. The method used to determine customer needs and expectations should consider the whole service experience. The application of this approach is likely to result in an accurate assessment of needs and expectations.
3. The method should be understandable and capable of being used by the service provider. Service providers are capable of identifying customer needs, as compared to management personnel, who remain physically and psychologically distant from the customer. Therefore, developing a method which meets this criterion will foster ownership of the customer profiling process.
4. Ideas which offer alternative methods of designing, providing and delivering service should be supported.
5. Design of the profile should be understandable and usable by all employees. The profile should be given to all the organization's customers.

Elements of the customer profile

The customer profile contains six elements which include search, arrival, pre-contact, contact, withdrawal and follow-up. The following discussion addresses each element in detail.

1. *Search*   This represents the first stage in the customer profile, where interaction between the customer and the service function becomes probable. Customer needs are focused on obtaining information.
2. *Arrival*   The stage prior to the customer making contact with the service provider. The customer is focused on accessibility to the service function.
3. *Pre-contact*   The stage where the customer is waiting to be serviced. Attention is focused on the surroundings.
4. *Contact*   The customer is in contact with the service provider and whether the customer's expectations are satisfied becomes of primary

importance. Factors such as the service provided in the preceding stages, interaction with customers or with the service providers influences the degree of customer satisfaction. The influence of other factors requires the level of service provided to be consistent.

5. *Withdrawal*   Customer contact with the service function is completed during this stage. The withdrawal stage is frequently disregarded by management. However, it should not be as it influences the customer's perception of the quality received.

6. *Follow-up*   This represents the last stage of the profile. Customer requirements at this stage include trust and understanding that their requirements will be fulfilled as specified during the contact stage.

The customer profiling model can be applied to any organization to develop a precise understanding of their customers. The stages presented in the model provide a general guideline to follow during this process. Specific actions and organizational procedures which constitute each stage can then be identified and analysed. Satisfying consumer needs and expectations within each of these stages depends upon the extent to which the five quality characteristics are met. The outcome of such a process is to develop a clear and consistent understanding of customer needs and expectations of the service encounter.

Factors which contribute to variability
The factors which contribute to variability with regard to managing the quality of a product are subject to less human input. Variability in this sense could be the result of untrained personnel, misuse of machines, faulty equipment, etc. The factors which contribute to service quality variability are increasingly subjective in nature, as they consist primarily of human interactions between the service provider and the customer. Correctly identifying the components of service which are of primary importance to the individual customer represents a formidable task. Ensuring that the service function is capable of consistently satisfying the five quality characteristics is imperative to customer satisfaction.

Consistency is made possible through identifying the factors which contribute to variability. Several common factors include the following.

- *The degree to which service quality goals are comprehended and practised by the service providers*   Simply publicizing goals will not ensure that employees are working toward their fulfillment. Clear, objective standards and procedures must be documented and perpetuated throughout organizational practices.

- *The training and education of the service providers*   Lack of training addressing communication skills, knowledge of the service support for a product or a product itself can create barriers between the customer and service provider.

- *The degree of honesty of the service provider*   The greatest contributor to consistent satisfaction with respect to honesty is the organization's ability to deliver and fulfill the contract or promise established by the service provider. Tactics such as misdirecting the customer to delay time or saying 'It's on the way' merely contribute to the customer's frustration and the organization's loss. Therefore, establishing honesty at the start of the relationship is a prerequisite to customer satisfaction. Failure to deliver the product or service as originally promised should be openly communicated to the customer.

- *The degree of communication between manufacturing and service support personnel*   The service support personnel have the greatest interaction with customers, therefore, it is important that information regarding the time to complete the product and factors which contribute to delivery delays such as excessive absenteeism, problems with suppliers or machine breakdowns be communicated to the service support personnel.
- *The ability to satisfy the customer's technological requirements*   The greatest impact upon delivery of a product which meets the consumer's technical requirements depends upon how well their initial specifications are defined, the degree of accuracy in relaying their requirements to manufacturing and the capability of operators and processes.

Preventing service quality problems

The most effective approach to preventing service quality problems from arising is to establish service procedures as part of the company's philosophy, provide training to employees on the delivery of services and institute preventive measures such as obtaining feedback from customers through the customer profile. The role of the customer profile is to assume a means of providing customer information on an ongoing basis.

Technological innovation has resulted in the introduction of service quality improvement through the application of 'facilitating goods', i.e. machines or automatic processes which allow for the replacement of a human service provider by a machine (Hensel, 1990). Facilitating goods can either fully replace the efforts of a person, or provide assistance. Examples of facilitating goods are automatic bank tellers, which are capable of fully replacing human effort, or the use of computer programs to assist an operator in obtaining customer information.

Standardizing tasks is another form of improving the delivery of customer services. Tasks which are performed repetitiously, such as determining customer requirements, should be performed accordingly to a systematic procedure. The use of forms or questionnaires consisting of a detailed outline for determining customer requirements should be used. The result of standardizing procedures allows for consistent and thorough methods of determining customer requirements.

Delivery of service quality

The design of any quality system should be functional on three levels. First, the system must provide a means of relaying management's expectations to service quality personnel. Second, the system must be designed to reflect the

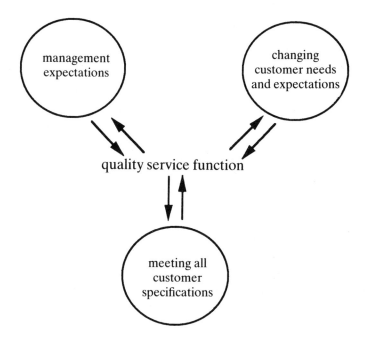

Figure 4.5 Service design: the three functional elements of quality service design.

changing needs of customers. Third, the system must provide a means of meeting all service specifications. Figure 4.5 summarizes the functional levels of service quality.

According to Hensel (1990), the design of the service quality system which fails to relay management's expectations to employees will result in the 'service quality gap'. The gap can be eliminated through establishing an organizational climate supportive of excellence in the delivery of service quality. The sphere of management's responsibility in creating such a climate extends to recruitment and selection of employees knowledgeable and experienced in service quality, developing procedures for training and motivating employees in the pursuit of excellence.

4.5 Quality issues in JIT

The previous discussions on quality addressed the methods of building in quality, the value of quality and the prevention of problems. This section summarizes a collection of information which assists in defining the philosophies and conventions of JIT.

4.5.1 Increasing customer responsiveness

Developing methods to meet customer demands effectively is what constitutes the very nature of JIT. Unfortunately, the name just-in-time is often misunderstood to mean an inventory program. The pull system, linkage through the kanban, streamlining of operations, reduction of waste and prevention of quality problems work together to meet customer requirements more effectively.

4.5.2 Continuous improvement

Effectively communicating the meaning of TQC and total employee involvement (TEI) requires one to grasp a complete understanding of the concept of continuous improvement (CI). Continuous improvement is 'a formal, integrated process which seeks to identify and implement operational improvements within a manufacturing organization on a continuous basis,' (Allor, 1988). Although CI is more readily recognized as being part of the philosophies and practices of a manufacturing organization, its application need not be limited to such organizations. Companies which provide services to customers can institute CI and make it a functional part of their organization.

Continuous improvement operates according to two basic premises: to eliminate waste or non-value-adding activities and to seek continuously to improve quality. Analogous to the success of quality problem prevention, CI must become an integral part of the organization's philosophy and practices, or the organizational culture. Regarding CI as a quality program will not ensure its success; indeed the short-comings of being labelled as a 'program' will largely contribute to its failure, since programs have characteristics which prohibit the acceptance and longevity of philosophies such as CI. Frequently, programs are viewed by employees and management alike as being short lived or temporary in nature and failure in obtaining the support and commitment of employees is common.

The prerequisite to continuous improvement involves a change in attitude. Unquestionably, changing attitudes represents the greatest obstacle to overcome. The current attitudes and beliefs held by many employees are continually reinforced through work practices by management, unions and plant workers. Breaking down the barriers to effective communication between management and employees and replacing our adversarial bargaining system with co-operative efforts lay the foundations for success.

The question remains 'How does an organization attempt to implement continuous improvement?' – the ensuing discussion presents the elements of a general implementation framework.

- *Change is initiated from the top-down*   Securing commitment from all will require management to set an example. Actions and effort must be consistent with the spoken word.
- *Establish continuous improvement as a formal organizational policy* Publicize the effort to inform customers and employees that continuous improvement is a means of achieving organizational goals.
- *Involve the union in the process as soon as possible*   Union involvement at this stage is the first step toward creating a co-operative effort and provides the opportunity for union representatives to express concerns openly.
- *Listen to employees*   Communication should be from the bottom-up. Employee involvement at the earliest stages will reduce resistance, facilitate information flow and make employees an integral part of the process.
- *Establish clear, objective goals for improvement*   Continuous improvement is an all-encompassing philosophy and must be made workable through the establishment of clearly defined and understandable goals. Failure to develop such goals will result in a frustrated workforce, aware of the must for improvement, but lacking the focus and standards necessary to gauge their success.

4.5.3 Total employee involvement: the key to JIT success

Total employee involvement is the collective efforts of all employees directed toward problem solving and improvement. TEI differs from many of the traditional forms of employee involvement as it seeks to involve all employees. The basic underlying principle of TEI is that employees who work closest with the customer, the product and the processes are most able to recognize how to improve these three elements.

TEI is realized through many methods used as a means of securing employee involvement. Suggestion systems represent one form of employee involvement. However, while they attempt to involve employees, they may fail in many respects because they are either not taken seriously or only a handful of employees will participate. The latter has been the main criticism of suggestion systems: many employees who have relevant suggestions fail to become involved in the process.

The main advantage of using TEI is that it provides a simple method of keeping employees interested in their work through establishing employee ownership. Employees are asked to become involved in the operations of the organization: to set its goals and ultimately its direction. TEI is the North American version of the Japanese 'team idea system' (Bodek, 1988). The team idea system uses the concept of applying employees' creativity to improve all facets of the organization. In effect, the result is a committed group of employees who are interested in their jobs. The use of TEI in an organization will not automatically secure the involvement of all employees. Employees must be made to feel comfortable with the idea of involvement, which is in part the responsibility of the cell leader or supervisor. The following present several actions and responses by cell leaders or supervisors which can present obstacles to securing TEI (Japanese Human Relations Association, 1988):

- viewing a suggestion as impossible;
- delaying review of suggestions;
- regarding the success of suggestions as culture bound;
- stating suggestions are impossible to implement;
- refusing to consider suggestions because something is already working – this approach does not allow for improvement; and
- disregarding a suggestion because it has been tried before and failed.

Employees who are reluctant to become involved, especially when others participate actively, should remember that in such organizations, it is often more difficult to remain on the sidelines than it is to submit a simple suggestion.

North American success with TEI will require patience and training, as it represents a change from the established organizational practices. Other prerequisites to its success include providing employees with the necessary resources to identify areas of improvement and make changes. Implementation of TEI can be accomplished through the development of teams which carry out 'small group improvement activities', or SGIAs (Stickler, 1990). The object of the teams is to define areas for improvement and implement improvement activities. Implementation of TEI and its ongoing success depends upon the following criteria.

- Organizational goals must be achieved. Activities should benefit the organization rather than focusing on individual needs.
- Direction must be provided through management. General guidelines and objectives must be set forth for employees to work within.
- Employees must be given the freedom and resources to work toward achieving the goals they have established with the general guidelines set by management.
- The role of management is to provide direction, whereas employees are responsible for the development of solutions and their implementation.

4.5.4 Total quality control

The Japanese interpretation of TQC involves removing quality control from the sole responsibility of designated specialists to all disciplines in an organization (Shingo, 1986). Thus, everyone in the organization would have a stake in managing quality. TQC is 'a philosophy aimed at increasing customer satisfaction through continuous process improvements' (Boyst,

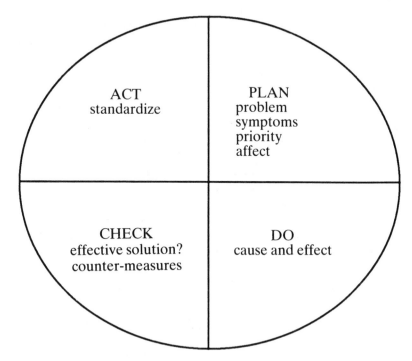

Figure 4.6 The Deming circle.

1990). The 'customer', as it applies to this definition, can be either internal or external to the organization. Total quality control is fundamental to JIT as it functions to eliminate the 'cause' of quality problems.

TQC contains three important elements which can be understood through analysing the individual meaning of 'total', 'quality', and 'control', and how each relates to the overall definition (Boyst, 1990). 'Total' denotes that everyone within the organization, just as the Japanese understood it to mean, is responsible for quality, especially where variability comes into play. Thus, the finance, marketing, manufacturing, personnel, engineering, production and materials personnel will play a role in the quality function. Similarly to TEI, total quality control commands the involvement of all. 'Quality' relates to understanding the causes of problems, correcting and preventing problems. 'Control' is the ability to affect the processes and product and experience results consistent with established standards.

The TQC process operates according to four basic principles, unlike that of traditional approaches to quality. The four principles, the components of the Deming Circle illustrated in Fig. 4.6, include plan, do, check and act (Sandras, 1988).

The process for TQC is unlike that of traditional approaches to quality as it applies a systematic method of problem solving and prevention. The role each component assumes in the problem-solving process is as follows.

- *Plan*   This involves identifying, prioritizing and assessing the impact of the problem. Assigning the problem to a group or individual to ensure it is rectified is fundamental to this stage.
- *Do*   The second component of the circle requires assigning a cause or causes to the problem and identifying symptoms.
- *Check*   This involves assessing the effectiveness of the solution. Failure to experience improvements indicates that either the cause or the effect of the problem was incorrectly identified. Counter-measures to the solution must also be checked. Thus, in the event the solution proves to be ineffective, efforts must be directed once again to 'do'.
- *Act*   The realization of an effective solution should lead employees to standardize the improvement by first identifying what other areas can benefit from this change. Implementation of counter-measures can be done in additional areas of the plant which are likely to experience the problem.

4.5.5 Quality circles

Quality circles are 'small groups of employees doing similar or related work which meet regularly to identify, analyse, and solve product-quality and production problems and to improve general operations' (Ross and Ross, 1982). They are presently a popular method of improving the quality of work life (QWL). Quality circles are identifiable through the purpose and action of members, as well as by several unique characteristics which they possess. Each group consists of a leader, and several members, usually eight to ten employees. Characteristics which assist in defining the groups include the following (Werther *et al.*, 1990):

- membership in the circles is voluntary for all members and the group's leader;
- training is provided to the members of each group to assist with problem solving; and
- problems are selected by group members through group consensus. Employees are given freedom to choose and select potential problems as through this process, they are more likely to be motivated to find a solution and remain within the group.

Quality circles, or as they are known in Japan, quality control circles, were first formalized by Kaoru Ishikawa in 1960. To understand the role circles have played in Japan's history, one must first understand the concept of quality as it applies to the Japanese and North America. Japan's concept of quality focuses on building in quality and the prevention of quality problems: concepts largely inspired and pioneered by Deming and Juran. Subsequent to World War II, the Japanese were faced with limited resources and a need to regain economic security. North America continued to focus on mass inspection and exported their expertise to the Japanese, who were ready and willing to learn. Thus, the Japanese learned of SPC and problem solving, with the formal quality control circle emerging as the outcome.

Today, the Japanese have expanded the use of the QC to areas such as the following (Ross and Ross, 1982):

- suppliers and subsidiary companies;
- applying the problem-solving skills of circle members to preventive maintenance, administration, purchasing and engineering;
- solving intradepartmental problems through the establishment of joint QCs; and
- providing advanced training which extends beyond initial problem-solving skills. Training of this nature involves correct use of advanced statistical methods and regression analysis.

North American companies began to adopt the idea in the 1970s. Although they functioned the same as for the Japanese, North American firms often referred to them as 'employee participation groups', or simply 'quality circles', with many organizations developing their own customized name. The first North American organization to adopt the use of QC was the Lockheed Missiles Space Company. The news of its success with quality circles rapidly spread and today, quality circles have assumed an important place in the quality of work life (QWL) for many North American employees. Focus on improving the quality of products and adopting the methods of building in quality and problem prevention will require the QC to play an ever-increasing role for many organizations.

The quality circle process
The success of QC requires a leader, co-ordinator, facilitator and other members who function together to achieve objectives. The objectives of the circle are to identify and solve quality problems and improve processes within their immediate area or work cell. All the circle members receive training related to problem-solving skills. Meetings between members occur at least once a week.

The identification of a problem and formulation of a solution then allows the circle members to present their ideas to management. Approximately 80% of a circle's suggestions are accepted by management, who must then provide the circle members with authorization to implement the suggestion (Werther et al., 1990). Failure to accept a suggestion requires management to offer valuable feedback, in order to ensure the continuing success of the quality circles.

The role of the QC members

The leader, co-ordinator and the facilitator each plays a unique role in the functioning of the QC. The responsibilities of each role are discussed below (Ross and Ross, 1982).

- *The QC leader*   The leader assumes a key position in the success of the QC, which depends upon how well the leader is able to promote group problem-solving success. Leaders who are able to achieve this success may possess the following leadership skills:
  - ability to resolve conflict,
  - success at encouraging member participation in problem solving,
  - ability to maintain member morale,
  - ability to develop and train co-workers, and
  - ability to secure commitment from members;
  and leadership characteristics:
  - possesses a positive attitude,
  - has growth potential,
  - exhibits creativity and innovativeness,
  - is a good listener,
  - likes to work with people, and
  - is worthy of belief.
- *Circle co-ordinator*   The co-ordinator assumes the responsibility of administrative duties and supervises the facilitator. The role may not be required, depending on the size of the organization. The facilitator usually assumes the responsibilities of the co-ordinator in smaller companies.
- *Circle facilitator*   The facilitator, in addition to that mentioned above, is responsible for co-ordinating and directing activities of the circle members. Functions of the facilitator also include:
  - maintaining documentation;
  - training circle members;
  - providing the link between management and the circle;
  - monitoring and assessing programs; and
  - facilitating communication.

The value of quality circles to an organization

The benefits associated with the efforts of quality circles are numerous. It has been established that they contribute to higher levels of efficiency, quality, productivity, safety, cost effectiveness and lower absenteeism. However, the main benefit of QCs is not the cost savings which can be experienced by implementation of solutions (Werther *et al.*, 1990). The main benefits of QCs are:

- increased employee commitment through participation and consensus decision making;
- increased sense of employee ownership and control;
- provides a mechanism to realize employee potential;

- improved communication between employees;
- increased motivation and employee morale; and
- an effective means of training.

The potential benefits an organization can experience through the use of QCs outweigh the costs. However, an awareness of the costs associated with QCs will provide a realistic picture of what QCs are capable of accomplishing. The most effective approach to implementing quality circles is to start with a realistic attitude. QCs do not provide quick-fix solutions to all organizational problems. Many problems will remain outside the responsibility of the circle members. Common costs and obstacles associated with the implementation of QCs include the following (Ross and Ross, 1982, Werther *et al.*, 1990).

- *The cost of training employees.*
- *Union concerns* Unions may present some reservations to management regarding the implementation of QCs and their use. Objections may include the following:
  - the use of QCs as a means of eventually eliminating the union;
  - increasing productivity levels to the point where it will produce adverse effects on the workforce; and
  - reducing the size of the workforce through increased productivity levels.

  The most effective approach to avoid union efforts of obstructing implementation efforts is to maintain open communication with union representatives. Sharing the objectives of the QCs will assist in clarifying management motivation.
- *QCs remove the worker from the job, reducing the time required to complete job tasks* The experience of most organizations with QCs is that workers are able to accomplish the same volume of work while participating in weekly meetings. This is a plausible outcome as the object of QCs is to develop more effective approaches to task completion.
- *Resistance to change* The implementation of QCs represents a change to the established work methods. Resistance is likely to be directed at management from supervisors and employees. Common concerns frequently address the increased level of responsibility of workers and reduced supervisory control.
- *Failure with previous attempts to increase the level of employee involvement* Past attempts may have resulted in failure; however, this need not be representative of the outcome of QCs. The success with QC implementation will require a positive attitude, commitment from all involved and a well-defined plan of action.
- *Failure to provide sufficient training to the members of the circles* This will result in incorrectly identifying cause, effect and formulation of solutions. The circle will lack the direction required to function constructively if the circle leader is not provided with adequate training.

- *Lack of management support* Failure of management to demonstrate commitment to the circles will result in failure. The circle members need management's support from provision of the necessary tools for problem solving to feedback on suggestions.
- *Setting unrealistic expectations for the QCs* The most effective approach to managing QCs is to allow them necessary time to develop and grow on their own. Expecting too much too soon will result in a group of frustrated and defeated employees.
- *Failure to establish specific, quantitative measures.*

Successful QCs contain all the features which are known to contribute to their success. Failing to address at least one of the obstacles to their implementation will interfere with the effectiveness of their long-term functioning.

4.6 Managing in-process quality

Managing in-process quality is executed through the use of SPC, training, fail-safe methods and quality circles. The problem-solving techniques used by quality circle members are applied to solving quality problems and addressing organizational-wide quality issues. Thus, problem-solving tools can be applied to solving problems associated with the quality of inputs, in-process quality and the quality of outputs, in addition to vendor development, customer profiling and reduction of the supplier base.

Problem-solving techniques aside from the statistical techniques described before include:

- methods for identifying cause and effect such as brainstorming and the nominal group technique (NGT);
- the 5 'whys';
- Pareto analysis;
- histograms;
- check sheets;
- flip charts; and
- cause and effect or Ishikawa diagrams.

4.6.1 Brainstorming and NGT

Brainstorming can be defined as 'a group of people using their collective imaginative powers to create ideas and solutions' (Ross and Ross, 1982). The objective of the regular meetings of the QC members is to identify problems and develop solutions. The process demands participation by all group members to avoid being guided by the opinion of a select few. Although this represents the ideal practice, in actuality, there will always be group members who are hesitant to offer their suggestions. The actions of members can be directed toward creating an open and positive environment which encourages participation. Members should:

- offer encouragement on a consistent basis;

- attempt to generate as many ideas as possible without being judgemental;
- foster a positive attitude toward suggestions; and
- attempt to make everyone feel welcome and involved in the process.

The NGT is another method of soliciting ideas from a group of individuals (Werther *et al.*, 1990). However, it is a silent idea-generation process and can be used to identify problems, inadequacies in training, etc. The process commences with a group of employees, managers or supervisors who privately list on a piece of paper possible causes of problems or solutions. The ideas are then shared with the group without being criticized or judged, until each person within the group 'passes' or runs out of ideas. Clarification of ideas occurs and group participants vote on the five ideas deemed to be the most important. NGT has been regarded as superior to brainstorming as it tends to encourage all members' ideas through the sessions.

4.6.2 The 5 'whys'

The 5 'whys' can be applied to any problem to determine its real cause. The underlying purpose of asking 'why' five times is to avoid attributing a false cause to the problem. The tendency for most people is to assign the first symptom or cause identified to be the root of the problem, whereas there may be several causes or symptoms to a problem.

The 5-why process requires an employee to consider all factors which may be part of the problem. Factors to consider include the tools and equipment used in production, work practices, the flow of work and WIP.

4.6.3 Pareto charts

Pareto charts assist in problem identification and analysis of the percentage of each cause which contributes to the problem. It is sometimes referred to as 'the separation of the vital few from the trivial many' (Ross and Ross, 1982). The concept is often regarded as the '80–20' rule, that is, the majority of the problem or 80% of it is the result of the impact of a minority or 20% of the causes. The 80–20 rule, however need not apply to all situations. For example, after careful analysis, it may be determined that 75% of the problem is caused by 25% of the causes.

The method of constructing a Pareto chart involves the following steps.
1. Collect data for a specified period of time for the causes or defects identified.
2. The data is then categorized as it relates to each cause or defect identified.
3. Construct the graph:
   (a) draw the horizontal (x axis), then two vertical (y axes), one at the left and one at the right;
   (b) place the causes or defect categories along the x axis, starting from the left in order of largest to smallest;

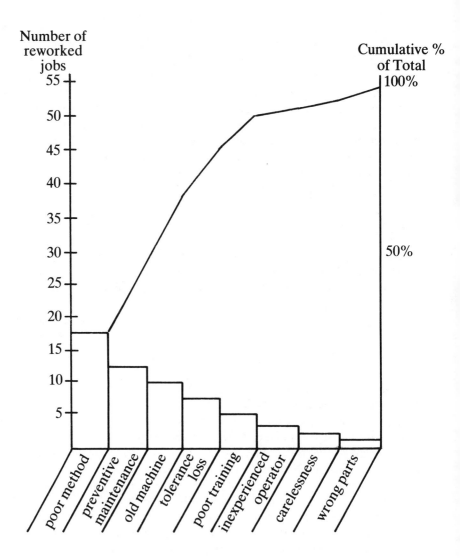

Causes of rework

Figure 4.7 A Pareto chart.

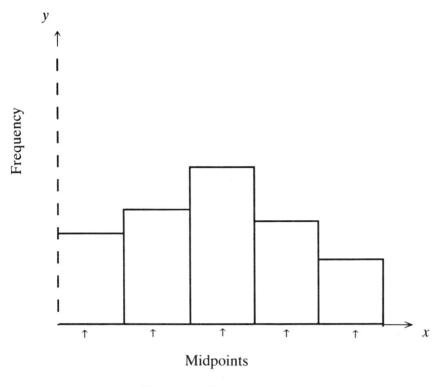

Figure 4.8 The histogram.

(c) place the number of occurrences for each cause or defect on the left y axis; and
(d) place percentages on the right y axis.
4. Plot the data in bars, of equal width.
5. Study the graph to understand the relationship between the cause categories and percentages. Figure 4.7 presents an example of a Pareto chart.

4.6.4 Histograms
Histograms are bar graphs used to show the frequency distribution of data and the variation within a process. The construction of histograms requires the collection of data; limits of midpoints are placed on the x axis and class frequencies scaled on the y axis. Figure 4.8 illustrates a histogram.

4.6.5 Check sheets
Check sheets offer an efficient method of collecting data that can be applied to any problem and is useful in illustrating patterns or trends. Check sheets are tables used to tally the frequency of defects or problems which occur.

Constructing a check sheet should entail the following:
- the use of visible, accurate data which can then be translated into a graph; and
- data which can be easily interpreted and understood.

Figure 4.9 depicts such a check sheet illustrating the frequency of factors which contribute to low employee morale.

Cell No. Reason for low morale	1	2	3	TOTAL
job security	||||			
poor employee relations	⦀⦀			
job stress				
wage freeze				
safety				
TOTAL				

Figure 4.9 Check sheet.

4.6.6 Flip charts

Flip charts are simply large, visible charts which are accessible to employees (Boyst, 1990). Markers should be located near the charts so employees can write in problems they have identified. The items placed on the charts should be discussed by the employees within each cell for approximately 15 minutes per day. Flip charts are effective in identifying quality problems and encouraging participation as employees feel comfortable using them.

4.6.7 Analysis of cause and effect

Analysing cause and effect has been identified as a six-step process (Japanese Human Relations Association, 1988). The process involves:
- idea identification;
- research;
- idea formulation;
- idea modification;
- implementing the improvement plan; and
- follow-up on the improvement plan.

Idea identification

The first step in the process requires that the problem is correctly identified. The root cause of problems must be correctly distinguished from mere

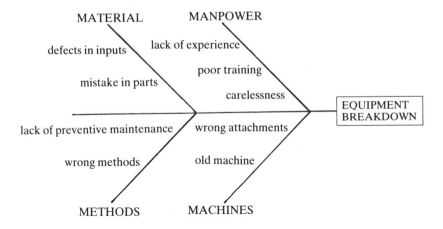

Figure 4.10 The cause and effect diagram.

symptoms. Employees should focus on improving quality through maintenance and defect reduction, reducing costs, improving productivity and delivery, increasing safety, and improving relations with fellow employees.

Research

The research stage in the process requires the application of the 5 'whys', cause and effect diagrams, Pareto analysis, histograms and checklists.

Understanding the problem

Circle members must develop a thorough understanding of the problem before they are capable of formulating a solution. The cause and effect or fishbone diagram is an effective method of organizing and analysing the root cause of problems. Figure 4.10 presents an illustration of a cause and effect diagram.

The method of construction involves five basic steps:

1. clearly identify the effect of the causes and write it to the right of where the remaining diagram will be placed;
2. identify all the factors which contribute to the cause, and categorize these factors by their relationship to one another into three groups – major, minor and intermediate causes;
3. construct the diagram to promote visibility, so that all causes are readily identifiable to employees;
4. display the diagram so that it remains visible and accessible to all employees to encourage further suggestions; and
5. relate the completed diagram to the actual condition.

The formulation of ideas

The formulation of ideas should assume the same process as for brainstorming possible causes of problems or defects. Several solutions to problems may exist. Thus, generating as many solutions as possible will provide the opportunity for selection of the most effective. Generating ideas for effective solutions requires food for thought. Engaging in 'what if' analysis will provide a variety of possible scenarios or outcomes to implementation of the solution. What if analysis can be used to address the outcome of the following (Japanese Human Relations Association, 1988):

- *elimination* of a task, movement, or material;
- *reversal* of equipment, workers or areas of the plant;
- *enlargement and reduction*, increasing flexibility or manoeuvrability;
- *linking and separating* tools and processes for greater flexibility;
- *addition and removal* of tools and tasks;
- *concentration and dispersion* of workers and processes;
- *replacement and substitution* of time and activities to improve productivity; and
- *changing the sequence* of operations.

Modifying ideas

Selection of the most effective solution will require circle members to evaluate each idea based on its cost effectiveness, time, labour and potential benefits such as application to other situations. Ideas should be evaluated according to the following breakdown.

- Tangible benefits: increased productivity, reduced costs.
- Intangible benefits: increased motivation, morale, quality, delivery.
- The ease of implementation: required labour, time, financial resources.
- The potential application to other areas of the plant, i.e. standardization.
- The affect on other facilities, workers, processes.
- The lasting effects or longevity of the solution.
- How well thought out is the solution?
- Has the solution been developed before?
- The amount of effort involved in the formulation of the idea.

The plan for implementation

The idea of ownership arises once again at this point. Employees should have control over identifying the problem, formulating solutions and implementing the solution once authorized by management. The steps required for successful implementation subsequent to approval include:

- obtaining necessary resources;
- defining individual member activities;
- defining an implementation schedule for the plan;
- communicating the implementation plan to all employees who will be directly or indirectly affected;
- including in the implementation schedule the use of a pilot program or project;
- anticipating implementation problems and solving them during the effort; and
- continually welcoming the advice of others.

Improvement plan follow-up

The follow-up or monitoring of the plan is the last step in the process. Follow-up is required to ensure that the goals set out prior to implementation are being achieved, the solution has impacted upon the work environment as expected and the benefits of the solution are being realized. The plan, once implemented, may require revisions and corrections, and may leave room for improvements, upon which adjustment and continual monitoring will be required.

5.

Total employee involvement

5.1 Teamwork

The result of organizational redesign as JIT implementation nears completion is a restructured organization with a customer-focused approach to
business. Teamwork and shared work effort will become central to this new
structure and focus, with employees learning new work methods and roles in
the organization. Many organizations will be faced with answering questions
regarding the most effective approaches to teamwork, how employees will
change from traditional work methods to ones which require group focus
and how such a change will become an integral and lasting part of the
organization. The following sections address these questions through identifying the role of management, cultural change, training and education and
methods of recognizing employee efforts.

The emphasis on participation in the North American manufacturing
environment has typically involved low involvement approaches such as the
formation of teams to address problem solving or teams developed for
special purpose activities. Total employee involvement (TEI) represents a
significant change relative to past endeavours and is distinct from traditional
approaches to employee involvement at two levels.

1. TEI requires universal participation. Participation is not limited to a few
   volunteer employees, nor is it limited to arbitrary occasions. TEI requires
   a consistent effort, on a continuous basis.
2. TEI will impact upon all aspects of the organization, from customer and
   vendor service and production to quality. Table 5.1 presents a summary
   of the evolution of employee participation in North America over the last
   70 years (Widner, 1989).

The organizational changes which occur through JIT redesign require a
different approach to teamwork, most likely to be reflective of the characteristics of self-managing teams. Lawler (1988) has identified the implementation of self-managing teams in terms of a high level of commitment
approach. Such an approach to employee involvement is directed toward
securing the universal participation of the employees on the plant floor. The
commitment approach is aptly named as it is based on the assumption that
if employees are going to be concerned about organizational performance,

Table 5.1 Evaluation of employee participation in North America over the last 70 years (Widner, 1989)

	Teams		
	Problem solving	Special purpose	Self-managing
Structure/function	• Employees volunteer • Meet 1–2 hours/week • Discuss ways to improve quality • Cannot implement ideas without management approval	• Design new technology • Meet with customers and suppliers	• Employees who produce a complete product • Job rotation, scheduling, ordering, are employee responsibilities
Results	• Cost reduction • Improved product quality • Dissolve after a few years	• Involve workers, unions in higher level decisions • Create a foundation for self-managing teams	• Increased productivity, quality and changed work organization • Creation of a flatter organization
Introduction	• 1920s and 1930s, small scale • Wide-scale acceptance in 1970s • Concept based on Japanese quality control circles	• Early to middle 1980s • Growth out of problem-solving teams	• Rapid spread in 1980s • Popular in 1960s and 1970s • Large-scale use in the future

they must possess an understanding of it, be able to influence performance, receive rewards for their efforts and possess the necessary resources (knowledge and skill) to affect performance. The organizational characteristics consistent with the commitment approach include the following. (Lawler, 1988)

- Jobs will be designed to require the use of work teams and job enrichment (cross-training) will become necessary.
- The organization's structure will be based on a customer-focused approach to business. Work groups will be arranged according to product line rather than function or department.
- Measures of performance will focus upon the need for key information related to actual business performance and achievement of goals.
- Employees will learn new skills and methods of work. Focus will be placed upon problem solving and business economics.
- Greater decision power will be distributed among employees, who will have increased authority over decision making in the areas of work methods, management decisions and have some input into strategic decisions.
- Rewards or recognition will be based according to skill. Employee ownership is emphasized and gain or profit-sharing plans are likely to be in place.
- The working environment in JIT organizations is likely to foster the following:
  - employment stability;
  - equality of treatment of employees; and
  - policies developed and administered through participation.

The extent of employee involvement will differ from organization to organization, specifically in the areas of decision-making authority and controlling the working environment. Despite these organizational differences, the approach to employee involvement is generally moving in the direction of increasing the amount of resources available to employees as well as the responsibilities which accompany these resources.

Involvement approaches include the use of teams. Teams can be defined as any group of people who work with one another to accomplish organizational objectives. JIT extends the meaning of 'team' to include all the people who associate with a company: suppliers, customers and employees. Employees within an organization will each play a significant role in the process of being a team member.

The process of instilling total company involvement will not simply happen on its own as a result of organizational redesign. Deliberate effort, or teambuilding, must be directed toward developing a team effort and organizational culture which encourages co-operative behaviour. Teambuilding is defined as 'the process of planned and deliberate encouragement of effective working practices whilst diminishing difficulties or "blockages" which interfere with the team's competence and resourcefulness' (Woodcock and Francis, 1981). Successful TEI has been identified with the following elements:

- well-defined company goals, values and beliefs which are made known to all employees;
- an organizational culture which promotes co-operative behaviour and emphasizes teamwork;
- a workforce which is accepting of teamwork;
- employees who possess a sense of ownership;
- a workforce which is provided with the necessary resources to execute tasks; and
- employees who are rewarded for their effort.

Teambuilding activities enable an organization to work toward TEI. However, they are not without their short-comings, and Woodcock and Francis have identified the advantages and disadvantages of teambuilding activities. The advantages include:

- employees learn new attitudes, acquire new skills and improve their personal effectiveness;
- the skills and knowledge of trainers and educators within an organization are relevant and appreciated;
- teambuilding is a rapid, enduring process, directly related to organizational goals and objectives;
- employees learn to appreciate teambuilding and realize benefits from the process; and
- the learning of one individual is reinforced by other team members.

Two disadvantages are identified:

- Negative initial experiences can adversely affect momentum for change through the development of poor attitudes and resistance.
- Problems can arise when an organization attempts to introduce teambuilding activities when it is not prepared for such a process. Organizational readiness is apparent when a company:
  - is not faced with other, more immediate problems;
  - possesses a culture supportive of teams;
  - has employees who are receptive to teambuilding efforts; and
  - can introduce teambuilding activities with the necessary training and skill requirements.

5.1.1 Management commitment to teamwork

Building TEI within an organization is only possible through management commitment. Fostering a sense of teamwork, co-operative behaviour and ownership are realizable, however, only when preceded through a change in attitudes. Although many attempts at change have been initiated through the efforts of lower level managers and employees, the most sweeping or pervasive changes occur through the direction, leadership and example provided by top management. Unfortunately, for many North American organizations, the relationship between employees and management is characterized by suspicion, threats and mistrust. TEI for these organizations will present itself as a formidable task, where success will be realized over time and through consistency of behaviour.

Essentially, management's responsibilities are twofold: to change attitudes and organizational culture. The process of changing attitudes is reciprocal in nature, whereupon management attitude changes will result in changed observable behaviour by employees, leading to employee attitude changes and eventually their changed behaviour. Management attitude changes toward the workforce include the following.

- Managers must believe employees want to work toward realizing organizational objectives.
- Employees want to perform their best and develop a sense a pride in their work.
- Although 100% of an organization's employees will not 'jump on the bandwagon' eventually, the majority of them will. Management must remember all employees do not want added responsibility and do not like to participate. Many employees may not know how to react and come to fear the change simply because it represents an untravelled and unpredictable course.

Management commitment, according to Huge (1987), manifests itself in varying degrees from 'low' to 'high' within different organizations. The level of commitment required for JIT employee involvement requires commitment to the degree where it becomes a religion in the organization. Commitment to this extent is described as follows.

- Commitment becomes internalized, that is, management's behaviour is consistent with the new philosophies.
- Management actions include regular 'audits' of the change process to establish it as an integral part of the organization.
- Management should eliminate obstacles to the change and communicate these actions on a regular basis to all employees.

The process of employee involvement has also been described as 'a people leveraging process,' (Clark, 1987). The process of people leveraging involves ownership, participation and the training and group activities which stem from such a process. The people leveraging process allows plant floor employees to become 'thinkers' of the process, rather than limiting their role to 'doers'.

Pervasive changes such as TEI do not have a grounded history in the North American organizational environment, thus, information regarding its success and problems is limited. Organizations can assess the impact of TEI upon employees and organizational objectives through evaluating employees' reaction to their increased involvement and responsibility, as well as analysing TEI contributions or hindrances to improvements in employee and overall organization performance.

Attitudes and culture are essential for laying the foundation to universal participation. However, employees must also be provided with the necessary resources and recognition in fulfilling their new roles, the topic of the following sections.

5.1.2 Employee education and training

Employee education and training are described as an important part of empowering the workforce to take action over their environment. Although regarded as a central role in achieving organizational objectives, employee involvement is frequently not utilized to its fullest potential simply because the role of training and education is underestimated (McGuire, 1990). Effective training and educating programs can assist an organization in achieving maximum potential from the workforce. Programs should address the concept of change, the overall concept of JIT, training for specific skills and interpersonal communication.

Providing education for change has been identified as a critical factor because education, more so than any other factor, has the most direct effect on people (Hanson, 1988). Education has been identified by Hanson to include three distinct categories:

- *generic* education, which introduces employees to basic concepts and principles;
- *application* education, which addresses the 'hows' of employee involvement; and
- *technical* education which serves to acquaint employees with information related to specific processes.

Ideally, education needs related to each category should be provided, however, it is not solely the provision of these which is important. The timing in which education is given is equally important. Education and training should be presented to employees to allow them sufficient time to anticipate needs and understand the concepts.

5.1.3 Factors of successful training and education programs

Training and education programs can be established internally or externally through workshops, seminars, etc. The success of these programs will depend largely on how relevant and appropriate the learning material is, how motivated employees are to learn and the method of instruction employed. In essence, the most effective learning processes are those which consider both content and process.

Content – the principles of learning

Learning principles spell out the guidelines for effective learning. Five learning principles have been identified as participation, repetition, relevance, transference and feedback. The effectiveness of the learning process is directly related to the use of the learning principles (Werther *et al.*, 1990).

1. *Participation* is the extent to which employees are able to become involved in the process of learning. Employees who learn through a participatory method of instruction, be it class discussion, role play, brainstorming exercises, etc., are likely to be highly motivated, to learn quicker and retain the material for longer periods of time.

2. *Repetition* is a learning principle which primarily functions to assist in transferring information into memory. The most apparent benefit of repetition is that it allows us to memorize information and recall it when required.

3. *Relevance* refers to how meaningful the information is to employees' work, or organizational objectives. Employees who are presented with relevant material will understand why it must be learned.

4. *Transference* relates to how well the information learned applies to the actual demands of the job. The more closely material matches the demands of the job, the quicker employees are able to learn.

5. *Feedback* is a means of relaying employees' performance back to them. Feedback provides employees with knowledge of their present performance, how closely that performance matches established objectives and whether or not their performance requires adjusting.

The approach to training and education an organization uses will depend upon whether or not they possess the necessary resources (knowledge, skill levels, available instructors) to fulfill needs internally, or if training needs will be more aptly met through external programs. Regardless of whether an internal or external training program is used, successful programs should give consideration to the following factors (Bourke, 1990).

1. *Needs analysis*   Needs analysis addresses the 'who' of training and education by identifying the training needs of the recipients of the program. Criteria such as the educational and experience level of employees, as well as their reasons for pursuing the program should be addressed. Essentially, a needs analysis can be conducted through discussion with employees, analysis of job description and proposed future needs.

2. *Stated objectives*   Education and training objectives indicate to employees what the required outcome of programs should be in terms of changes in behaviour, knowledge and skill levels which are stated in objective terms. Effective objectives should provide a means of evaluating the effectiveness of training programs and therefore should:
   - provide a description of the level of competence required at the end of the program;
   - describe what the learner will be able to do upon completion;
   - be realistic, meaningful and relevant;
   - include criteria for actual performance;

- identify the conditions under which performance is achieved; and
- provide evaluation and testing.

3. *Motivation for learning*   Motivation with respect to learning addresses the degree to which employees are enthused about learning, changing their behaviour in line with expectations, focusing their attention on and acceptance of subject matter. Employee motivation to learn can be enhanced through increasing the relevance and meaning of program material.

    Previously it was stated that teambuilding success will be negatively affected if it is not presented as a positive initial experience for employees. The same holds true for the effectiveness of training and education programs. Relying on instruction methods which involve participants through exercises and discussion will maintain employee interest in the program.

4. *Clarity of information*   The effective approach to education and training is to present information to employees in an understandable and familiar fashion. Discrepancies between what is presently occurring within an organization and what is expected from future performance can be made more 'real' to employees by applying information to existing problems.

5. *The learning environment*   The most successful training and educating programs tend to structure the learning environment into one which is non-threatening, encourages participation and is challenging for the employees. Feedback or reinforcement on employee performance serves to inform employees of their learning progress.

5.1.4 Incentives for employees

The nature of incentive offered to employees is linked to an organization's culture; in its values, objectives and organizational strategy. The reward system present within a company reflects and reinforces the values and norms of corporate culture, and reward systems can be used to change an existing culture to bring it in line with a new organizational direction (Kerr and Slocum, 1987). Incentives are offered to employees primarily as a vehicle to stimulate motivation for cost reduction or increasing productivity, and rewarding employees for their success at doing so. Employee acceptance of incentive systems stems from the values which management espouses. The majority of North American workers view incentive systems to include the reward of money; recognition which is realized through bonuses or increases in basic pay.

Financial incentive systems

Incentive systems which reward employee performance through increases in basic salary, stock dividends, or bonuses form what is known as financial incentive systems. Many forms of financial systems exist, including those which reward on the basis of piecework, production bonuses, commissions, maturity curves and production incentive plans. Financial incentive systems are powerful tools when chosen properly; they not only assist in changing corporate culture, but enable an organization to achieve its objectives. Factors to consider when choosing an incentive system within a JIT environment include the following.

- Linkage between the incentive system and actual performance.
- Compatibility with short- and long-term objectives.
- Degree of employee acceptance of the incentive plan.
- The incentive system's impact upon productivity, cost and waste.

The common belief regarding financial incentive systems providing the most direct link between performance and reward fails to consider the distinction between the various plans. Although, reward through financial incentive systems does provide more visible linkage between performance and reward relative to basic pay, some plans are more effective than others.

Types of financial incentive systems

Many types of financial incentive systems exist and they share common benefits and drawbacks. The types of these systems will be considered, then their associated benefits and drawbacks (Werther *et al.*, 1990).

1. *Piecework* incentive systems reward performance on a per unit basis. Frequently, an employee's performance is stagnated due to the impact of group norms. Group norms operate through peer pressure to control the level of individual output. Similarly, it may be difficult to measure actual individual output because the employee's ability to control output is limited, especially if the employee is working on an assembly line.

2. *Production bonuses*, in addition to a basic salary, are paid to individual employees who are successful at exceeding a pre-established level of output or time savings.

3. *Group incentive plans* reward a group of employees. There are three possible group plans.
   (a) *Production incentive plans* which reward groups of employees for exceeding specified output levels.
   (b) *Profit-sharing plans* which disperse company profits among a group of employees. Successful profit-sharing plans impact positively upon an organization in that they assist in creating trust and a sense of 'common fate' among plant floor employees and management. Unfortunately, many attempts at profit sharing are rendered ineffective as a result of the effect of external variables on performance such as competitors and economic conditions. Employees, in a sense are punished if they receive less or no bonus for some reason beyond their control such as a recession. The plan itself does not provide the clearest link between performance and results, which is further diluted when profits are diverted into employee retirement plans, reducing any reinforcing value the plan may offer.

(c) *Stock ownership plans* are increasing in popularity at an increasing rate. The growth in popularity of the plan is a result of the benefits employees and organizations as a whole receive from its use. Organizations which make use of stock ownership plans are able to surpass competitors in growth rate, return on equity and profit margins.

4. *Cost reduction plans*, such as those designed to reward employees for controlling labour costs, provide an increasing amount of control for employees. Frequently, cost reduction plans seek employee input on how labour costs (or other cost contributors) can be reduced. Cost reduction plans can be divided into three types including the Scanlon Plan, Rucker and Improshare plans. Although these three plans differ in their administrative function, they allow for increased employee control through direct input.

The pros and cons of financial incentive systems
Regardless of the type of financial incentive system employed, there are a number of advantages and disadvantages associated with their use. The advantages include providing direct linkage between work and reward and increasing employee motivation. Incentive systems, as compared to increases in basic salary, provide a visible means of linking employee effort with reward. Reward reinforces desired behaviour, thus desired behaviour is likely to continue. Financial reward systems can increase employee motivation and this motivation in itself is responsible for a number of benefits, which include decreased turnover and recruitment expenditures.

The disadvantages of financial incentive systems include increasing administrative costs, the creation of inequities between employees, and union resistance. Administration of financial incentive systems entails the need to develop standards and measures of performance. Frequently, these standards and measures are difficult to establish given the nature of many jobs. Standards can be imprecise and difficult to measure resulting in the creation of inequities or perceived discrepancies among employees. For example, the resulting incentive system may place employees' salaries at a level higher than their supervisor, or pay employees equally when the level of effort involved is unequal.

Union resistance to financial incentive systems can pose a problem with respect to administration. Resistance of financial incentive systems is based on the contention that work standards will increase and more stress will be placed upon employees to work for the same pay. Group peer pressure is frequently the result of union resistance and functions to restrict all employee output to a certain level. The emergence of peer pressure interferes with the objectives of financial incentive systems, eliminating any potential benefits. In essence, companies should seek the participation of unions if embarking upon a financial incentive system is probable.

An additional problem has been associated with financial incentive systems concerning their long-term impact on employees. Employees who are rewarded consistently through a form of financial system gradually come to expect that reward. The absence of a reward can impact negatively upon employee motivation, morale and commitment to the organization.

Monitoring the success of incentive systems

Whether employees are rewarded financially or not for their efforts, incentive systems must all be capable of meeting organizational objectives. The presence of employee resistance and apathy are indicators the chosen plan has not fulfilled its expectations. Perry (1988), has developed a method of testing the effectiveness of an incentive plan. The method simply involves asking questions related to the plan's organizational effectiveness and answering these questions with the available data and information provided through feedback. The questions include the following, although assessment need not be limited to these.

- Does the plan capture attention? Capturing employee attention is evident through increased discussion of activities and pride in early successes.
- Do employees understand the plan? Ensuring employees understand the plan entails employees being able to explain the function of the plan, and their requirements under the new system.
- Is the plan improving communication? Employees should possess an increased understanding of the organization's mission, plans and objectives.
- Does the plan offer incentive in a timely manner? Employees should be rewarded for desired performance, not just any performance.
- Has the company's performance improved? Improvements in performance are evident through increased profit, market share and work methods, as well as reductions in waste.

5.2 JIT discipline

JIT discipline includes employees' work ethic, attitudes towards jobs and the approach to work procedures. Standards will be higher and greater emphasis will be placed upon consistently achieving these standards or even surpassing them. Employees must learn and become comfortable with taking an active role in day-to-day activities. Although these changes seem relatively basic, the fact remains they are very difficult to realize as they represent a significant departure from past organizational practices and employee approach to work.

5.2.1 Employee work ethic

Employee work ethic is influenced strongly by social/cultural factors, motivating factors and the work itself. Organizations which are able to function effectively, employ individuals who are highly motivated, committed, and are willing to put 100% effort into the job. Ideally, all organizations would like to maintain such a workforce; however, high absenteeism and turnover rates are common problems for many companies and have been identified as an outcome of a decline in the work ethic. Although some sceptics argue that JIT places much undue stress and tension on workers to perform, JIT can offer the employee an environment which is consistent with their expectations of the workplace, relative to traditional organizations. The main reason for this rests with a social/cultural explanation. North American people are conditioned to a culture which offers them a high degree of choice and flexibility in their lives. The likelihood of an employee being satisfied and highly motivated within an organization which does not provide the same degree of choice is relatively low (Gray and Starke, 1988). The result is high absenteeism and turnover as employees become discontented with their jobs and seek new employment in line with their expectations.

JIT functions to decrease the gap between employees' expectations and the actual workplace. Focus has been placed upon making the organization a more attractive place to work. The most recent attempt has included improving the quality of work life (QWL) of employees through participative management, development of employees, social integration, growth and security of the organization. JIT practices parallel the areas of focus in the QWL effort. Organizational changes which occur through JIT allow for the following.

- *Increased employee participation in decision making*   Employees learn they have the capacity to control their immediate environment and make changes which affect the organization's ability to satisfy the customer.
- *Development of the workforce*   Employees become 'thinkers' rather than just 'doers' through acquiring new skills and knowledge. New skills allow employees to perform a variety of work, rather than focusing on one specialized skill. Performing a variety of jobs such as through job rotation reduces monotony and boredom by providing employees with interesting work.
- *Increased teambuilding*   Teamwork and group co-operation are required in a JIT environment. Contact and affiliation, through teamwork, assist in reducing worker alienation, improving openness between employees and developing an egalitarian environment.
- *Growth and security of the organization*   The competitive advantages of JIT, as discussed in previous chapters, place the organization in a position where it is able to sustain or even expand its workforce. Worker concern over job security issues does not have to play a primary role.

Although the above are effective means of addressing the problems which result in employee absenteeism and turnover, focusing on motivation can result in furthering organizational effectiveness. Motivation is a term which has been used to describe productive employee behaviour, and motivated employees are vital to organizational effectiveness because it is through them that innovation, productivity and higher quality standards are achieved.

5.2.2 JIT and employee motivation

Effective employee performance is determined through a combination of ability and motivation. Allocating the necessary resources for JIT implementation and putting them into place is half of the implementation effort. However, in the absence of motivated employees, all the education, training, financial resources and expertise provide no substitute for the results of a motivated workforce.

Motivation for JIT implementation, as critical as it is to success, can present itself as a formidable task. Resistance, rather than motivation is frequently the response to JIT. Landvater (1987) suggests that understanding the principle elements of human behaviour are prerequisite to JIT implementation, and identifies three areas where elements of human behaviour must be taken into account.

1. *Motivating people* Effective means of motivating employees can include financial incentives in addition to avoiding the use of 'management by electrocution'. Punishing employees for mistakes should be replaced with fostering employee involvement, allocating control to employees, providing them with feedback on performance and recognition.
2. *Changing behaviour in an organization* Changing employee behaviour can be achieved through a reinforcement model of behaviour, where consistency plays a fundamental role. The model involves three forms of reinforcement: positively reinforcing or rewarding desired behaviour; ignoring undesirable behaviour to extinguish it; and administering punishment with discretion, for punishment will reduce the occurrence of negative behaviour – however, it may also be followed by negative side-effects.
3. *Developing teams who work well together* Effective teambuilding is based upon:
   - exposure, or allowing employees to experience a different perspective;
   - providing leadership training to employees – such training serves to reduce problems, such as supervisor reluctance to surrender their traditional role; and
   - providing employees with real problems to solve.

Forms of motivation can be divided into two categories: intrinsic and extrinsic motivators (Gray and and Starke, 1988). Intrinsic motivation results from the potential of intrinsic rewards, or feeling of accomplishment from an interesting and challenging job. Extrinsic motivation, results from expectations of receiving extrinsic rewards such as promotion, pay or recognition. Although both intrinsic and extrinsic rewards are effective means of motivating employees, the appropriateness of the reward is dependent upon the job itself. JIT functions to increase employees' intrinsic motivation through allocating greater control over their working environment.

The suggestion system has also been identified as a motivational tool for employees (Japanese Human Relations Association, 1988). Suggestion systems, when implemented and managed correctly, provide an avenue to instill meaning in employee work and fulfill potential. Workers learn their value to the organization through the suggestion system, when management listens to suggestions and implements them for the betterment of the workplace.

5.2.3 JIT work procedures

JIT work procedures involve the way employees perform their work. The approach to work within a JIT environment will involve significant changes in attitude and behaviour and effective practices will run contrary to traditional practices, affecting everything from production methods to labour relations. Employees must learn new, desired behaviour, that is continuously supported by management. Management must show its support in changing behaviour through the methods of dealing with employee mistakes and attitudes (Cheng, 1990). The level of effectiveness in handling mistakes, will determine employees' motivation for change. Mistakes should not be handled in a punitive manner; rather, they should be focused upon as a learning experience. Managers should treat employees and mistakes in a consistent manner, while remembering that JIT work procedures are new to all employees.

Management's attitude toward employees should focus upon building employee morale. Patience is also crucial to changing work practices. Traditional work methods have been supported and practised for many years; therefore, the change is likely to take considerable time for employees to develop an understanding of and appreciation for new work methods.

5.2.4 JIT vs. traditional work practices

Attention has been focused upon the Japanese to determine the factors which have contributed to their economic and productivity success. Japanese style of management, production practices, attitudes, approaches to employee involvement, communication and quality have been recognized as contributors to this success. Although much focus is placed upon these work procedures, there remain questions as to whether or not North American success can be achieved through similar approaches. The most significant determinant of this success is whether or not cultural differences prevent the transfer of such work practices. For example, Japanese work ethic greatly differs from that of North America. North American work ethic is more highly reflective of individualism, the focus on leisure and challenge of authority, relative to the Japanese. JIT success will require companies to identify and work with problems within their organization which hinder the adaptation of new work practices.

Comparison of traditional work practices and those required for JIT include the following (Cheng, 1990; Shingo, 1986):

1. *Production methods* Traditional approaches to production embrace large lot sizes, safety or buffer stocks to ensure smooth production, long set-up times, focusing on machine productivity, stopping the production line only when absolutely essential and assigning quality problems to the quality control department. The changes required for JIT production include reducing lot sizes, eliminating safety or buffer stocks, methods to reduce set-up times, focusing on the human input rather than machines to increase productivity, embracing the idea that stopping production is desirable and making quality a universal concern.

2. *Quality issues* Traditional views toward quality differ not only in who is assigned responsibility for quality, but in the approach toward ensuring a product does in fact have quality. JIT requires quality be built in through production, whereas traditional approaches view quality as an after-the-fact process of inspection.

3. *Communication* Communication in traditional organizations involves a top-down process, where managers exert control over the working environment. JIT requires a bottom-up approach to communication, where production floor employees assume new responsibility and value within the organization. Employees and management share in controlling the environment as employee suggestions are referred to management and feedback is given to employees.

4. *Employee involvement* Traditional approaches to employee involvement have typically included suggestion systems and small groups of employees formed to address problems. High level approaches to teamwork must be adopted to reach all levels of an organization and allocate greater control to teams.

5. *Employment and labour relations* Japanese labour relations have been identified as a critical factor in their economic and productivity success. Success has been attributed to the relationship between unions and management, which has facilitated the achievement of increasing productivity and competitive levels, as well as meeting employees' needs for job security and equity (Anderson *et al.*, 1989). The relationship necessary for JIT has been described as one of co-operation, rather than adversarial. The use of no lay-off policies and the growth and stability organizations are expected to realize over the long term with JIT holds promise for addressing many employees' employment concerns.

5.2.5 JIT standards and measurements

Standards, in accordance with measurements provide the means of monitoring performance. Standards are established levels of performance, or means of carrying out work, which can be assessed through specific methods of measurement. Objectives are established, employees given the necessary resources (training and tools) to obtain the objectives and performance evaluated to ensure the objectives are being met.

Effective performance measures must be accurately defined and continually updated to ensure they are measuring what is actually meant to be measured. Measurements can be developed for any performance objective, including production and employee involvement. Regardless of what is being measured, all effective performance measurements include the following characteristics (Roman, 1988).

- *Valid* This refers to how comprehensive and correct performance measurements are. Valid measures significantly relate to performance or other criteria. Information necessary to give a 'true' result of performance should be included so as not to obscure results.
- *Accurate* Performance measures should include all data, correctly calculated.
- *Timely* Measurements must make use of timely data.
- *Believable* Performance measurements must be believable, since providing believable results to employees is necessary for initiating improvements.
- *Supported by management* Performance measurements should be supported by management. Attention should be focused on improvements to realize long-term objectives, not manipulating numbers or results to meet the short-term objectives.
- *Supported by employees* Support from all employees can be gained through giving the workforce control over the design of measurements and collection of data, while allowing employees to identify problems with the overall success of the measurements.
- *Understandability* Employees should all possess an understanding of the measurements to prevent misuse.

The most apparent measures are those which measure production activities and quality, such as number of defects, set-up times, lot sizes and cycle times. Monitoring and updating data on the number of employees trained, degree of employee participation and use of consensus decision making, provide examples of how a company's progress with total employee involvement can be measured (Souza, 1987).

6.

Implementing JIT manufacturing

Planning and organizing activities mark the beginning efforts of JIT implementation, with the development of a strategy and operational plan being the result. Implementation of JIT is described as an incremental rather than step-by-step process, where upon continual effort, completion is gradually realized over a number of years with continued effort on improvement. The strategy and operational plan provide the tools necessary to commence and complete JIT implementation.

6.1 Developing an implementation strategy

The development and application of an implementation strategy provides the most appropriate vehicle for implementation, as it allows an organization to manage change effectively. The strategy is the result of the strategic planning process, which provides the means of bridging the gap between current organizational status and where the organization would like to be, as specified in its mission statement. Strategic planning enables the company to identify potential areas of impact, acquire and allocate resources, specify actions according to a specific time frame and plan for contingencies. The strategy cannot be defined narrowly, rather, it must incorporate and plan for the affects of change upon all levels and departments within an organization. Development of the strategy, consistent with a systems approach, should be the efforts of a multidisciplinary team, educated and trained in the concepts of JIT.

Prior to embarking upon JIT implementation, an organization should assess its readiness. The best strategy in the world will not ensure success unless management is prepared to undergo changes first itself. Recognition, acceptance and adoption of new roles, commitment and attitudes are prerequisite to the development of a strategy. Managers must be prepared to be leaders of the change to JIT, recognize the value of employees to the organization and encourage innovation through employee involvement (Mayne, 1987). The obstacles to goal achievement must also be identified and removed, whether it is formal organizational policies and practices or employee behaviour which has the potential to impede progress.

The process of developing an implementation strategy involves assessing the internal and external environment. Evaluation of internal factors includes the organization's strengths, weaknesses and problems, while external factors include customers, suppliers, unions, and government. Internal assessment enables an organization to determine the adequacy of resources and identify and solve problems which interfere with implementation. Analysis of the external environment assists in determining how customers, suppliers, unions and government can assist in the implementation process, or present potential obstacles.

Implementation actions should be defined according to a set timetable, with methods of monitoring implementation established. According to Starke *et al.* (1988), an organization must establish strategic control points or critical areas which must be monitored in order to achieve organizational objectives. Strategic control points possess five basic characteristics.

1. Strategic control points monitor key operations or events.
2. Strategic control points are established to identify problems at their point of origin.
3. Strategic control points should be capable of indicating the level of performance for many key events.
4. Strategic control points should make use of key information in order to be effective.
5. The selection of strategic control points should be balanced. The controls placed on tangible functions, such as production and sales should be balanced with those placed on intangible controls, such as employee development. The two should be balanced such that too strict controls are not placed upon production and too lenient controls placed upon employee development.

6.2 An operational plan for implementation

Once an organization formulates an implementation strategy, an operational plan for implementation should follow. Operational plans formulate the day-to-day activities and address the specifics of implementation such as who is involved, or the allocation of tasks, when activities are to be completed and how completion of activities is to be realized. Although operational goals are specific to each organization, common goals of JIT include provisions for universal commitment, education and training, cellular plant layout and design, preventive maintenance/housekeeping activities, vendor development, customer communication, TQM, waste identification and reduction, participation, cross-training and job rotation, set-up time reduction and scheduling (Landis, 1987). An operational plan for implementation is likely to address these goals.

Who is involved in the implementation process?

Defining roles in the implementation process is critical to JIT success. Although employees will be assigned individual roles within the implementation process, recognition and effort directed toward common goals is essential. The appropriateness of roles stems from the training and background employees already possess. For example, the responsibility of organizing and co-ordinating training effort can be effectively carried out by the human resource department, with input from production employees.

The organization can benefit directly through the guidance offered from outside assistance who possess a proven track record and experience in JIT implementation. Mayne (1987) recommends such assistance be secured primarily for two reasons: to guide implementation efforts or ensure the organization is on the right track; and to provide a channel of communication.

Implementation effort is further facilitated by the use of an implementation leader: an employee who dedicates full-time attention to JIT implementation (Bently, 1988). The implementation leader functions as a project manager, facilitator of communication between top management and production floor employees, as well as initiator of planning and organizing activities. Given the significance of this role in the implementation effort, interpersonal skills and knowledge of JIT are prerequisite to the selection of a leader.

When JIT implementation activities are performed

JIT implementation presents the organization with a multitude of activities to perform. Although these activities can be readily identified through an organization's objectives, the sequence of activities to be executed may not be as readily apparent. Bently (1988) suggests implementation efforts commence with activities most likely to set the foundation for, or drive the remaining implementation efforts. Housekeeping has been identified as one of these activities. Commencing activities with housekeeping introduces the organization to neat and orderly work conditions, while creating a climate which promotes desired behaviour. The benefits which flow from such an environment include:

- management illustrating its commitment to JIT implementation by providing employees with the necessary time and resources to put housekeeping activities into place;
- the introduction of neatness and orderliness stimulating waste reduction and achievement of operational goals;
- the visibility provided through housekeeping allowing many issues and problems to surface; and
- housekeeping activities setting the stage for other implementation activities such as material handling, redesign and work methods.

Ensuring implementation activities are being carried through and ultimately completed on time requires the use of controls, or measurements for monitoring progress. The operational plan should establish a detailed time frame for each activity, as well as the system of measurement which will be used to monitor its progress. Timeliness of activity completion in itself serves as a measurement.

How JIT implementation activities are performed

Specifying how JIT implementation activities are to be completed involves the allocation of resources and development of processes. The use of an established method for carrying out JIT implementation activities should serve as a tool or general guideline for directing and ensuring all necessary steps within a specific process have been performed. Given that processes fulfill these two objectives, they should be well defined and comprehensive.

6.3 Data collection and measurement systems

Data collection and measurement systems supplement the operational plan for JIT as they provide the mechanisms to collect all information on a continual basis, as well as provide the means with which to compare actual performance to established standards. Data collection systems must provide information that is timely, relevant, consistent and complete. Employees should receive training to utilize the system properly, as its effectiveness is as much a function of the system itself as it is the user. Common data collection systems include databases, where all information is fed into and retrieved when needed from the database by use of a computer, or manual standardized procedures where data is gathered and located in designated areas.

Measurement systems for JIT serve two purposes: providing the basis for monitoring implementation activities, monitoring or tracking the progress of work; and providing a standard for improvement activities. Although an organization is likely to have measurement systems in place prior to JIT implementation, these traditional measurements are not likely to reflect JIT organizational requirements. JIT measurement systems differ from traditional measurement systems on three levels: they must relate to organizational strategic objectives, provide information which reflects the organizational direction and relate the organization's performance in terms of improvement (Weaver, 1987).

Measurement systems for JIT must be accurate, effective and meaningful. Grieco (1988) has established accurate measures for JIT to be compatible with a 'total business concept', or the view of an organization operating as a system or integrated whole. Total business concept measurements provide information related to performance at the cell level as well as for the organization as a whole. JIT measurement systems based upon the total business concept will provide an organization with the following:

- accurate information – measurement systems which are capable of providing information free of errors will save the organization valuable time and effort in the long run;

- information about the waste present in purchasing and manufacturing activities;
- information which relates actual performance to pre-established plans; and
- awareness of the timeliness of information from manufacturing and purchasing activities.

The actual performance measurements for JIT can be grouped into several categories including those which measure inventory, delivery performance, quality, production and data accuracy/ paperwork reduction measurements. Measurements such as these provide examples of effective measurements; however, their application within an organization may vary, depending upon the nature of an organization's product or service line. Each class of measurement is discussed below.

1. The inventory turnover ratio provides a measure of cost of sales to investment in inventory and measures the performance of the organization as a whole.
2. Measurements for delivery must provide information regarding cost and time. Delivery measures provide the organization with information regarding performance with respect to the customer (delivery of the product on the specified date), the receipt of inventory from vendors (receipt of material on the specified date) and the processes which occur in between the activities of shipping and receiving.
3. Quality measurements include the number of defects from incoming materials, the percentage of scrap and rejects. Effective control measures include the use of SPC to monitor in process quality.
4. Production measurements can be grouped into three categories: machine up time, or a measure of actual rates of productivity as compared to planned productive time; lead times; and throughput times. Lead times identify the discrepancy between actual, as compared to planned, lead time. Excessive material handling and long queue times are frequently the sources of long lead times, therefore, the factors which contribute to these should be analysed and eliminated. Throughput time provides a measurement for balancing the flow between operations.
5. Data accuracy and paperwork reduction – the integrity, accessibility and commonality of the database serves as a means of eliminating 'multi-cate' paperwork. Databases which are accurate and updated are capable of providing all employees with the required information.

Measurements can also be established to monitor improvements in worker participation and flexibility (Shapiro, 1990). Given the importance of worker participation and flexibility in JIT, establishing meaningful measurements capable of indicating performance levels in these two categories will benefit the organization. Traditional methods of measuring employee involvement include measurements for suggestion systems,

such as number of suggestions submitted and total number of suggestions approved per time period. Shapiro suggests more appropriate
measures such as total dollars awarded per approved suggestion would be
more meaningful, however, an organization should also consider what
motivates employees to participate. Employees who participate because
they genuinely believe their input will lead to improvement, rather than
financial reward, will require a different measurement to maintain their
interest. Measurement systems should therefore assess how efficiently
suggestions can be evaluated and feedback given to the employee.
Transferring the task of approving suggestions to an immediate supervisor
or cell leader can facilitate the feedback process.

Application of measurement systems consistent with a total business
concept enable an organization to receive benefits it would otherwise not
experience with traditional measurements. The benefits include:

- reduced material costs and improvements in product design as a result of
  relationships with suppliers and integration of engineering, purchasing,
  design, planning and production;
- improved quality through the delivery of defect-free parts;
- improved administrative efficiency as a result of reduced paperwork and
  improved communication; and
- increases in productivity from improved flow of WIP, elimination of
  waste, quicker set-up and lead times.

Additional benefits are received from the use of employee involvement
measurements. Management's approach to monitoring improvements in
employee involvement not only provides a means of measurement, but has
the potential to encourage employee participation by fulfilling their needs.

6.4 Pilot projects

Pilot projects for JIT and quality circles are frequently adopted by many
organizations because they provide the opportunity to experiment and test
new ideas. Pilot projects for JIT involve selecting areas of the plant, either
through product line or component part and applying JIT concepts to those
areas. Several JIT pilot projects can be chosen in parallel, operating
independent of each other.

Quality circle pilot projects serve the same purpose as JIT projects;
however, their implementation is less involved as it functions primarily
as a part of employee involvement and quality. Planning for quality circle
pilots involves three main elements to be included in the operational
plan. The main components of a QC pilot project address establishing
standards, substantiating the benefits or costs and expanding efforts to
other areas of the plant.

Pilot projects for JIT and QCs offer benefits to the organization,
however, they do possess some limiting characteristics. The advantages
include the following.

- The pilot project allows problems to surface which had not previously been considered. Employees and managers can work through these problems and learn from their experience. Lessons learned can be applied to other implementation efforts.
- The operational plan for implementation can be applied and its effectiveness evaluated prior to full-scale implementation. The pilot project provides the opportunity to revise the strategy and plan in the light of problems which were not considered previously.
- Pilot projects gradually ease the company into implementation. The result of this relative to full-scale implementation, is to allow employees to become accustomed to the idea of change.

The most common disadvantage of pilot projects includes limiting the benefits received to a small area of the plant and the experience with the project to a few employees. Overcoming this limitation is possible through establishing several pilot projects in parallel. Establishing several projects which run independently of one another also increases the organizations chance of success (O'Connor, 1990). Failure or excessive problems associated with one pilot project have no bearing on the success of the other projects and the organization is less likely to abandon future implementation efforts.

6.5 Dealing with employee resistance and unions

Implementation of JIT will not necessarily follow a smooth course, as obstacles are likely to be encountered. The most relevant and significant fundamental cause of implementation difficulties rests with employee resistance to the JIT change. Managers must realize employees are the most valuable organizational asset, for it is through them the goals and continuation of the company will be realized ultimately. The earliest stages of implementation should mark the beginning of a new relationship with employees, characterized by trust and equality.

Although it may be difficult or even impossible to prevent the full or partial impact of some obstacles to implementation, it is important to realize the methods in which they are handled are critical determinants of success. Management's approach should be proactive, rather than reactive. The proactive approach entails management leading the implementation effort through putting into place mechanisms to address employee concerns. Examples of proactive approaches include involving employees, managers setting examples through 'doing as they say', consistency of behaviour and providing employees with education and training. Involving employees in the implementation effort must extend beyond simply obtaining employee input for the change, although this in itself cannot be disregarded. Rather, involving employees must include seeking employee approval and providing them access to information previously not shared. Information regarding available resources and progress toward goal achievement is necessary to keep employees informed in the activities of the business. Sharing with employees to this extent will present the greatest difficulties for management, especially if the previous working environment was characterized with 'us versus them' attitudes and closed-door discussions.

Setting examples through management actions and consistent behaviour primarily serve to develop trust in the management/employee relationship and set standards that clearly apply to all within the organization. Employees will gradually come to realize management is committed and prepared to make changes which affect them. Through consistent behaviour, management sets implicit standards or norms and enables employees to recognize this is how it is going to be. Employees can then establish realistic expectations of JIT, and assess their own behaviour and attitudes.

Providing employees with the necessary education and training equips them with the knowledge and skill required to work effectively in the new environment. Management demonstrates its commitment through dedicating resources to improving employees. These proactive approaches share common attributes. First, they attempt to strengthen the working relationship between management and employees. Second, each demonstrates a degree of commitment to employees, either through dedicating resources as in education and training or introducing employees into what is generally regarded as areas of management concern. Third, they serve to promote equality in treatment between management and employees through the creation of organization-wide standards and sharing of information.

Dealing with unions

The relationships which exist between management, employees and unions· will each in part determine the level of support for JIT. Given the role unions play within the contemporary organization, obtaining their support to JIT will be fundamental to preventing obstacles and ensuring long-term success. Several key factors play a role in establishing the necessary formula for success of JIT in unionized organizations. Among these factors include the impact of JIT upon the workforce, the nature of North American union/management relations and the psychological processes which operate in the negotiating process. The manner in which management deals with obtaining support and building trust with unionized employees will establish the longevity of JIT in the workplace.

JIT in its ideal sense can contribute to the realization of positive results for an organization as a whole. Labour unions share the same concerns as management with respect to the organization's customers, products or services. The customer is regarded by union members as the most important aspect of the organization, for without the customer, the organization would not exist. Thus, improving work methods and providing the customer with a better product or service are principles valued by unions. Union members regard JIT as a means of increasing organizational competitiveness, however, their reservations of JIT address the negative impact of the change upon the workforce. In consideration of JIT, unions weigh the positive and negative factors and the fact that JIT realization within the workplace will not always occur according to the ideal principles established in textbooks.

Concern over potential loss of jobs and the resulting added stress on employees to perform have been identified as two outcomes of JIT which prevent unions from supporting the effort. The goal of JIT is to work smarter, not lay off substantial portions of the workforce. Redeployment of workers to other areas of the plant is the preferred course of action. Management commitment to redeployment of workers and the establishment of no lay-off clauses function to alleviate concerns over job losses and have been recognized as effective means of securing union support for JIT.

The relationship between management and unions will differ from organization to organization. However on a large scale, the relationship which characterizes union/management relations has been described as adversarial, where trust and co-operation are for the most part absent. Many union members believe management's willingness to commit itself is one of the most significant determinants of whether JIT will withstand obstacles or simply fade away and be labelled as yet another fad over the course of time. Commitment in this sense involves management sharing information and issues with employees consistently and not simply selecting the issues it chooses to share.

The relevance of management commitment is carried forward into JIT from past attempts at implementing QCs and other employee involvement strategies which stem from quality of work life (QWL) efforts. Many attempts at these employee involvement schemes have faded away and resulted in failure. Unwillingness to share with employees and make them an equal partner in the organization has contributed to the mortality rate of involvement efforts. Many organizations and employees were able to benefit from such employee involvement approaches while they endured. However, their ultimate failure has prompted many to question whether any approach to implementation in the absence of an equal partnership will result in lasting effort.

Although JIT represents an all-encompassing effort which has an organization-wide impact when compared to past attempts at employee involvement, these previous efforts provide a substantial amount of information which can serve as a learning experience in the future. It has been shown that QWL innovations such as increased co-operativeness and productivity among workers are not so much the result of employee involvement as they are an outcome of union/management co-operation (Anderson et al., 1989). Identifying and eliminating the factors which prohibit co-operative relations between unions and management will be necessary to realize success with JIT. The adversarial system or lack of trust between the two parties is one such factor; however, past inequities and their influence upon co-operation can also play a substantial role in the negotiating process. A history of disagreement can cause people to bring with them bitterness, mentality to oppose and expectations of seeking gains over the other party, which all function to destroy any co-operative effort.

Securing support from all involved in the operations of the organization is crucial to JIT long-term success. Labour unions represent a special case as gaining their support will enable an organization to develop co-operative relations with employees and secure their enthusiasm required for the change. While the relationship between union members and management will be unique to each organization, there are steps management can take to lessen resistance and gain support, as follows.

- Involve the union from the initial stages of implementation and throughout the life of the JIT effort. Immediate involvement will indicate to union members that management is serious about the effort and will take the necessary steps to ensure its success. Union involvement throughout the life of the effort is necessary because changes within the organization will occur continuously.
- Establish the union as an equal partner in the implementation process, sharing all concerns and issues. Management can not be selective if obtaining true support is important.
- Seek to redeploy workers to other areas of the plant where their skills will be more fully utilized. Establishing 'no lay-off' clauses can substantiate the union's belief in management's commitment to employees.
- Both union's and management should become aware of the hidden biases and attitudes which can interfere with negotiations and discussions of JIT. Becoming aware is the first step toward controlling the influence these biases have upon co-operative efforts.

Consideration of new competitive levels nationally and internationally, will make JIT a concept embraced by many in the future. JIT not only represents a new way of doing business, but it also provides the opportunity to improve relations between all involved. Many who embrace the concept will discover its success will largely be determined by the people in the system, not the manufacturing resources.

7.

Industrial case study

The following industrial case study provides an opportunity for the reader to view the application of the ideal concepts presented in the preceding chapters: to examine the role of workers, changes in organizational culture, areas of application consistent with, and deviating from the ideal concepts. The vast majority of literature has focused on manufacturing environments. Our case study presents implementation in a job shop environment, with the company's JIT effort designated as TQM. Despite the difference in name, Company A has focused on the same elements of a typical JIT system, touching on issues ranging from education to production and implementation.

7.1 Introduction

Company A, a non-unionized organization, operates in the aerospace industry and provides repair and overall services for three types of gas turbine applications: industrial power units, turbo prop aircraft and helicopters. The company has undergone major changes beginning seven years ago when their hierarchical structure was replaced with one favouring decentralization. Reorganization, however, did not allow the company to realize the benefits it had originally anticipated. Confronted with increasing competition from new and existing competitors, Company A adopted TQM as a vehicle to increase their competitive position within the industry and complement their decentralized structure.

TQM implementation for Company A is an 18 million dollar program, with resources allocated amongst the acquisition of expertise, comprehensive training programs and implementation activities. TQM implementation at Company A is known to its employees, customers and suppliers as the 'world best' project. The effort is promoted through visibility, such as the employee and visitor ID badges which publicize the company's philosophy: a 'world best' company
- is totally committed to quality;
- focuses directly on customer needs and expectations (internal and external);
- views all activities as processes which can be continuously improved;
- requires universal participation – everyone, everywhere, teamwork; and
  - seeks perfection as the goal.

The remaining report will introduce the reader to Company A's experience with TQM: their unique approach to implementation, production and quality issues, teamwork, future plans and learning experience. Four cells – the reduction gearbox cell, the A56 power section cell, the A56 supply cell and the reworks exhaust cell – have served as the basis for the information in the case study and are representative of Company A's overall approach to implementation. Each cell consists of 8 to 20 employees, responsible for performing repair and overhaul services to an engine and its related components. These four cells will serve to address specific case topics deemed central to implementation. The case topics include

- the role of employees;
- implementation strategy;
- cell design;
- training;
- monitoring and measuring progress;
- production issues;
- quality issues;
- relationship with suppliers;
- relationship with customers;
- teambuilding issues; and
- learning experience.

7.2 TQM project

7.2.1 Development of the TQM project

The idea to implement TQM at Company A was conceptualized by the parent company. Company A employees developed a proposal for implementation which was presented to the parent company, and based upon this proposal, Company A became one of six subsidiary companies selected to implement TQM. Company A began its TQM project in March of 1990, after several months of planning and organizing.

The program was designed with the purpose of completely changing all facets of the organization to be consistent with the philosophy of TQM. The main goal of the effort was eventually to realize an altogether new approach to repair and overhaul, with significant improvements in meeting customers' needs and expectations. The company looked toward its customers and competitors within the industry itself to key in on specific areas of improvement. A customer survey was developed and administered to potential and existing customers. The results assisted the company in identifying the primary measures of competitiveness within the industry, which are based upon a company's ability to meet due dates, or due date compliance, operate with the shortest turn times possible and maintain or improve quality standards.

Due date compliance, turntime reduction and improving quality standards have served as objectives for TQM implementation. The company has focused on reducing turntime to a total of 15 days in order to ensure due date compliance 100% of the time.

7.2.2 The repair and overhaul process

Awareness of the repair and overhaul process at Company A is necessary to understand the role TQM plays in meeting organizational objectives. Company A has broken the repair and overhaul process into three cycles where distinct tasks are performed on each engine or subcomponent inducted into the company. Figure 7.1 provides an illustration of the kinds of jobs performed and how turntime is calculated in each cycle. Cycle 1 includes the dismantling, cleaning and inspection of engines and sub-assemblies. Through these activities, employees determine the work required for each engine or sub-assembly and provide an estimate to the customer. Upon verification of the estimate, the engine or sub-assembly is sent to Cycle 2.

Cycle 2 involves the work performed in reworks and accessories. Reworks functions to repair and replace sub-assemblies or parts and determine if parts need to be subcontracted out for repair. Each engine or sub-assembly sent to reworks will require a unique service; therefore, no set sequence of jobs can be established. Repaired or replaced parts are then placed together in a kit, and transferred to Cycle 3. Cycle 3 involves sub-assembly and final assembly, building of major components, testing and inspection activities.

Company A operates in a job–shop environment, where the level and nature of the work to be performed is not known in advance. Each job to be

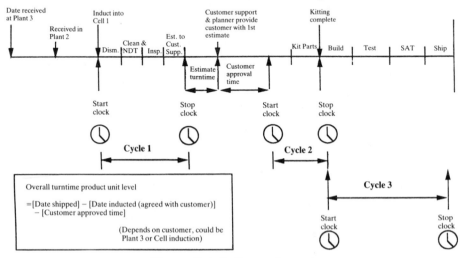

Figure 7.1 Cell turntime.

performed is unique; there is no set sequence of operations or processes to be carried out as in a manufacturing environment. Offsetting variation is realized through level loading Cycle 1. For example, four engines may arrive during the same day, however, the company may load one engine every four days. The initial delay reduces the level of WIP as all value adding activities are performed closest to the due date. Negotiating with customers also enables the company to manage induction levels more effectively.

7.2.3 Implementation of TQM

The redesign has focused upon the implementation of work cells, with individual product lines being broken down into components and each component and related support service organized into separate cells. The TQM initiative began with the design and implementation of four work cells. Presently, the company has in place 15 of the planned 32 cells.

Cellular redesign has meant significant changes to the organization. Change has affected the role of employees, the physical layout of plant and equipment, and the general approach to work. Managing this change to a TQM environment has been initiated through the observed behaviour of the company's president and managers, who have taken proactive approaches toward implementation. The proactive approach has included 'walking the talk', involving employees and maintaining open communication. Willingness to listen and act upon employee suggestions has substantiated management belief in employees and their commitment to TQM. Additional changes have involved new ownership of the company which occurred in October of 1991. Although this new ownership is not expected to affect TQM implementation, employees must now adjust to a results-oriented style of management in which accountability and return on investment are vigorously pursued.

Employee roles as well as their relationship to one another reflect the changes in the physical environment. The TQM effort has resulted in the creation of a project manager, interdisciplinary teams, cells composed of teams of employees headed by a cell leader, and involvement from an external consulting firm.

Employees at all levels of the organization play a central role in the TQM process. The success of TQM implementation at Company A is dependent upon the active involvement of all employees. Therefore, employees must 'buy into' the process. The buying-in process is facilitated by having employees become actively involved in the design of their immediate work area. Each must 'sign off' indicating their acceptance of it. Employees must also learn to become active participants in decision making, take initiative and realize they have the capability to affect their environment. For these reasons, employees have felt TQM impact upon their jobs through increased responsibility and involvement.

A project manager was established, whose job is critical to adopting TQM methods. The project manager's job is dedicated to providing the guidance and co-ordination for the implementation effort by working closely with the consultants, directors and cell members. One of his most critical responsibilities is to facilitate communication between the task forces, cell members and the directors of the organization. Through the project manager, proposals and related budgets established by cell members are submitted and reviewed. Other duties of the project manager include establishing the task forces and co-ordinating their activities through schedules, budgets and planning, resolving issues or bringing them forth to a change council, and monitoring implementation progress through operations and post-implementation audits.

Employees who perform the work within each cell have assumed greater importance to the organization. The employees who work most closely with the engines and components are now recognized as possessing an in-depth understanding of the products and knowledge of what can be done to improve the repair and overhaul process. Employees receive job rotation training and are able to perform two or more of the operations required within each cell. Cell members partake in daily meetings with their cell leader to discuss production related matters such as housekeeping, priority work, problems which have surfaced, planning and scheduling. Employees can announce any suggestions or problems which have occurred, or ask questions during the meetings. Cell members also design their working area board and make the necessary changes to perfect the functioning of the cell.

Cell leaders who head each cell are responsible for implementing the cell design, monitoring and co-ordinating training efforts and managing the employees and processes within a cell. Cell members have recognized the cell leader's ability to direct implementation efforts, as well as the relationship with employees as crucial to the success of the overall cell. Many cell members have attributed their motivation to work toward success to the level of positive feeling felt for the cell leader. Several cell members felt their willingness to accept the change to TQM was the result of their friendship and openness with the cell leader. Traditional management roles such as hiring and firing employees and dealing with employees' personal problems are also carried out by the cell leader.

The cell leader is responsible for relaying the progress of the cell and weekly performance to the director, facilitator and project change manager. Weekly performance is documented through the cell leader's report, which provides the basis of discussion during the weekly meetings. Creating and maintaining the cell operations manual is an additional responsibility of the cell leader. Information regarding the type of tasks performed in each cell and the activities which constitute each task are collected and documented in the cell operations manual.

Several of the cells require an additional member to perform the duties of a cell planner. The cell planner is mainly responsible for building schedules, gathering data related to the cell's performance and posting the data, ensuring production is able to meet schedules, informing fellow employees, planning activities on a weekly basis and co-ordinating the work activities. Although the role of the cell planner is vital to cells such as the reworks exhaust cell, not all cells have a planner. The need for a cell planner is primarily determined by the volume of work which flows through the cell.

A multidisciplinary team of employees form the task forces, who execute three main functions: designing the cells, following through with implementation and conducting cell audits. Each task force is composed of a leader and other members, with the leader's role within the team distinguished from others through the assignment of additional responsibilities. The members of the task force, as well as Company A management, receive TQM awareness training from the consultants. This training served as a basis for implementation, where the task force applied scientific methods developed by the consultant firm to execute the redesign.

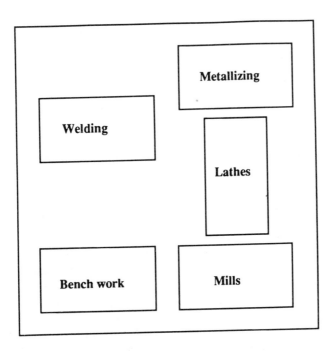

Figure 7.2 Functional layout.

The consulting firm was brought into the company during the initial stages of the redesign to assist the employees with the effort. Several employees of the consulting firm, one for each of the company's product lines, were hired on a full-time basis to work with the in-house implementation teams. The consulting firm became an integral part of the implementation process, training employees, directing the company's efforts and evaluating their progress.

The physical redesign of the plant involved the design and implementation of work cells. This contrasted significantly compared to the former method of performing repair and overhaul services. The former method was based upon a functional approach, where employees' responsibilities and arrangement of the plant were defined according to a functional layout. Presently, the layout of the plant floor is consistent with a product-oriented approach, where work cells have being established to meet individual product line needs. Each work cell is organized according to natural product groupings, where equipment and employees are allocated to each cell according to its needs. The reworks exhaust cell in Figs. 7.2, 7.3a and 7.3b present an example of a functional vs. product-oriented layout. Many of the parts spend up to 90% of their turntime in reworks; therefore, in order to meet the company's overall objective of reducing turntime to a total of 15 days, reworks was redesigned to reflect this need.

The design and implementation of cells was executed through the use of a systems approach. A generic outline or procedure known as the 'five step approach', and input/output analyses, provide the tools which the company used to design and implement the cells. These tools enabled the company to take into consideration all factors which affect the cell's functioning and capability. An analysis of the company's internal and external environment was carried out, regarding skills, targets, budgets, available machinery, competitors and market analysis to determine these factors.

The five step approach involves the process of defining a cell, analysing the cell, designing jobs, establishing control systems and finally, developing an implementation plan. Cell definition involves the analysis of part characteristics and natural groupings. Natural groupings occur when processes related to a product can be placed together within a cell and simultaneously facilitate continuous improvement and ownership of the process. Thus, processes which can be naturally grouped together will serve to reduce the physical flow of WIP between processes (time and distance) and promote ease of transfer. Cell definition also addresses the size of teams and shared resource conflicts.

An analysis of the cell occurs in two steps known as steady state design and dynamic design. Together, these two steps address the elements of the cell which do not change and those which do change, respectively. Steady state design takes into account the average number of employees and machines per cell, development of the preliminary floor plan, defining

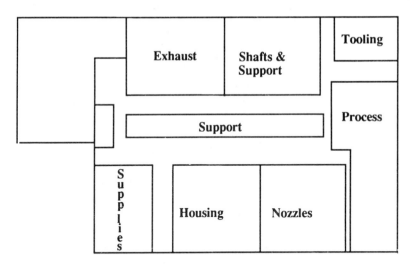

Figure 7.3a Product-oriented layout: reworks.

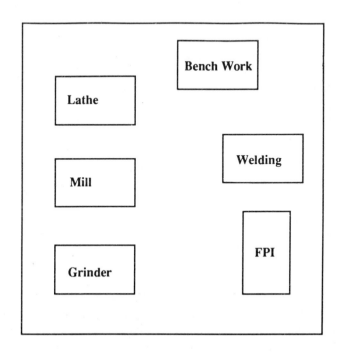

Figure 7.3b The reworks exhaust cell.

bottlenecks, applying market forecasts and the degree of employee owner-ship of the cell. Dynamic design addresses how to accommodate variations such as bottlenecks, limiting processes, development of a final floor layout and labour requirements. In short, dynamic design functions to design in or design out variations.

Job design assisted in determining the tasks to be performed in each cell, design the work shifts and establish cross-training requirements. Control systems are put into place to measure the performance of the cell, monitor implementation progress and establish timetables. The completion of a cell's design sets the stage for the development of an implementation plan. The plan addresses the timeliness of implementation, the creation of a design handbook and operations manual, resource and training require-ments and the allocation of financial resources.

7.2.4 Measuring and monitoring progress

Company A has been monitoring and measuring TQM implementation through meetings where problems are addressed, and the use of an implementation and operations audit. The implementation and operations audits are formal procedures used to assess the cells and highlight areas for improvement. The audits follow evaluation criteria which apply to a specific set of categories. For example, audits assess how well employees within the cell conduct housekeeping and maintenance procedures, maintain and update visual aids, complete training requirements, adhere to safety speci-fications, follow through with implementation and participate.

Audits are conducted periodically, with employees unaware of when they will be performed. The first audit is conducted with half a day's warning, the second and third audit are conducted without any advance warning. The purpose of random checks is to ensure employees are consistent with cell maintenance and improvement activities.

The audits serve to make visible the areas of the cell which do not conform to the planned design. Once these areas are identified, cell members are required to complete implementation. Scoring the varying elements of each category involves two steps: to provide a numerical score ranging from 0–5 (5 being perfect), and provide suggestions for improvement.

The audit allows for changes to be made to its format, to increase its relevance to a particular cell or update its currency. The result of the audit is made visible to all cell members by posting the results on the performance board. Employees voice their opinion of the audit and discuss the results at weekly meetings. Methods for addressing improvement activities of the cell are addressed and actions planned during the meetings. The employees then follow through with the activities to complete implementation or improve-ment activities.

The employees monitor completion of the required changes documented by the audit through the use of a cell audit action sheet. The action sheet is a systematic approach to identifying the cell category/feature, the required action, its due date and who is responsible for the action.

The difference between an implementation audit and an operations audit entails how far advanced the cell is in its implementation. Implementation is considered complete when a cell receives a score of 60 or better on the audit, however, it is only after the score exceeds 80–85% that an operations audit is used. Although the two audits are similar in the categories they assess, operation audits assess the cell's operational performance and promote continuous improvement.

The implementation and operation audits provide Company A with a standardized method of assessing the effectiveness of their progress. Other means of assessing progress lie with the impact of TQM on the company in terms of resource utilization. An example of this is provided through employee involvement. Although the company had a formal suggestion system in place for many years prior to the TQM initiative, it is not until the redesign was in place that employee suggestions and input into the job have come to light. Two of the most prominent developments as a result of employee involvement are the blade room and the gearbox test stand. Both of these developments have made significant contributions to turntime reduction and cost savings for Company A. Table 7.1 presents a summary of these savings.

The blade room was designed and built on site to transfer the stripping and inspection activities of engine blades to the responsibility of employees rather than a subcontractor. This in-house capability has reduced the amount of travelling and transfer of the blades from an external subcontractor, reducing the number of quality problems and cost through ownership of the process.

The idea to design and build the gearbox test stand was inspired by the redesign task force. The gearbox test stand has enabled Company A to reduce the waiting time required to perform testing activities in the absence of a test stand.

TQM has contributed toward innovative ideas in meeting objectives and goals. For example, since the redesign was initiated, many new ideas have been developed to reduce turntimes effectively. Innovations include the introduction of control mechanisms such as gateway control systems, production scheduling tags and production scheduling boards. These three

Table 7.1 Summary of savings

	TQM Savings	
Suggestion	Turntime (days)	Cost ($)
Blade room	5–8	15–20 000
Gearbox test stand	1	2 000

innovations function through visibility to drive measures of performance, prioritize and control jobs and accumulate data on subcontracts, spare part shortages and process interruptions, respectively.

7.2.5 Preparing employees for TQM

Company A's approach to training has attempted to make the employee an integral part of the process. Objectives of training include training employees to understand the TQM concept and apply its principles to the job, training for a variety of jobs to make job rotation a reality and training which reflects the requirements of the job. Company A has directed large sums of financial resources toward training its employees to prepare them for TQM and realize the training objectives. The 1991 expenditure for training, excluding the training received through the consultant firm amounted to $435 000.

The training employees receive, in addition to the initial TQM training, can be selected from a number of in-house or external training programs. Formal and informal procedures are used to evaluate the effectiveness of training, identify training needs and employee interests and co-ordinate the training schedules within each cell. Each procedure represents an effective way of ensuring the delivery of education. The informal procedures include employee/management discussions. Open communication allows employees to voice their training concerns with their cell leader, or instructors. The formal procedures include the use of an employee developmental plan, skills record and training schedules, standardized tracking forms and a seminar evaluation form.

The employee developmental plan and skills record and training schedule

Cell members' training needs are identified through the use of an employee developmental plan and a skills record and training schedule. The employee developmental plan serves to assist employees in identifying their interests and specific training needs.

The skills record and training schedule functions as a part of the concept of visibility. Each cell posts a large chart listing the cell member's name and the tasks which must be performed within each cell. The skills record also functions to identify the training gap: the discrepancy between the required levels of training within a cell and the actual training levels.

Upon achievement of the fifth level of training, employees are able to assist in the training and development of their co-workers. Many of the company's employees viewed the opportunity to learn from one another as a beneficial and necessary aspect of the job. For example, many employees recognized they were able to learn many aspects of the job which would otherwise not be addressed through an external education programme and learning from one another promoted a team effort, necessary for a product-oriented approach.

The cell leader is responsible for maintaining the schedule, assisting employees with identifying their training needs, as well as co-ordinating the training schedule. Cell leaders must be skillful at balancing the needs of the cell with training needs. Absences due to training can interfere with the cell's ability to meet the production schedules. Thus, cells must be fully functional while simultaneously allowing for employee absence to fulfill training requirements such as job rotation.

The standardized tracking form

The standardized tracking form is developed for each task performed within a cell. The purpose of the form is to identify all the training requirements for each job. The information collected is applied to the design of in-house training programs and functions to standardize training procedures and reduce duplication of training through elimination of overlapping activities.

The seminar evaluation form

The in-house instructors and training co-ordinators at Company A require employees, upon the completion of a training program, to fill out the seminar evaluation form to communicate how well the training program prepared its employees to perform their jobs. Information from employees is assessed and the course is adjusted to reflect the job requirements. Employees believe their input into course content serves to increase the relevance and transference of course material.

7.3 TQM production issues

The TQM effort at Company A has changed many of the production practices the company had performed in the past. Table 7.2 presents

Table 7.2 Production practices

Production activity	Prior TQM	TQM
Housekeeping	Work of outside cleaning staff, not Company A's responsibility	Shared and conducted by employees
Preventive maintenance	Separate maintenance department	Shared and conducted by employees
Visibility	Unaware of the concept	Organization-wide promotion
Production control	Functional design	Cellular design
Continuous improvement	Not promoted	Accepted, employees work with the concept

a summary of the changes which have occurred with respect to production practices.

TQM implementation has brought with it a new focus on housekeeping at Company A. The company views housekeeping as an integral component of turntime, quality and safety. Given that Company A no longer advertises, housekeeping is also key to customer perceptions during sponsored plant tours. Prior to TQM, the company relied on an outside cleaning staff to perform the housekeeping activities. Currently, employees perform almost all housekeeping activities which are closely monitored by the implementation audit.

Housekeeping has become a shared and continuous effort where focus is placed upon six broad categories of housekeeping including training, orderliness, clear access, identification, co-operation and cleanliness of each cell. Each employee within a cell receives training on housekeeping to relay its value to work performance. Co-operation is also viewed as a necessary element of housekeeping. It is based upon the cell members' ability to share the housekeeping activities with neighbouring cells. The areas of question include shared equipment and floor space.

Several employees who are responsible for the housekeeping activities regard many of them unnecessary and trivial, such as removing the dust off the floor each time a lathe is used. Instances such as this are regarded with a difference in opinion by managers, who believe employees' initial reactions should change with time. The implementation audit serves to keep in check many of these housekeeping activities: to ensure employees are consistent in maintaining specified housekeeping standards.

Prior to the company's TQM implementation, preventive maintenance was primarily thought of as 'maintenance' and was largely the responsibility of a separate department. The activities the maintenance department carried out were checking oil and cooling fluid levels of equipment and responding to emergency situations. Today, first-level 'preventive' maintenance by employees who use the equipment has been adopted and applied to the company's practices.

Preventive maintenance activities include training employees to properly clean, maintain and respond to machine breakdowns. Operators clean, oil and carry out routine maintenance activities on their own machines. The cells are able to benefit from these preventive maintenance measures as operators work most closely with the equipment and therefore have developed a 'feel' for the machines.

Documentation, which includes maintenance check-off sheets is another element of preventive maintenance practices. Each sheet is placed near each machine for easy operator access. The sheets ensure that oil levels are checked daily, coolant levels checked weekly and both changed when required. In addition, sheets stating the type of oil and coolant required for various parts of the machine accompany the check sheet. Diagrams of equipment are posted near some machines, with symbols indicating where the various cooling and lubricating agents should be placed.

Employees recognized the benefits of these preventive maintenance procedures to include consistent care of machines with the result being fewer fire fighting instances. Posting checklists and machine maintenance manuals near machines ensures employees do not forget to perform maintenance procedures. Detailed diagrams allow employees to reference the proper maintenance procedures, rather than resulting in guesswork.

The concept of visibility is now highly promoted throughout the organization. Prior to TQM, the employees of Company A had no working knowledge of the concept, its purpose or how it could benefit the organization. Visibility has been applied through the cellular design, the use of windows, breaking down physical walls which hinder communication and workers' ability to see one another, as well as abolishing separate offices and compartments which serve to seclude employees. Windows are used to maintain visibility between groups of employees where offices must be built. The company believes eye-to-eye contact is an important element of visibility and has expended $20 000 to remove a wall blocking worker communication and contact with one another.

The production scheduling board, another aspect of visibility, is designed and updated by employees within each cell. Each board functions according to a colour coded system to indicate whether a unit is behind schedule, on schedule, or ahead of schedule. Figure 7.4 presents an example of a production scheduling board. The black areas indicate the present date, or where a unit should be according to schedule. The shaded areas indicate the actual place of the unit within a cell. Shading in the areas before the black square indicate the unit is behind the planned schedule. Shading which occurs after the black square indicates the unit is ahead of planned schedule. The effectiveness of the board rests with its design. Its large

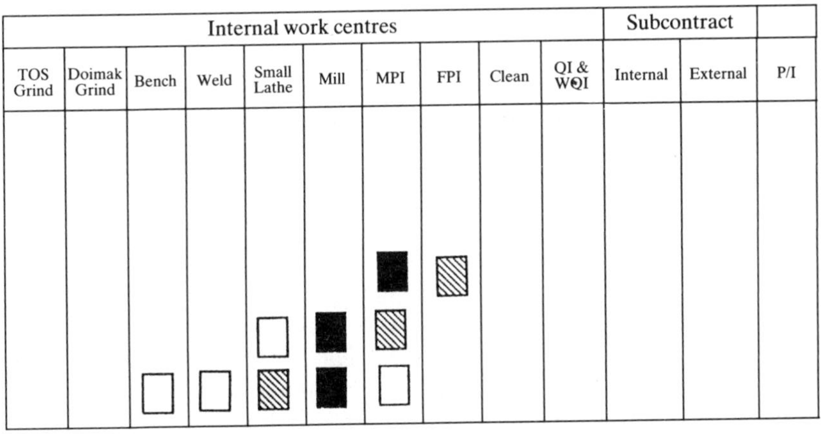

Internal work centres										Subcontract		
TOS Grind	Doimak Grind	Bench	Weld	Small Lathe	Mill	MPI	FPI	Clean	QI & WOI	Internal	External	P/I

Figure 7.4 The production scheduling board.

size and positioning within a cell allows employees to determine at a glance priority work.

In addition to the production scheduling board, a performance tracking board is used to provide visible information to the employees within a cell regarding the specific areas targeted by the redesign and continuous improvement. The board is updated weekly with the information collected from daily measures of performance. The measures of performance, as they apply to each cell are clearly displayed on the board to keep all employees informed and aware of the cell's progress.

Production control is now consistent with a product-oriented approach. Engines and sub-assemblies flow through the three cycles of repair and overhaul according to the product-oriented layout, rather than functional. Given that jobs are prioritized and driven according to due date, a 'true' pull system cannot be used, rendering the use of kanbans inappropriate. The company uses a combination of push and pull as the products flow through the three cycles. Engines and sub-assemblies, according to their due dates, are pushed through Cycle 1 into the cleaning, dismantling and inspection activities. Induction levels are level loaded through scheduling and co-operation with the customer to avoid the occurrence of bottlenecks. Parts and subcomponents are then pushed into Cycle 2 or the various operations of reworks, where they are repaired or subcontracted out. Cycle 3 allows parts and sub-assemblies to follow a pull system given that variability at this stage is reduced or eliminated. The parts and subcomponents arrive at Cycle 3 already kitted where the required work to be performed is known or predictable.

The concept of continuous improvement has been largely accepted and promoted as a part of Company A's TQM effort; however, it has generally been applied to design and implementation aspects, with the mature cells beginning to direct the concept toward their everyday practices. Employees are constantly trying to improve their individual performance and direct much of their effort toward improving visibility, housekeeping, preventive maintenance and fulfilling training objectives. The use of the implementation audit and intercell rivalry serve as motivating factors for continuous improvement within individual cells. Cells compete with one another to see who will score the highest on the implementation audits.

7.4 Quality issues

Although the company is progressing steadily with TQM implementation efforts, many of the quality aspects deemed as an integral part of TQM in the ideal sense have not yet been addressed. However, the company has set goals for itself to achieve within the next year or two. Company A's quality goals include focusing on vendor development and redesign of the quality department, determining the costs of quality and implementing company-wide self-inspection.

Focusing on vendor development
Company A currently has no formalized plan to focus on vendor development. However, the company has anticipated that the relationships it currently maintains with vendors will be enhanced through a mutual understanding of company requirements and expectations. The absence of a formal plan with respect to vendor development has not meant the company has remained static in its approach toward vendor selection and the relationships it maintains with suppliers. The redesign of the quality department as well as the development of the vendor certification survey has changed the company's method of dealing with vendors.

Redesign of the quality department in accordance with TQM measures has resulted in the development of strategic business units. Previously, the quality department conducted periodic audits of the various quality functions and stored the results in a filing cabinet. Decentralization has meant the company was able to become closer to the vendor through the establishment of three areas related to separate product lines. Vendors are now able to deal directly with quality employees. The use of the three business units has allowed Company A employees to become aware of the impact of problems; however, it has not resulted in a decrease in the vendor base. The reasons attributed to this are twofold: TQM implementation in the quality department is still in its early stages, thus it may be too soon to realize a decrease; and decentralization has meant that many contracts have been established with new subcontractors rather than focusing on the development of existing subcontractors.

Previous to the development of the vendor certification survey and decentralization of the quality department, Company A conducted a periodic audit on subcontractors. The primary purpose of the periodic audit was to resolve problems and issues when they arise between the two parties involved. The audit functioned to update approvals, focus on new processes/capabilities, provide a copy of the quality assurance manual to subcontractors, put in place the procedure traceability of material throughout the plant and ensure compliance. The application of the vendor certification survey has provided the company with a proactive approach of ensuring vendor standards meet established requirements. Problems are prevented by initially screening out subcontractors who are not willing or able to meet the company's standards. The survey examines vendor acceptance and attitudes toward TQM; whether subcontractors are currently total quality companies or have future plans to become total quality companies.

Determining the costs of quality
Company A is currently embarking upon a project to assess the factors which contribute to the cost of quality, specifically opportunity costs. The objectives of the project are to eliminate the causes which contribute to the

realization of opportunity costs and enhance the company's competitive position in the market.

The area which is receiving much focus is the testing of engines and components. An engineer has been assigned to the duty of identifying and tracking the factors responsible for test failure. Two approaches are possible to reduce the effects of this: build better engines/subcomponents; and improve the process of troubleshooting the causes of failure. Failure to pass first test means the company must begin repair over again and absorb the cost in doing so. Through analysing opportunity costs, the company hopes to have engines pass test the first time, every time.

Engineers are documenting all measurable parameters of the engine and apply scientific logic to troubleshooting. Past attempts have included a process described as 'black magic', where upon an engine failed on test, engineers would examine the engine, change something, then run it again hoping it would pass test. Eventually, an engineer would discover the cause of the failure. The process is called black magic because the engineer was unable to quantify the effects the change or changes made to the performance of the engine. Presently, engineers document all the measurable parameters of the engine and apply scientific logic to troubleshoot engines. The result of the new process is the development of a troubleshooting guide to enable engineers to pinpoint the cause of failure immediately. Parallel to this troubleshooting guide, a custom build standard is being created to serve as a guide to build engines to maximize performance, significantly reducing the test failure of future engines.

Company A has sought to reduce opportunity costs through recapturing the cost of repair reprocessing. The objective behind this is to process components correctly the first time as reprocess failure results in a substantially reduced margin on components. Improper surface preparation of a component prior to metallizing is illustrative of process failure. Preventive measures have been taken to reduce or eliminate this from occurring. The company has intervened through increasing accountability of performance by giving ownership of the process to the employees, while establishing standard procedures for the surface preparation activities. Measuring the number of reprocesses inspires the technician to pay close attention to work while simultaneously providing the necessary tools to perform the work properly.

Implementation of self-inspection

Company A's TQM effort has resulted in the recent development of a pilot project to implement self-inspection. One employee, trained in the area of inspection was selected and is currently receiving training in TQM. The purpose of the pilot project is to enable the trained employee to identify defects, follow up on their cause and provide awareness training to other employees. The self-inspection pilot project will serve as a test for the organization. If the project proves to be successful, the company will apply self-inspection to other areas. The use of self-inspection will differ significantly from the company's current method of inspection which entails the use of an independent inspector, that is, the use of a trained employee to inspect others' work. Company A recognizes the potential benefits of self-inspection to include decreased quality problems and deployment of employees to other areas where they are needed.

7.5 Teamwork building issues

Company A recognizes teambuilding efforts as a naturally occurring phenomenon among its employees. Formal systems have not been established, although the company strongly encourages team effort. Generally, cell members are looked upon as a team, with cell leaders having their own meetings. Given the importance of involvement and participation in a TQM system, several of the cell leaders have developed unique means of encouraging cell member involvement. While everyone attends meetings, it is often only the outgoing cell members who participate in discussion. Recognizing that each individual within the cell has something valuable to offer the group, two cell leaders have developed their own means of involving everyone in the discussion. Attempts have been made to involve everyone in discussion through gradually making everyone feel comfortable with the process. During discussions, everyone must take turns keeping record of the points discussed. The record keeper or secretary must then repeat the list out loud. The cell leader feels by having everyone take turns at speaking out loud, quiet or reserved employees will gradually lose their inhibition and eventually participate actively in the discussion.

The supply cell leader takes it upon himself to draw out the opinions of the employees who are reluctant to participate by asking them for their suggestions. The environment is supportive and encouraging of all discussion. Recent development in teambuilding effort includes a 'learn at lunch session'. Ideally, employees volunteer their time at lunch to sit in on a session conducted by a cell leader. Topics include measures of performance, company instructions and problem-solving techniques.

Peer pressure or going along with the group has been recognized as another aspect of teambuilding. The company is introducing new systems and programs, as with TQM. The employees who have not been exposed to these new systems will feel left out if they do not participate while others around them do. Conformance to the group rather than going against the grain has been identified as the most painless way to handle the change. Thus, employees will jump on the bandwagon to reduce the stress of change.

Employees have recognized a change in the company with respect to teambuilding and TQM. Company A is now moving in the direction where they are trying to enhance teambuilding. Prior to TQM, the topic was never mentioned. Today, employees hear of teambuilding issues all the time.

Employee work ethic: direct vs. indirect labour

The work ethic of employees differs, depending upon what kind of work one performs. The employees responsible for the production side of the business view their work and the way it has changed as a result of TQM very positively, noting how their jobs have become increasingly interesting. The office and technical employees of the company, or those regarded as managers possess a different point of view regarding TQM implementation and its impact upon their work. Many feel the pressure and stress placed upon them to complete the implementation and the associated increased level of work. Focusing efforts on implementation has resulted in other aspects of the job being neglected in favour of establishing TQM systems. One employee, who prided himself as being a perfectionist, well practised at completing his work on time, stated he had a difficult time accepting that he was unable to complete all the work when required.

7.6 Learning experience with TQM

Employees recognize the problems they have encountered with TQM implementation simply as learning experiences and have cautioned against its use as a quick-fix solution to organizational problems. Although planning and organizing efforts in the initial stages of development can serve as a check on potential problems, difficulties are apt to arise regardless, as they are a natural part of the implementation process. The difficulties Company A has experienced with the implementation process involve employee resistance, general lack of co-ordination, focusing too heavily on the process of implementation and adjusting to the physical layout of a cell.

Employee resistance to TQM has been experienced in the attitudes and behaviour of a few employees. Employee resistance has been felt from production employees as well as those who occupy supervisory positions. Many employees come to challenge the process. Although this challenge can be beneficial, to the degree that it forces people to consider alternatives and new ideas, in its destructive form, it results in the blocking of the implementation process and development of co-operative relationships.

Employee resistance has been described as a natural reaction to the change. The problem is difficult to contend with because it is human nature to resist change. Although it is difficult to avoid completely, the manner in which it is handled is critical to eventual success. Job security issues have resulted in many employees' gradual acceptance of TQM, but, at the same time, fail to prompt employee enthusiasm for the change. Company A has described a proactive approach to managing change as the most effective. This approach includes lessening employee fear through increasing training and the level of employee involvement in the process of change. Through an employee development plan, employees assume an active role in identifying their training interests and weaknesses.

Employees are also reassigned to other areas of the company. Redeployment as well as the belief that increases in the volume of work made possible through TQM will provide employees with jobs. Inasmuch as Company A has managed to subdue employee resistance, it has become less of a problem and more of a limiting factor of TQM implementation.

Company A has experienced difficulties in co-ordinating the implementation effort. Role overload can be a consequence of TQM if care is not taken to assess the level of work increases and employees' capability to effectively manage the increase. Assigning the co-ordinating activities to a cell facilitator is one method which Company A has elected to deal with the co-ordination problems.

Failure to involve all the people who will work within a cell during the design stage has contributed to modifying the original cell design. The problem of insufficient communication between task force members and cell members was evident with the cells first implemented. The design process would have benefited from employee input as the plant floor employees are most familiar with the environment and would have been able to communicate the workability of the original design. Employees now assist in the design stage and must buy into the process by signing off. Signing off by all employees who will work within the cell stipulates acceptance and sets the stage for actual implementation.

Adjustment to the physical layout of a cell has been identified as a necessary part of implementation. Although cell implementation may be considered complete, there are minor problems which occur and when corrected, assist in fine tuning the process. Adjustment problems can include complications of equipment which cause delays, poor co-ordination and insufficient training. Costs associated with the rearrangement of equipment such as stopping production, disrupting the workforce and increasing power supply are common outcomes of the equipment arrangement process which can prevail until the system is completely fine tuned. The quality of the initial cell design will determine the amount of readjustment activities required subsequent to physical implementation. Therefore, the initial design of the cell must take into account all factors which will affect implementation.

Focusing too heavily on the mechanics of the implementation process rather than on the objectives has also been recognized as a problem. Employees focus on perfecting the process, whereas focusing on how to meet objectives such as 'how can we improve overhauling of engines', becomes neglected. Becoming 'lost' in the process, rather than using the systems as tools to assist in achieving goals is one problem which employees felt could be corrected through refocusing of effort.

Increased competition or intercell rivalry, has been identified as an unhealthy drawback of TQM to the extent that it causes employees to lose sight of the systems approach. Each unit or component part must come together as a whole, thus employees must remain committed to the achievement of the overall established goals. Competition between cells within limits, however, is not purely negative. Cell member preoccupation with perfection of the functioning of their cell relative to other cells, is partly responsible for motivating employees to complete implementation as soon as possible.

Although it is too early in implementation to realize most of the expected benefits, employees feel TQM at Company A will result in positive payback. Employees, both managers and cell members, recognize that the benefits of TQM outweigh the costs. Although most benefits are realized over the long term, some became apparent immediately, while others were realized within two to four months of implementation. Through their experience with TQM, employees recognized ownership of the process, increased visibility, reduction in waste, changed organizational structure, flexible workforce, increases in the workforce and increased ability to compete through reduced turntimes as the most apparent benefits of TQM.

Employee ownership of the process was enacted through securing employee involvement in TQM implementation. The signing-off process allowed employees to expressly state whether they agreed with the design or not. Ownership is further enhanced through employees' active participation in decision making and improving the day-to-day operations of the cell. Employees recognized their jobs had become more interesting and felt more control over their ability to affect the environment.

Ownership has also enabled the company to address the problem of apathy which was apparent with the lack of initiative in handling documents. Frequently, a document holding up production would sit in several employees' in-baskets for days or sometimes weeks. Typical response from employees included 'it wasn't in my in-basket so it's not my fault'. Although the company recognized this mentality as very difficult to change, ownership and measuring performance has shed some light on the matter. Employees, now monitored for its delivery, take initiative and ensure the document or part is not held up needlessly.

Increased visibility has allowed problems and the causes of problems to surface. The shaft and support cell presents an example of the benefits which can be received from visibility. TQM allowed employees to determine the service provided by a local subcontractor was responsible for long turntimes in the cell, as the service was not being performed expeditiously, placing delays on the downstream processes. Housekeeping procedures have also enhanced visibility through the reduction of unnecessary material and efficient storage of tools and parts.

Company A has successfully eliminated wastes such as accumulated inventory, travelling time and redundant activities. The use of cells has enabled the company to reduce the amount of time WIP is spent travelling from one process to the next. Presently, fewer employees are required to perform the same jobs which allowed the company to deploy workers where they would be more beneficial to the repair and overhaul process. Although waste reduction has allowed the company to benefit directly, it has also contributed indirectly to the securing of new contracts.

The change in organizational structure has benefited the company with respect to clearer lines of communication and defined roles. Employees have found since the introduction of TQM, not only are they more clear of whom to approach with their problems or suggestions, but the result is increased effectiveness in the manner problems and suggestions are dealt with.

Employees have attributed the use of TQM with a net increase in the workforce of 40 employees. Although employees were released from employment with the company, either through attrition or poor performance by failing to become part of the process, employees have generally benefited from the use of TQM. Increases in the workforce have had positive signalling affects upon existing employees.

The use of Company A's extensive training program has served to introduce employees to the overall TQM concepts, as well as provide training in specific skill areas. The provision of cross-training to create a flexible workforce has benefited the organization through increased awareness of the product, increased ability to execute tasks and higher levels of mental alertness and motivation attributed to performing a variety of jobs.

Although quality has benefited indirectly from the introduction of new housekeeping and preventive maintenance procedures, each has served to enhance and facilitate the execution of tasks and thus contributes to reducing turntimes. Proper maintenance of equipment and production control has allowed employees to reduce variability due to machine breakdowns and prioritized jobs.

The redesign of cells has also allowed the company to work toward its objective of reducing turntime. Through their efforts with TQM, Company A has successfully managed to reduce turntime from 65 to 30 days. The implementation of work cells and TQM work methods have contributed to turntime reduction by:

- identifying the causes and working with the causes of variation;
- providing training to employees to facilitate job rotation;
- reducing queue time;
- increasing employee ownership of the cell;
- making visible, production control;
- standardizing procedures; and
- increasing innovation on the repair and salvage of parts.

TQM is being employed at Company A to a level never seen before by many of the employees and has been described as a costly endeavour which requires time, work, money and commitment to realize its benefits. It extends beyond merely understanding the concepts, but being able to apply the concepts to a specific environment. TQM is not a step-by-step process, rather, it is situation oriented. The approach which proves successful for one company may result in problems for another.

References

Allor, P. (1988) How to implement a continuous improvement programme. *APICS Conf. Proc.*, 713–15.

Anderson, J., Gunderson, M. and Ponak, A. (1989) *Union Management Relations in Canada*, 2nd edn., Addison-Wesley Publishers, Toronto.

Andrew, C. (1987) Extending JIT into distribution. *APICS Conf. Proc.*, 698–701.

Artes, R. (1987) Demand management for a JIT environment. *APICS Conf. Proc.*, 263–5.

Aus, W. (1987) Case study: on-time delivery – 100% customer service is not too expensive. *APICS Conf. Proc.*, 169–71.

Bechtel, T. (1987) Hands on: manufacturing lead-time determination. *APICS Conf. Proc.*, 651–3.

Bently, D. (1987) Emphasis on total quality management for JIT success. *APICS Conf. Proc.*, 20–3.

Bently, D. (1988) How to plan and control JIT implementation. *APICS Conf. Proc.*, 497–8.

Bodek, N. (1988) Total employee involvement (TEI). *APICS Conf. Proc.*, 752–6.

Bourke, R. (1990) Excellence in education: tops in training. *APICS Conf. Proc.*, 703–6.

Boyst, W. (1990) TQC: the problem-solving side of JIT. *APICS Conf. Proc.*, 292–4.

Broh, R. (1982) *Managing Quality for Higher Profits*, McGraw-Hill Inc., New York.

Brooks, R. B. (1987) How to integrate JIT and MRP II. *APICS Conf. Proc.*, 407–11.

Bruun, R. (1987) How to improve on-time delivery using operation sequencing. *APICS Conf. Proc.*, 62–4.

Buker, D. (1987) Ten steps to class A MRP II. *APICS Conf. Proc.*, 120–124.

Buker, D. (1988) 10 steps to JIT. *APICS Conf. Proc.*, 507–8.

Burns, S. (1987) Customer networking: how to manage your customer's demand. *APICS Conf. Proc.*, 299–302.

Burt, D. (1989) Managing suppliers up to speed. *Harvard Bus. Rev.*, **67** (4), 127–34.

Cheng, T. C. E. (1990) A state-of-the-art review of just-in-time production. *Adv. Manuf. Eng.*, **2**, 96–101.

Cheng, T. C. E. (1990) Some thoughts on the practice of just-in-time manufacturing. *Prod. Planning and Control*, **2**, 167–78.

Civerolo, J. (1990) Demand pull: what are the prerequisites for success? *APICS Conf. Proc.*, 467–71.

Clark, M. (1987) Getting people involved in JIT. *APICS Conf. Proc.*, 188–91.

Claunch, J. (1988) Setup reduction: exposing the hidden capacity. *APICS Conf. Proc.*, 144–7.

Darress, W. (1988) Getting our maintenance-JIT together. *APICS Conf. Proc.*, 316–20.

Deakin, E. (1988) Focus on industry, supplier management in a just-in-time inventory system. *J. Accountancy*, December, 128–33.

Dilworth, J. (1989) *Production and Operations Management,* 4th edn., Random House Inc., New York.

Duffy, A. (1987) SPC: What it is and how to make it work. *APICS Conf. Proc.*, 15–19.

Edwards, J. (1987) Integrating MRP II with JIT: an update. *APICS Conf. Proc.*, 399–403.

Everett, D. (1987) How to implement kanban. *APICS Conf. Proc.*, 65–7.

Ford, Q. (1987) DRP/MRP: distribution JIT. *APICS Conf. Proc.*, 672–6.

Fuller, T. and Brown, J. T. (1987) JIT myths and opportunities. *APICS Conf. Proc.*, 395–7.

Garwood, D. (1990) Flexibility is job 2. *APICS Conf. Proc.*, 568–9.

Giunipero, L. and O'Neal, C. (1988) Obstacles to JIT procurement. *Ind. Marketing Mgt*, **17**, 35–41.

Goddard, W. E. (1986) *Just-In-Time*, Oliver Wight Ltd. Publications, Inc.

Gray, J. L. and Starke, F. A. (1988) *Organizational Behaviour Concepts and Applications*, 4th edn., Merrill Publishing Company, Ohio.

Grieco, P. L. (1988) Monitoring JIT/TQC performance levels. *APICS Conf. Proc.*, 270–2.

Hale, C. D. and Karney, B. (1987) How to professionally qualify your suppliers. *APICS Conf. Proc.*, 590–6.

Hall, E. H. (1989) Just-in-time management: a critical assessment. *Acad. Mgt Exec.*, **3** (4), 315–18.

Hall, R. W. (1987) *Attaining Manufacturing Excellence*, Dow Jones-Irwin, Illinois.

Hamre, R. F. (1988) The real cost of nonconforming inventory material. *APICS Conf. Proc.*, 303–5.

Hanson, P. C. (1988) Managing change: the real issue of implementation. *APICS Conf. Proc.*, 719–20.

Hay, E. J. (1988) *The Just-In-Time Breakthrough*, John Wiley and Sons, New York.

Heard, E. L. (1987) Responsiveness: the next battleground. *APICS Conf. Proc.*, 479–83.

Heiko, L. (1989) Some relationships between Japanese culture and just-in-time. *Acad. Mgt Exec.*, **3** (4), 319–21.

Helle, P. F. (1988) Pulling JIT along with your MRP II project. *APICS Conf. Proc.*, 490–1.

Hensel, J. S. (1990) Service quality improvement and control: a customer based approach. *J. Bus. Res.*, **20**, 43–54.

Huge, E. C. (1987) Building top management commitment to JIT/TCQ implementation. *APICS Conf. Proc.*, 368–72.

Japanese Human Relations Association (1988) *The Idea Book, Improvement Through Total Employee Involvement.*

Johnson, A. (1986) MRP? MRP II? OPT? CIM? FMS? JIT? Is any system letter perfect? *Man. Rev.*, **75** (9), 22–27.

Juran, J. M. (1988) *Juran's Quality Control Handbook*, 4th edn., McGraw-Hill, New York.

Kapoor, V. K. (1987) Focused factories: a simple idea with a big payback. *APICS Conf. Proc.*, 468–71.

Kerr, J. and Slocum, J. W. (1987) Managing corporate culture through reward systems. *Acad. Mgt Exec.*, **1** (2), 99–108.

Kidd, J. and Reinbolt, L. (1990) Delivery reduction time at Bourns: a case study. *APICS Conf. Proc.*, 121–4.

Kinsey, J. W. (1987) Push JIT vs. pull JIT. *APICS Conf. Proc.*, 58–61.

Kinsey, J. W. (1990) Just-in-time and quality at the source: implementing a performance advantage. *APICS Conf. Proc.*, 295–8.

Klein, J. A. (1989) The human costs of manufacturing reform. *Harvard Bus. Rev.*, **67** (2), 62–6.

Lancendorfer, H. and Siegel, D. I. (1988) Measuring supplier performance using cost factors. *APICS Conf. Proc.*, 247–51.

Landis, G. A. (1987) Specific skills required to successfully implement JIT in a manufacturing environment. *APICS Conf. Proc.*, 327–30.

Landvater, D. (1987) How to conquer the most difficult part of JIT: motivating people. *APICS Conf. Proc.*, 186–7.

Lawler, E. E. (1988) Choosing an involvement strategy. *Acad. Mgt Exec.*, **2** (3), 197–204.

Lee, S. M. and Ebrahimpour, M. (1987) Just-in-time. *Mgt Dec.*, **25** (6), 50–4.

Lubben, R. T. (1988) *Just-In-Time Manufacturing: An Aggressive Manufacturing Strategy*, McGraw-Hill, New York, USA.

Lucht, L. H. (1988) Implementing TQC. *APICS Conf. Proc.*, 287–9.

Martin, A. and Sandras, W. A. (1990) JIT/DRP: key to high-velocity customer response. *APICS Conf. Proc.*, 337–8.

Mayne, L. B. (1987) JIT implementation: making it happen in the west. *APICS Conf. Proc.*, 236–9.

McGuire, K. J. (1990) The people side of JIT. *APICS Conf. Proc.*, 277–80.

Monden, Y. (1983) *Toyota Production System*, Industrial Engineering and Management Press, Georgia USA.

Nelson, M. (1990) The JIT supplier relationship: war and pieces. *APICS Conf. Proc.*, 350–2.

Novitsky, M. P. (1988) DRP & JIT. *APICS Conf. Proc.*, 380–3.

O'Connor, B. J. (1990) JIT implementation. *APICS Conf. Proc.*, 134–8.

Oversmith, G. E. (1987) The manager's role in the quality improvement process. *APICS Conf. Proc.*, 12–14.

Oversmith, G. E. (1988) Developing employee ownership of the quality improvement process. *APICS Conf. Proc.*, 267–9.

Pallas, M. (1989) Managing suppliers up to speed. GM's evaluation procedure, *Harvard Bus. Rev.*, **67** (4), 130.

Perry, N. J. (1988) Here come richer, riskier pay plans. *Fortune*, December 19, 50–4.

Peters, A. M. (1990) Supplier quality training (SQT): the next step after supplier audit. *APICS Conf. Proc.*, 670–3.

Plossl, K. R. (1987) The vital role of integrated engineering in JIT success. *APICS Conf. Proc.*, 85–9.

Potter, P. A. and Buker, D. W. (1988) Visibility: the key to manufacturing control. *APICS Conf. Proc.*, 171–3.

Raeker, R. H. (1987) Toward the achievment of manufacturing excellence with a JIT-modified MRP II system. *APICS Conf. Proc.*, 386–9.

Reeds, J. D. (1988) Purchasing's role in achieving supplier total quality management. *APICS Conf. Proc.*, 528–32.

Rhyne, D. M. (1990) Total plant performance advantages through total productive maintenance. *APICS Conf. Proc.*, 683–6.

Roman, R. J. (1988) Can you believe that? *APICS Conf. Proc.*, 633–5.

Ross, J. E. and Ross, W. C. (1982) *Japanese Quality Circles and Productivity*, Reston Publishing Company Inc., New York.

Sandras, W. A. (1988) Total quality control: the other side of JIT coin. *APICS Conf. Proc.*, 273–7.

Schonberger, R. J. (1987) *World Class Manufacturing Casebook, Implementing JIT and TQC*, The Free Press, New York.

Schultz, T. R. (1987) Lead time: enemy #1 to managing demand. *APICS Conf. Proc.*, 308–10.

Sepehri, M. (1987) Science of just-in-time. *APICS Conf. Proc.*, 421–3.

Shapiro, M. N. (1990) Meaningful measures. *APICS Conf. Proc.*, 628–30.

Shingo, S. (1986) *Zero Quality Control: Source Inspection and the Poka-yoke System*, English translation by Productivity Inc., USA.

Sipes, J. W. (1987) How to benefit from MRP and JIT. *APICS Conf. Proc.*, 390–2.

Souza, S. A. (1987) Performance measurements: successful application to JIT, *APICS Conf. Proc.*, 393–4.

Spencer, M. S. (1990) The JIT, MRP, OPT choice: how to CIM with the sharks. *APICS Conf. Proc.*, 561–4.

Starke, F. A., Mondy, R. W., Sharplin, A. and Flippo, E. B. (1988) *Management Concepts and Canadian Practice*, 2nd edn., Allyn and Bacon Publishers, Toronto.

Stelter, K. (1987) How to define work centers for maximum benefit in the changing MRP II/JIT environment. *APICS Conf. Proc.*, 79–80.

Stickler, M. J. (1990) Continuous improvement guaranteed (but only with TEI). *APICS Conf. Proc.*, 328–31.

Suzaki, K. (1987) *The New Manufacturing Challenge*, The Free Press, New York.

Thorne, F. L. (1988) Mixed model scheduling: a foundation for flexibility and responsiveness. *APICS Conf. Proc.*, 473–5.

Townsend, P. L. and Gebhardt, J. E. (1986) *Commit To Quality*, John Wiley and Sons, Inc., New York.

Voss, C. A. (1987) *Just-In-Time Manufacture*, IFS Publications, Bedford.

Waliszewski, D. A. (1987) JIT starter kit for design engineering. *APICS Conf. Proc.*, 93–5.

Walton, M. (1986) *The Deming Management Method*, The Putnam Publishing Group, New York.

Weaver, R. L. (1987) Manufacturing excellence: a strategy for competitive advantage. *APICS Conf. Proc.*, 225–8.

Wenzel, S. (1987) Flexible work force: a foundation for JIT. *APICS Conf. Proc.*, 510–13.

Werther, W. B., Davis, K., Schwind, H. F. and Das, H. (1990) *Canadian Human Resource Management*, 3rd Canadian edn., McGraw-Hill Ryerson Ltd., Toronto.

Whittle, S. and Foster, M. (1989) Customer profiling: getting into your customer's shoes. *Mgt Dec.* (6), December, 27–30.

Widner, T. (1989) The payoff from teamwork. *Business Week*, July 10, 56–62.

Woodcock, M. and Francis, D. (1981) *Organizational Development Through Teambuilding*, Gower Publishing Company Ltd., London.

Index

Acceptance sampling 145
Adversarial system 152, 192
Andon 27, 70
Automation 70
Autonomous control 70, see also
    Jidoka
Autonomous maintenance 37
Autonomy
    individual 11
    team 11

Bill of materials 45, 58, 93, 94
Brainstorming 62, 142
    definition 160

Categorization 21
Cause and effect diagrams 160,
    164-65 (see also Ishikawa
    diagrams)
Cell audit action sheet 202-203
Cellular manufacturing 71, 116
    benefits of 57
    defined 46
    multiple machines 51
    prerequisites to 57-58
Checklists 145
Check sheets 160, 163-64
Clamping 68-69
Cleaning 23
Clearing 21
Closed loop system 90
Colour coded containers 25
Communication 215
Competitive responsiveness 74-75
Conformance 140
Continuous improvement 6, 7, 10,
    17, 205, 208

definition 152
Continuous production 17
Control boards 26
Control charts 144
Conventional organizations 8-9
Cost of quality 209
    appraisal 140
    nonconformance 127, 140
    nonconforming material 141
    opportunity costs 209-10
    process failure 210
Counter measures 30
Cross-training 71, 78, 81, 119
Culture 2, 168
Customer 155
    delivery 73
    employee as 41, 47, 156
    expectations 137-38
    orientation 41, 147-48
    profile 120
    profile model 148
    relationship with suppliers
        102-103, 109-111
    requirements 137-38
Customization of products 72
Cycle analysis 112
Cycle time 49, 74-76, 88

Demand pull 3, 6, 23, 40-41, 82, 83
Deming Circle 155-156
Deming, W.E. 123 -124, 156
Diagrams 26
Discipline 23
Disposal notice cards 27-28
Distribution requirements planning
    (DRP) 115, 121-122

Emotional resistance 12, 153, 190,
    212-213 (see also resistance to
    change)
Employee absenteeism 179
Employee involvement 169, 184,
    203
Employee ownership 81, 91,
    166, 214
    definition 133-134
Empowerment 11
External set-up activities 66-69

Facilitating goods 150
Failsafe methods 25-26, 70-71
    145, 160
Fishbone diagram 165
Final inspection 145
Financial incentive systems 175-178
Five why's 30, 62, 160, 161
Flexible manufacturing
    defined 59
    systems 77
Flexible workforce 17 (see also
    multi-functional workers)
    implementation of 54-57
Flip charts 160, 164
Flow charts 116
Focused factory 56, 77-82
Foolproof 31, 53
Forecasting 120-121
Fourteen points 123-124
Fraction defective chart 143-144
Functional layout 46-48

Group peer pressure 177

Handling 14 (see also waste)
Histogram 160, 163
Housekeeping activities 18, 82
    142, 143, 145, 186, 205-206,
    214, 215

Iceberg analogy 127-130
Implementation audit 208

Implementation leader 186
Incentive systems 175-177
    types of 176-177
Incoming inspection 142
In-process quality 160
Intercell rivalry 208, 213-214
Internal setup activities 66-69
Intrinsic motivation 180-181
Inventory 16, 27
Ishikawa diagrams 160, 164-165
    (see also cause and effect)
Ishikawa, K. 156

Japanese cultural characteristics 2-4
    contrast to North America 11,
        114
    team idea system 153
    work ethic 2-3, 181-182
Japanese management philosophy 2
Japanese manufacturing plants 113
Japanese work ethic 181
Job rotation 53-54, 145
Job security 12, 212
Job shop 18, 194, 196
Juran, J.M. 156
Just in Time:
    benefits 10-11
    defined 1
    goals 7-10
    implementation strategy 184-187
    limitations 10-12
    prerequisites 17-18
    rationale for 12
    support 5-6

Kanban 6, 79, 82, 83, 95, 208
    benefits 91
    functions of 83-84
    hybrid method 43-44
    implementation 89, 91
    obstacles to 91
    plant preparation 85
    production ordering 83
    pure kanban 43

rules 84-85
withdrawal 83

Lead time 71-72, 89-90
Learning principles 173-174
Line balancing 57
Line imbalance 58
Locating 23
Lot sizes 89, 111
Lower control limit 143

Machine breakdowns 30
Management commitment 134,
    171-173
Management influence 18
Manufacturing lead time 90
Market responsiveness 71
Master schedule 45, 94
Material on hold 21
Measurement system 187
Mixed model scheduling 72-73
Mixed production levelling 88
Monthly reviews 28
Motion 14 (see also waste)
Motivation, defined 179
    types of 180-181
MRP, MRPII 6-7, 82, 92-93, 112,
    117, 121
    integration with JIT 94-96
Multi-functional skills 53
Multi-functional workers (see also
    flexible workforce) 6
Multi-process handling 53
Multiple sourcing 103

Nominal group technique (NGT)
    160-161
Nonconformance 127, 140
Nonconforming material 141
Non-repetitive manufacturing 76
Non-value added 130, 136, 139
North American cultural
    characteristics 11

Ohno, Taiichi 2, 30
Oil embargo 2
One-at-a-time production 67
Operations audit 202-203
Operations sequencing 117
Operator's five senses 30
Operator instructions 26
Opportunity cost 209-210
Organizational culture 125-126,
    134, 152
Organizational flexibility 19
Overproduction 14-15 (see also
    waste)
Over-usage 14-15

Parallel operations 67-68
Pareto analysis 160, 161-162
Pareto chart 162
Participation 24
Peer pressure 211
People involvement 5
Performance measures 183, 188-189
Performance scheduling board
    207-208
Performance tracking board 208
PERT (see Program evaluation and
    review technique)
Pilot product 92, 111
Pilot projects 189-190, 210
Plant evaluation 17
Plant layout 6, 46, 197, 200-202
Pokayoke 53, 145
Preventive maintenance 25, 28, 142,
    143-145 205-207 215
    implementation 34
    procedures 29, 31
    relationship with JIT 31-33
    software 39
Proactive approach 190-191
Problem solving teams 61
Process analysis 49
Process design 138-139
Process failure 210
Process improvement 50-51

Processing 16
Product defect 16
Production control 82, 205, 208
Production levelling 85-88
Production practices 205
Professional qualification 105
Profit center 82
Program evaluation and review
    technique 67-68
Progressive organizations 8-9
Pull system 40, 208
    advantages/disadvantages of
        42-43
    contrast with push systems 41
    prerequisites 44-45
Purchasing 99
Push system 41, 208

Quality 7
    assurance 132
    at the source 7, 140
    contrast to traditional 7
    cost categories 127
    defined 124
    design 136
    service 146
Quality circles (QC's) 5, 55, 160
    benefits 158-159
    costs 159
    defined 156
    employee roles 158
    function 157
    history 156-157
    resistance to 159
Quality continuum 140-141
Quality delivery 106
Quality gap 126
Quality of working life (QWL) 156,
    157, 179, 192
Queuing time 16

Rabbit chase 49
Range chart 143-144

Rational resistance 12 (see also
    resistance to change)
Repetitive manufacturing 17-18, 76
Resistance to change 5-6, 126, 159,
    190-191
Responsiveness 74-75, 152
Role overload 213

Safety stocks 11
Sailboat analogy 85-86
Schedule stability 23
Self-inspection 6, 52, 142, 145,
    210-211
Self managing teams 168
Sensory inspection 143
Service quality 146
    characteristics 146
    cost categories 147
    quality gap 151
    variability 149
Set-ups 51
Set-up time 57, 63, 71, 116
    adjustment activities 67
    external/internal setup activities
        66-69
    reduction 59, 62
    reduction techniques 66-69
    rules for 62-66
Seven wastes 14-16, 116
Signal markers 25
Simplifying 21 (see also workplace
    organization)
Single sourcing 103-104
Small group improvement
    activities 154
Small lot sizing 89
Spreader model 72
Standardized operations 145
Standardizing 67, 72, 150
Standards 183
Statistical process control (SPC) 95,
    142, 157, 160, 188
Storage 21-22
Strategic business units 209

Strategic control points 185
Suggestion systems 134, 153,
    181, 203
Supermarket analogy 83
Supplier resistance 99, 101, 102,
    104
Supplier selection criteria 105-108
Systems perspective 125

Teambuilding 170-171, 211
Teams 132-133, 135
    defined 170
Teamwork 17
Time buckets 88
Tooling 21
Total business concept 187
Total employee involvement 35,
    152, 153, 168, 183
    contrast with traditional
        approach 168
Total people involvement 5
Total productive maintenance 116
    benefits 37
    defined 34
    contrast with preventive
        maintenance 36
    elements of 34-35
    implementation of 36-39
Total quality control (TQC) 36, 38,
    95, 121, 152
    defined 154
Total quality management
    defined 124
    benefits 214-215
Toyota manufacturing plants 2
Toyota production system 5
Traditional manufacturing 82-83

Traditional purchasing 99-100
Training 6, 8-9, 12, 53, 160, 173,
    204-205, 215
Training gap 204
Transportation 16
True work cells 49
Type 1, Type 2 errors 143

Union involvement 191
Union management relations 192
Union resistance 177
Union support 5
Upper control limit 143

Value added 13-15, 62, 96, 127, 142
Vendor certification survey 209
Vendor development 208, 209
Visibility 71-72, 82, 145, 204, 205,
    207, 214
Visible signals 4

Waste 14-15, 118, 214-215
    categories of 14-16, 116
What if analysis 166
Work cells 25, 197
    benefits 48, 51-53
Work ethic (see also Japanese
    cultural characteristics)
    employees 178-180, 212
Workplace organization 21, 116
Work practices,
    comparison of traditional vs. JIT
        181-182
Work orders 29-30

X-bar 143-144